PRAISE FOR *Blood, Sweat, and Pixels*

"Making video games is one of the most transformative, exciting things I've done in my two decades as a freelance writer. Making video games is also an excruciating journey into Hellmouth itself. Jason Schreier's wonderful book captures both the excitement and the hell. Here, at long last, is a gripping, intelligent glimpse behind a thick (and needlessly secretive) creative curtain."

—Tom Bissell, author of *Extra Lives* and *Apostle*, and writer on the *Gears of War*, *Uncharted*, and *Battlefield* franchises

"So many of the cultural problems both within the game industry and among fans come down to a lack of realistic public understanding of the tribulations of development. Jason opens a crucial door into an abnormally secretive industry, in the brave hope of teaching us a little more about its flammable alchemy."

—Leigh Alexander, author and tech journalist

"A meticulously researched, well-written, and painful at times account of many developers' and studios' highs and lows. May need to make it required reading for the developers at my studio."

—Cliff Bleszinski, creator of *Gears of War* and founder of Boss Key Productions

"The stories in this book make for a fascinating and remarkably complete pantheon of just about every common despair and every joy related to game development."

—Rami Ismail, cofounder of Vlambeer and developer of *Nuclear Throne*

"Jason Schreier brilliantly exposes the truth about how video games are made. Brutal, honest, yet ultimately uplifting; I've been gaming for thirty years, yet I was surprised by every page. Turns out what I didn't know about my favorite hobby could fill a book. This book! Can't recommend it enough to any serious fan of this generation's greatest new art form."

—Adam Conover, executive producer and host of truTV's *Adam Ruins Everything*

BLOOD, SWEAT, AND PIXELS

BLOOD, SWEAT, AND PIXELS

The Triumphant, Turbulent Stories Behind How Video Games Are Made

JASON SCHREIER

HARPER

NEW YORK • LONDON • TORONTO • SYDNEY

BLOOD, SWEAT, AND PIXELS. Copyright © 2017 by Jason Schreier. All rights reserved. Printed in the United States of America. No part of this book may be used or reproduced in any manner whatsoever without written permission except in the case of brief quotations embodied in critical articles and reviews. For information, address HarperCollins Publishers, 195 Broadway, New York, NY 10007.

HarperCollins books may be purchased for educational, business, or sales promotional use. For information, please e-mail the Special Markets Department at SPsales@harpercollins.com.

FIRST EDITION

Designed by Leydiana Rodriguez

Library of Congress Cataloging-in-Publication Data

Names: Schreier, Jason, author.
Title: Blood, sweat, and pixels : the triumphant, turbulent stories behind how video games are made / Jason Schreier.
Description: First edition. | New York : Harper Paperbacks, [2017] |
Identifiers: LCCN 2017015481 (print) | LCCN 2017034583 (ebook) | ISBN 9780062651242 (ebk) | ISBN 9780062651235 (paperback)
Subjects: LCSH: Video games. | Video games—Economic aspects. | Video games industry. | Video games—Design. | BISAC: BUSINESS & ECONOMICS / Industries / Computer Industry. | GAMES / Video & Electronic.
Classification: LCC GV1469.3 (ebook) | LCC GV1469.3 .S37 2017 (print) | DDC 794.8—dc23
LC record available at https://lccn.loc.gov/2017015481

17 18 19 20 21   LSC   10 9 8 7 6

For Amanda

CONTENTS

BLOOD, SWEAT, AND PIXELS

INTRODUCTION

Say you want to make a video game. You've got this killer idea—it's about a mustachioed plumber who has to rescue his princess girlfriend from a giant fire-breathing turtle—and you've convinced an investor to give you a few million dollars to make it happen. Now what?

Well, first you need to figure out the exact number of people you can afford to hire. Then you need to call up some artists, some designers, some programmers. You'll need a producer to keep things running smoothly, and a sound department to make sure the game has, you know, *sounds*. Can't forget to hire some quality-assurance testers to check for bugs. And a marketing savant—how else will everyone know about your future best seller? Once you're all staffed up, you'll need to make a strict schedule that determines how much time your team will spend on each part of the game. If all goes well, you'll develop a demo for E3 in six months, then be "feature complete" by the end of the year.

After a few months, things seem to be going well. Your artists are drawing all sorts of cool enemies for your plumber to fight: ghosts, mushrooms, that sort of thing. The designers have sketched out some clever levels that will guide the player through raging volcanoes and fetid swamps. The programmers just figured out a fancy rendering trick that will make the dungeons look more realistic than anything you've seen before. Everyone is motivated, the game is making progress, and you're handing out stock options like they're free newspapers in the subway.

One morning, you get a call from your producer. Turns out that rendering trick is useless, because it knocks your game's frame rate down to ten frames per second.* The playtesters keep getting stuck on the volcano level, and your marketing guy is grumbling about how that might affect your Metacritic score. Your art director insists on micromanaging the animators, which is driving them *crazy*. Your E3 demo is due in two weeks, and you know there's no way you can get it done in less than four. And suddenly the investors are asking if maybe you can slash that $10 million budget down to $8 million, even if you have to let go of a few people to make it happen.

A week ago, you were fantasizing about the speech you'd make at The Game Awards after taking home Game of the Year. Now you're wondering if you'll ever even finish.

I once had drinks with a developer who'd just shipped a new game. He looked exhausted. He and his team had been right near the goal line, he said, when they were hit with a revelation: one of the game's biggest features wasn't actually fun to play. The developer's team had to spend the next few months "crunching," working eighty- to one-hundred-hour weeks to scrap the feature and overhaul everything they had done to that point. Some of them slept in the office so they wouldn't have to waste time commuting, because every hour spent in the car was an hour not spent fixing

---

* A game's frame rate is the frequency at which images are displayed on the screen. Our eyes are trained to play games at a baseline rate of thirty frames per second; when the frame rate dips lower than that, everything in the game starts to look choppy, as if it's being run on an old projector.

bugs. Up until the day they had to submit a final build, many of them doubted they'd be able to release the game at all.

"Sounds like a miracle that this game was even made," I said.

"Oh, Jason," he said. "It's a miracle that *any* game is made."

In the years I've been reporting on the world of video games, that's been a common theme. Developers everywhere, whether at tiny independent studios or publicly traded corporations, talk frequently about how difficult it is to design and produce games. Walk into any San Francisco bar during the annual Game Developers Conference (GDC) and you're bound to find groups of weary designers trying to one-up each other with stories of coding binges and caffeine-fueled all-nighters. War metaphors are common—"tales from the trenches" is a ubiquitous expression—as are choruses of complaints that the outside world doesn't get it. One surefire way to annoy a game developer is to ask, in response to discovering his or her chosen career path, what it's like to spend all day playing video games.

But even if you accept the premise that video game development is grueling work, it's not easy for those of us on the outside to see why. People have been making games since the 1970s, haven't they? With decades of lessons and experience to draw from, shouldn't game development have grown more efficient? Maybe it made sense for developers to crunch in the late 1980s, when gaming was the domain of teens and twentysomethings who gorged on pizza and Diet Coke as they coded all night and slept all day, but decades later, video games fuel a $30 billion industry in the United States alone.* Why do game developers still have so many stories about staying at the office until 3:00 a.m.? Why is it still so difficult to make video games?

---

* According to data from the Entertainment Software Association, the US video game industry generated $30.4 billion in 2016.

To try to answer these questions, I went out and engaged in my favorite activity: bothering people who know way more than I do. I spoke to around one hundred game developers and executives, both on and off the record, asking them an endless number of nosy questions about their lives, their jobs, and why they sacrifice so much to make video games.

There are ten chapters in this book, each telling the story behind how a different video game was made. One chapter visits Irvine, California, for a look at how the Kickstarter-funded *Pillars of Eternity* helped Obsidian Entertainment recover from its darkest days. Another chapter heads to Seattle, Washington, where the twentysomething Eric Barone shut himself alone in a room for nearly five years to create a serene farming game called *Stardew Valley*. Other chapters tell stories about *Dragon Age: Inquisition*'s technological nightmare, *Uncharted 4*'s brutal time crunch, and even the mystery behind LucasArts' much-hyped *Star Wars 1313*.

As you read, many of these stories may strike you as anomalous—games that were hampered by drastic technology changes, directorial shifts, or other wild factors beyond the developers' control. It's tempting to think, while reading these stories, that these games were all made under abnormal sets of circumstances. That these people were just unlucky. That the developers of these games might have averted hardship if they had followed industry standards and avoided common pitfalls, or if they had made smarter decisions from the get-go.

Here's an alternative theory: *every single video game* is made under abnormal circumstances. Video games straddle the border between art and technology in a way that was barely possible just a few decades ago. Combine technological shifts with the fact that a video game can be just about *anything*, from a two-dimensional iPhone puzzler to a massive open-world RPG with über-realistic graphics, and it shouldn't be too shocking to discover that there are no uniform standards for how games are made. Lots of video games look the same, but no two video games are created the same way, which is a pattern you'll see throughout this book.

But why is it so hard to make them? If, like me, you have never tried to develop a commercial video game before, you might find it helpful to review a few possible theories.

1. They're interactive. Video games don't move in a single linear direction. Unlike, say, a computer-rendered Pixar movie, games run on "real-time" graphics, in which new images are generated by the computer every millisecond. Video games, unlike *Toy Story*, need to react to the player's actions. As you play a video game, your PC or console (or phone, or calculator) renders characters and scenes on the fly based on your decisions. If you choose to walk into a room, the game needs to load up all the furniture. If you choose to save and quit, the game needs to store your data. If you choose to murder the helpful robot, the game needs to identify (a) whether it's possible to kill the robot, (b) whether you're powerful enough to kill the robot, and (c) what kind of awful sounds the robot will make as you spill its metallic guts. Then the game might have to remember your actions, so other characters know that you're a heartless murderer and can say things like, "Hey, you're that heartless murderer!"

2. Technology is constantly changing. As computers evolve (which happens, without fail, every year), graphic processing gets more powerful. And as graphic processing gets more powerful, we expect prettier games. As Feargus Urquhart, the CEO of Obsidian, told me, "We are on the absolute edge of technology. We are always pushing everything all the time." Urquhart pointed out that making games is sort of like shooting movies, if you had to build an entirely new camera every time you started. That's a common analogy. Another is that making a game is like constructing a building during an earthquake. Or trying to drive a train while someone else runs in front of you, laying down track as you go.

3. The tools are always different. To make games, artists and designers need to work with all sorts of software, ranging from common programs (like Photoshop and Maya) to proprietary apps that vary from studio to studio. Like technology, these tools are constantly evolving based on developers' needs and ambitions. If a tool runs too slowly, is full of bugs, or is missing pivotal features, making games can be excruciating. "While most people seem to think that game development is about 'having great ideas,' it's really more about the skill of taking great ideas from paper to product," a developer once told me. "You need a good engine and toolset to do this."

4. Scheduling is impossible. "The unpredictability is what makes it challenging," said Chris Rippy, a veteran producer who worked on *Halo Wars*.* In traditional software development, Rippy explained, you can set up a reliable schedule based on how long tasks have taken in the past. "But with games," Rippy said, "you're talking about: Where is it fun? How long does fun take? Did you achieve that? Did you achieve enough fun? You're literally talking about a piece of art for the artist. When is that piece of art done? If he spends another day on it, would that have made all the difference in the world to the game? Where do you stop? That's the trickiest part. Eventually you do get into the production-y side of things: you've proven the fun, you've proven the look of the game, and now it becomes more predictable. But it's a real journey in the dark up until that point." Which leads us to . . .

---

* In game development, a producer's job is to coordinate schedules, wrangle the rest of the team, and ensure that everyone is on the same page. As Ryan Treadwell, a veteran producer, once told me, "We're the people who are responsible for making sure that a product gets made."

5. It's impossible to know how "fun" a game will be until you've played it. You can take educated guesses, sure, but until you've got your hands on a controller, there's no way to tell whether it feels good to move, jump, and bash your robot pal's brains out with a sledgehammer. "Even for very, very experienced game designers, it's really scary," said Emilia Schatz, a designer at Naughty Dog.* "All of us throw out so much work because we create a bunch of stuff and it plays terribly. You make these intricate plans in your head about how well things are going to work, and then when it actually comes and you try to play it, it's terrible."

In all the stories in this book, you'll see several common themes. Every game is delayed at least once. Every game developer must make tough compromises. Every company must sweat over which hardware and technology to use. Every studio must build its schedules around big trade shows like E3, where developers will draw motivation (and even feedback) from throngs of excited fans. And, most controversially, everyone who makes video games has to crunch, sacrificing personal lives and family time for a job that seems to never end.

Yet many of the people who make video games say they can't imagine doing anything else. When they describe that feeling of being on the cutting edge of technology, of building interactive entertainment that's unlike any other medium, of working with a team of dozens or even hundreds to create something that millions of people might play, it all adds up to an unshakeable belief that for all the turbulence, for all the crunch, for all the

---

* The role of a designer can vary from studio to studio, but in general, it's a designer's job to make decisions about how a game will function. These decisions range from major (what kind of weapons will the player use?) to minor (how will the game distinguish between doors that the player can open and doors that just stay locked?).

unadulterated bullshit that developers often have to go through, making video games is worth it.

So about your plumber game (*Super Plumber Adventure*). It turns out there are solutions to all your problems, though you might not like them. You can cut your budget by outsourcing some of the animation work to a studio in New Jersey. It might not look as good, but it'll be half the price. You can ask the level designers to add some extra platforms to the volcano level so it's a little less punishing. When they object, remind them that, hey, not everybody loves *Dark Souls*. And you can tell the art director that the programmers have their own jobs to do and really don't need to hear his opinions on chiaroscuro in video games.

Hitting that E3 deadline might be a little tougher, but what if you ask your employees to stay late for a couple of weeks? No more than two weeks, of course. To make up for it, you'll buy them dinner, and maybe even offer them nice bonuses if the game gets a 90 on Metacritic.

You'll also have to cut out a few features. Sorry, sorry. I know— they were awesome. But it's not like your plumber really *needs* to transform into a raccoon. You can save that for the sequel.

REPORTING NOTE

The stories in this book are based on interviews I conducted with roughly one hundred game developers and other industry figures between 2015 and 2017. Most of those people spoke on the record. Others spoke on background, requesting anonymity because they were not authorized to participate in this book and did not want to risk damaging their careers. You'll probably notice that most of the people who speak in this book are male, which is a depressing (and unintentional) reflection of an industry that has, for decades now, been dominated by men.

Except when otherwise noted, anything you see in quotation marks was said to me directly. This book does not contain re-created dialogue. All the anecdotes and details in this book come directly from the accounts of sources, and all were corroborated by at least two people whenever possible.

Some of this reporting was based on trips to studios and homes in Los Angeles, Irvine, Seattle, Edmonton, and Warsaw. I paid for my own travel and did not accept accommodations from any companies or developers, although I did say yes to a few lunches, which seemed kosher. Well, the lunches weren't kosher. What I mean is that it seemed ethically accep—You know what, let's just get on with the book.

PILLARS OF ETERNITY

The most important question in video game development has nothing to do with making video games. It's a simple question that has stymied artists for centuries and put an end to countless creative endeavors: *How are we gonna pay for this thing?*

In early 2012, Feargus Urquhart, the CEO of Obsidian Entertainment, found himself unable to come up with an answer. Obsidian, a relatively small game development studio based in Irvine, California, had spent the past year working on a fantasy role-playing game (RPG) called *Stormlands*. They'd never made a game quite like this. It was weird, ambitious, and, most important, funded by Microsoft, whose game producers had decided they wanted a massive, exclusive RPG to launch alongside their next console, the Xbox One. Around fifty of Obsidian's ~115 employees were working on the game, which meant it cost a lot of money. Which was fine—as long as Microsoft kept sending checks.

Urquhart had grown accustomed to financial pressure. He'd been working in games since 1991, first as a tester at the publisher Interplay, then as a designer, then as the boss of the powerhouse developer Black Isle Studios, which a suddenly cash-strapped Interplay dismantled in 2003. That same year, Urquhart founded Obsidian with a few other Black Isle veterans, and they quickly learned that running an independent studio was like juggling dangerous objects. If they didn't have a new contract ready to go as soon as the last one had finished, they were in trouble.

Urquhart has thin, light brown hair and a stocky build. He speaks quickly, with the authoritative tone of someone who's spent decades pitching games. Over the years he's played a part in creating some of the most beloved RPGs in gaming, like *Fallout* and *Baldur's Gate*. While speaking on panels and to the press, he's always candid about the difficulties of running an indie studio. "The life of an independent developer is, every morning you wake up wondering if your publishers are going to call and cancel your games," Urquhart said. "I wish I was more of a sociopath or psychopath and I could just completely ignore the fact that there's this guillotine pointed at my neck all the time. But I can't. And I don't think a lot of developers can, and unfortunately there's that constant threat, and that threat is used a lot. It's used all the time."

On the morning of March 12, 2012, Urquhart's cell lit up. It was the *Stormlands* producer at Microsoft, texting to ask if Urquhart could hop on the phone. Right away he knew what was about to happen. "It's the text from the girlfriend who's going to break up with you," Urquhart said. "I just got on the call knowing what it was going to be."

Microsoft's representative was frank: they were canceling *Stormlands*. Effective immediately, fifty of Urquhart's employees no longer had work.

The producer didn't say why Microsoft was axing the game, but it had become clear to Obsidian's top staff that development was not going smoothly. There was an inordinate amount of pressure, not just to make a good RPG, but to make a good RPG that could sell Xbox Ones. *Stormlands'* ideas had felt disjointed to Obsidian's staff, and, at least from Obsidian's point of view, Microsoft's expectations were impractical.

As some former *Stormlands* developers described it, the game was full of ambitious "high-level" ideas, many driven by Microsoft's vision of what should be in an Xbox One launch game. The Xbox One was all about the Kinect, a motion-sensing camera that could recognize full-body gestures, so what if *Stormlands* let you use Kinect to haggle with shopkeepers? The Xbox One would support "cloud computing," allowing each player's console to interact with Microsoft-owned computer servers, so what if *Stormlands* had big, massively multiplayer raids that would let you meet up with other players on the fly? These ideas all sounded interesting on paper, but it was unclear whether any of them would work in a game.

Different people who worked on the game point to different reasons for *Stormlands'* ultimate demise—some say Microsoft was too ambitious; others say Obsidian was too petulant—but everyone agrees that by the end, the project had gotten unwieldy. "Expectation after expectation after expectation got piled onto the game," Urquhart said. "It turned into this thing that everybody was scared of. I think in fact even we were scared of it."

Urquhart hung up the phone, trying to figure out what this would mean for his company. The standard burn rate for a game studio was $10,000 per person per month, a number that included both salaries and overhead costs, like health insurance and office rent. Using that number as a baseline, keeping all fifty *Stormlands* developers employed would cost the studio at least $500,000 every month. By Urquhart's count, Obsidian had already put $2 million of its own money into *Stormlands* on top of what it had received from Microsoft, and the company didn't have much left to spare. With only one other game in development—*South Park: The Stick* *of Truth*, which was having its own financial crisis thanks to the slow meltdown of its publisher, THQ—Obsidian just didn't have the cash to keep all those people employed.*

Feargus Urquhart gathered Obsidian's other four owners and went to a Starbucks down the road, where they spent hours huddling over a big list of names, trying to figure out whom to keep and whom to let go. The next day, Urquhart called an all-hands meeting. "It started out fine," said Dimitri Berman, a lead character artist. "People were joking around. Then Feargus came out all dead looking."

Choking back tears, Urquhart told the company that Microsoft had canceled *Stormlands* and that Obsidian would have to lay people off. The staff trickled back to their desks, wondering which of them were about to be escorted out of the building. For hours, they all just had to wait there, nervously watching as Obsidian's operations guy prepared severance packages for those who hadn't made the cut. "He comes around with a manila folder, and he walks around, and he tells you to pack your bags," said Adam Brennecke, a programmer on *Stormlands*. "And he escorts you off the premises and he sets up a time when you can come back and get your belongings. He's just walking around and you're thinking, 'Don't come into my office, don't come into my office.' You're watching him and then you see and you're like, 'Fuck, there goes one of my friends.'"

By the end of the day, the company had been gutted. Obsidian laid off around twenty-six of the people who had worked on *Stormlands*, including one engineer who had been hired just a

---

* THQ stopped operating nine months later, in December 2012, selling off all its projects in a bankruptcy auction the following month. *South Park: The Stick of Truth* went to the French publisher Ubisoft.

day earlier. These weren't incompetent or inadequate employees; they were beloved coworkers. "It was fucking terrible," said Josh Sawyer, the director of *Stormlands*. "It was horrible. It was probably the worst day of my career. . . . It was the biggest layoff I had ever seen."

Since 2003, Obsidian had survived as an independent studio, bouncing from contract to contract as its staff took freelance work to keep the lights on. The company had been through brutal cancellations before—like *Aliens: Crucible*, a Sega-published RPG whose demise also led to big layoffs—but none had hurt this much. None had left Feargus Urquhart with so few options. After nearly ten years, those remaining at Obsidian were starting to wonder: Was this the end?

Four hundred miles north, as Urquhart and his crew tried to recover from catastrophe, the staff of Double Fine were popping champagne. Double Fine, an independent studio in San Francisco led by the illustrious designer Tim Schafer, had just found a way to revolutionize the video game industry.

For decades, the video game industry's power balance had been simple: developers made games; publishers paid for them. Although there were always exceptions—venture capitalists, lottery winners, and so on—the bulk of video game development was funded by big publishers with deep pockets. Publishers almost always had the leverage in these negotiations, which could lead developers to agree to some rigid deals. For the role-playing game *Fallout: New Vegas*, for example, the publisher, Bethesda, offered Obsidian a $1 million bonus if the game hit an 85 (out of 100) on Metacritic, a website that aggregates review scores from across the Internet. As the reviews started pouring in, the Metacritic number swung up and down several times before finally settling at 84. (Obsidian did not get its bonus.)

Traditionally, independent studios like Obsidian and Double Fine had three ways to stay afloat: (1) finding investors, (2) signing contracts with publishers to make games, or (3) funding their own video games with war chests they'd hoarded via options one and two. No decent-size indie studio could survive without relying at least partly on money from outside partners, even if that meant dealing with cancellations, layoffs, and bad deals.

Double Fine had found a fourth option: Kickstarter, a "crowdfunding" website that had launched in 2009. Using this website, creators could pitch directly to their fans: *You give us money; we'll give you something cool.* During Kickstarter's first couple of years, users of the site were hobbyists, hoping to earn a few thousand dollars to shoot short films or build neat folding tables. In 2011, however, the projects started getting bigger, and in February 2012, Double Fine launched a Kickstarter for a point-and-click adventure game called the *Double Fine Adventure.**

It shattered every record. Previous Kickstarters had been lucky to break six figures; Double Fine raised $1 million in twenty-four hours. In March 2012, just as Microsoft was canceling *Stormlands*, Double Fine's Kickstarter concluded, having raised over $3.3 million from 87,142 backers. No other crowdfunded video game had earned even a tenth of that. By then, Obsidian's staff were all paying attention.

With Kickstarter, a developer wouldn't have to rely on any other companies. Independent studios wouldn't have to sign away

---

* Double Fine would release this game as *Broken Age* in 2015, following a painful three-year development cycle that the studio documented in a series of excellent short films.

the rights to their intellectual properties or give up royalties to big publishers. Instead of pitching to investors or executives, game developers could make a case directly to fans. The more people they could get on board, the more money they'd make.

The crowdfunding revolution had begun.

Back down in Irvine, Feargus Urquhart and Obsidian's other co-owners started talking about their next move. They still had *South Park: The Stick of Truth* in development, but they knew that wasn't enough. If *South Park* ran into more trouble, or if they couldn't find a new project when it was over, the company would simply run out of money. Obsidian needed to diversify. And even after laying off so much of the *Stormlands* team, the studio still had two dozen developers who needed work.

Thanks to the *Double Fine Adventure* and other high-profile projects, the Kickstarter bug had spread throughout Obsidian. Several employees were high on the idea of crowdfunding, including two top veterans: Adam Brennecke and Josh Sawyer. Both had worked on *Stormlands*—Brennecke as a programmer, Sawyer as the director—and both thought that Kickstarter would be the perfect fit for a work-for-hire studio like theirs. During meetings, as management tried to figure out the company's next step, Brennecke and Sawyer kept bringing up the *Double Fine Adventure*. If Tim Schafer could make $3.3 million, why couldn't they?

Urquhart shut them down. He saw crowdfunding as a desperation move. He thought there was a strong likelihood that they'd flop, that they'd be embarrassed, that nobody would give them a dollar. "Even if you feel like you have the greatest idea," said Urquhart, "and you really believe in it, and you would put money into it, you still wonder if anybody's going to be there." Instead, he asked Sawyer, Brennecke, and the remaining *Stormlands* developers to start putting together pitches for outside investors and publishers.

As spring turned into summer, Obsidian offered its services to almost every big publisher in gaming. The studio's leadership talked to Ubisoft and Activision about doing big series like *Might & Magic* and *Skylanders*. They spent some time pitching (and briefly working on) their own version of Bethesda's ill-fated *Prey 2.** They even took a few of their ideas for *Stormlands* and transformed them into a new pitch called *Fallen* that was spearheaded by one of Obsidian's co-owners, Chris Avellone.†

None of those pitches went anywhere. Big publishers had reasons to be conservative: the Xbox 360 (released in 2005) and PlayStation 3 (2006) were near the end of their life spans, and a new console generation was on the way, but analysts and pundits were predicting that console gaming was doomed thanks to the rise of iPhones and iPads. Publishers didn't want to invest tens of millions of dollars into big games without knowing that people would actually buy the next-generation Xbox One and PS4.‡

By June 2012, many at Obsidian were sick of failing. Some had already left the studio, while others were considering calling it quits. Those who weren't making *South Park* felt like they were stuck in development purgatory, moving from pitch to pitch with no real work in sight. "Nothing was going anywhere," said Brennecke. "Even the pitches we were doing, I don't think anyone was

---

* Originally developed by the Wisconsin-based Human Head Studios, the project known as *Prey 2* bounced around several times before ultimately getting rebooted by Arkane Studios as *Prey*, which came out in May 2017.

† *Fallen* would later morph into an RPG called *Tyranny*, which Obsidian released in November 2016.

‡ As we'll see in several of the chapters in this book, the analysts were way off. The PS4 and Xbox One were both quite successful.

really into." Feargus Urquhart started having breakfast meetings with the company's lawyer to talk about what it might look like if they had to pull the plug, in case they couldn't find another project by the time they'd finished *South Park*.

Then Josh Sawyer and Adam Brennecke came to Urquhart with an ultimatum: they wanted to launch a Kickstarter. They preferred to do it with Obsidian, but if Urquhart continued to stonewall, they'd quit, start their own company, and do it themselves. To sweeten the pot, Sawyer added that he'd be happy to keep working on pitches for publishers, as long as *someone* at the company started planning a Kickstarter.

It helped that other Obsidian veterans had also expressed a great deal of interest in crowdfunding, including Chris Avellone, who had been publicly praising Kickstarter for months, even going as far as to poll Obsidian fans about what kind of project they'd want to help fund.[*] Urquhart relented, and within the next few days, Adam Brennecke was locking himself alone in an office, trying to come up with the perfect Kickstarter.

One thing became immediately clear to everyone who was left at Obsidian: they needed to make an old-school RPG. Much of the company's DNA came from Black Isle, the studio that Feargus Urquhart had operated back in the Interplay days, which was best known for developing and publishing RPGs like *Icewind Dale*, *Planescape: Torment*, and *Baldur's Gate*. These games had several things in common. They were all based on the world and rules of *Dungeons & Dragons*; they all put a huge focus on story and dialogue; and they all used a fixed, "isometric" camera that would let you play with an angled perspective, as if you were looking

---

[*] Avellone had even partnered with Brian Fargo, the founder of Interplay and a longtime friend of the company, on the Kickstarter for a game called *Wasteland 2*.

down at a chessboard. Since they all used the same base technology, called the Infinity Engine, they all felt similarly to play.

Nobody was making games like that anymore. Isometric RPGs had gone out of favor in the mid-2000s, replaced by games with 3-D graphics, voice acting, and far fewer conversations. Publishers were mostly trying to chase megahits like *The Elder Scrolls V: Skyrim*, the Bethesda-developed 2011 RPG that had sold over thirty million copies.* Gamers had been grumbling about this trend for quite some time. Anyone who'd grown up playing Black Isle's isometric RPGs agreed: those games were classics, and it was a shame that the game industry had moved past them.

Obsidian didn't have the *Dungeons & Dragons* license, so they couldn't blast magic missiles or sojourn in the Underdark, but the studio did have several people with experience working on games like *Icewind Dale* and *Baldur's Gate*, and they knew that making an isometric RPG would cost far less money than trying to develop a brand-new 3-D game. If they kept their team small and somehow managed to raise a couple million dollars on Kickstarter, even selling just a few hundred thousand copies could turn Obsidian's fortunes around.

Adam Brennecke spent the next two months working on a pitch, compiling PowerPoint presentations and spreadsheets in preparation for what they were now calling *Project Eternity*. He brainstormed with Josh Sawyer, Chris Avellone, and other veterans at Obsidian including Tim Cain, a designer best known for his work on the original *Fallout*. Before they could launch the Kickstarter, they needed to nail down every detail, so they spent weeks mapping out a schedule, a budget, and even reward tiers. "There was a lot of debate," said Brennecke. "Do we have a physi-

---

* This figure is according to Todd Howard, the director of *Skyrim*, who mentioned it in a November 2016 interview with the website *Glixel*.

cal box? What goes in the physical box? Do we do a collector's edition? What items go in the collector's edition?" You'd get a box by pledging at the $65 tier on Kickstarter, they decided. For the snazzy limited edition, which came with a cloth map, you'd have to pay at least $140.

In August, Brennecke sat down with Obsidian's owners and gave them the full pitch. This would be "D&D without the bullshit," he told them. *Project Eternity* would take the best parts from those old-school RPGs that everyone loved, but it'd ditch the features that felt obsolete after the last ten years of innovation in game development. Brennecke told them he'd budgeted for a Kickstarter goal of $1.1 million, but he secretly thought they could hit $2 million. "Obsidian employees want to make this game," he wrote. The owners agreed. They said Brennecke could put a small team together and launch the Kickstarter in September.

From there, Brennecke pulled Josh Sawyer away from the dreary world of pitching and asked him to start designing the game. They knew *Project Eternity* would be set in an original fantasy world, but what would it look like? Brennecke had thought it'd be cool to do something that focused on human souls, so Sawyer riffed on that. In the world of *Eternity*, souls wouldn't just be metaphysical ideas; they would be tangible sources of power for people. Your main character would be a gifted Watcher, with the ability to peek into other people's souls and read their memories. "I came up with that sort of concept as, that's what the player character's going to be," said Sawyer. "Where does it go from there? We'll figure it out."

You'd start off by customizing your character. You'd pick a class (fighter, paladin, wizard, and so on), a race (traditional fantasy fare like humans and elves, or one of *Eternity*'s original races, like the divinely enhanced "Godlike"), and a smattering of skills and spells. Then you'd get to go out into the world of Eora and explore. You could go on side quests, recruit companions, and fight monsters using the gear and weapons you'd acquire along the way. Combat would unfold in real time, but in the vein of classic RPGs, you'd be able to pause at any time to zoom out and figure out a strategy. Like those old games, this one would be on computers only. No consoles. *Eternity*, as Obsidian envisioned it, would take the best ingredients from *Baldur's Gate*, *Icewind Dale*, and *Planescape: Torment* and put them all together in one delicious stew.

For the next few weeks, Adam Brennecke and Josh Sawyer met daily with their small Kickstarter crew. They pored over every word, every screenshot, and every second of their video pitch. They battled against last-minute second-guessing from some of the owners—Was this *really* a good idea? What if nobody showed up?—and on the morning of September 10, 2012, they launched a teaser countdown on the Obsidian website, promising big news in four days. "This was FINALLY our chance to sidestep the publisher model and get financing directly from the people who want to play an Obsidian RPG," Chris Avellone wrote in an e-mail to me that week. "I'd much rather have the players be my boss and hear their thoughts for what would be fun than people who might be more distant from the process and the genre and frankly, any long-term attachment to the title."

Around the same time, a separate team at Obsidian was working on a pitch for the Russian publisher Mail.Ru, one of the largest Internet companies in Eastern Europe. Mail.Ru had been watching the success of the game *World of Tanks*, which brought in hundreds of millions of dollars in revenue a year primarily from fans in Europe and Asia, and the publisher was eager to make its own online tank game. Although multiplayer tank games weren't Obsidian's MO—Obsidian was, as Urquhart liked to say, the "dorky RPG guys"—the company's owners saw it as an opportunity for a stable stream of income, so they dreamed up what would later be called *Armored Warfare*.

Toward the end of 2012, *Armored Warfare* would turn into an important financial security blanket for Urquhart and crew. What it meant was that they weren't gambling *everything* on Kickstarter. Just a few things.

On Friday, September 14, 2012, a group of Obsidian employees gathered at Adam Brennecke's desk and hovered behind him, waiting for the clock to hit 10:00 a.m. They'd run into a scare an hour earlier, when a big red text alert had informed Brennecke that there was an ambiguous "problem with the campaign," but a quick call to Kickstarter HQ had resolved the issue just in time. At exactly ten o'clock, Brennecke hit the launch button. When the page loaded, the ticker was already at $800. *How the hell?* Brennecke hit refresh. They were over $2,700. Then $5,000. Within a minute, they had broken five digits.

If you were to have visited the offices of Obsidian Entertainment on September 14, 2012, you might not have realized you were at a game development studio. There was very little game development happening there. What you'd have found instead was dozens of people mashing F5 on their keyboards, watching the *Project Eternity* Kickstarter raise hundreds of dollars per minute. In the afternoon, realizing that they weren't going to get much work done, Feargus Urquhart took a group of staff and went to Dave & Buster's across the street, where they ordered a round of beers and proceeded to stare silently at their phones, refreshing Kickstarter. By the end of the day they'd hit $700,000.

The next few weeks were a whirlwind of fundraising, updates, and interviews. *Project Eternity* raised its original goal of $1.1 million a day after the Kickstarter went live, but Urquhart and his crew weren't content settling for the minimum—they wanted to raise as much as possible. More money wouldn't directly translate to a better game, but it would mean that they could afford to hire more people and take more time on the project (which would probably lead to a better game).

As Brennecke scrambled to produce a regular stream of Kickstarter updates, the team began to add stretch goals—features they'd add to the game if they hit certain funding thresholds. It became a tricky balancing act. There was no way to know how much each feature would cost before the game had entered production, so they simply had to estimate. Feargus Urquhart wanted to put a second major city in *Eternity*, for example, but how could he and his team possibly know how much time it would take to build a second city when they hadn't even started making the first one? So they guessed, promising that if the Kickstarter hit $3.5 million, they would add a second city to the game.

On October 16, 2012, the final day of their Kickstarter campaign, the staff of Obsidian held a party to celebrate their success. The whole company gathered in a conference room—much as they had seven months earlier, when they found out *Stormlands* had been canceled—and hooked up a camera so they could broadcast their reactions on an Internet stream. They drank, sang, and watched the final dollars pour in. When the countdown hit zero, they had raised $3,986,794—nearly four times their Kickstarter goal and double what Adam Brennecke, the most optimistic of the bunch, had hoped they could get.

With additional backing they received on PayPal and the Obsidian backer website, their final budget was around $5.3 million.*

---

* Fulfilling and shipping Kickstarter rewards like T-shirts and portraits would drain hundreds of thousands from that sum, so the actual budget was closer to $4.5 million.

Urquhart's company had gambled that fans would show up and pay big for the type of classic RPG that publishers would never fund, and those fans had delivered. In just half a year, thanks to *Armored Warfare* and *Project Eternity*, Obsidian's trajectory had reversed. The company was no longer on the edge of collapse. They finally felt free to do what they wanted to do, rather than what a publisher wanted from them.

Now they just had to make a game.

A week after the Kickstarter ended, once the dust had settled and the hangovers had eased, Josh Sawyer released a short video update to backers. "The Kickstarter's over," he said. "Thanks. But now it's time to work."

Work, for Sawyer and the rest of the team, meant entering pre-production, the period of development when they'd try to answer fundamental questions about *Eternity*. They knew they wanted to make a game that felt like *Baldur's Gate*, but if they couldn't use the *Dungeons & Dragons* rule set, what would their characters look like? What kind of skills would each class have? How would combat play out? How many quests would be available? How big would the world be? What sort of graphic techniques would the artists use? Who would write the story? How big would their team get? When were they going to release the game?

Josh Sawyer, a history buff and an avid cyclist with striking tattoos of poetry running up both arms, had taken the role of project director, the same job he'd had on *Stormlands*. Colleagues describe him as a director with a strong vision and a tendency to stick to that vision, no matter whom he rubs the wrong way. "Josh by far has the highest percentage at making the right decision the first time," said Bobby Null, the lead level designer. "Eighty or eighty-five percent [of the time] he makes the right call. . . . When he needs to, he'll fight the fight all the way up as far as it needs to go, which is not an easy fight sometimes to have when we're talking about fair amounts of money."

In the opposite corner for many of those fights was Adam Brennecke, who took on the dual roles of executive producer and lead programmer. Brennecke, an easygoing soccer player with expressive eyebrows, liked to describe himself as the "glue guy"—the person in charge of ensuring that *Eternity*'s pieces would all fit together. He was also responsible for the budget. During the first few weeks after the Kickstarter ended, his job was to plan a schedule and figure out exactly how much money the team could spend on each part of the game. It made him a natural foil for Sawyer, who was looking to squeeze in as many ambitious ideas as possible.

Early in preproduction, Sawyer stood his ground on big decisions; most significantly, the size of the game. The old Infinity Engine games, which the team had been playing during spare afternoons for inspiration, had worlds that were divided into individual map screens, each full of objects and encounters. The largest of these games, *Baldur's Gate 2*, had nearly two hundred unique maps. To plan *Project Eternity*'s scope, Sawyer and Brennecke would need to figure out how many maps the game would have. Brennecke had settled on 120, but Sawyer disagreed. He wanted 150. And Sawyer wouldn't relent, even though they all knew it would cost more money. "The way I view the relationship between production and direction is there intentionally should be a little bit of antagonism," Sawyer said. "Not hostility—but the director at some level is saying, 'I want to do this, I'm writing this check.' Production holds the checkbook."

Thanks to crowdfunding, Brennecke had over $4 million in that checkbook, which was a lot of money for a Kickstarter project. But compared with modern major video game budgets, which can cap out at hundreds of millions of dollars, it was minuscule. Using the standard $10,000 per person per month burn rate, the *Eternity* budget could maybe feed a team of forty working for ten months. Or a team of twenty working for twenty months. Four million dollars could even fund a team of two people working for two hundred months—although Kickstarter backers might not enjoy waiting seventeen years for their game.

That was all on paper, though. In real life the math was never that clean. A development team would expand and contract based on what it needed every month, and the budget would adjust accordingly. Brennecke would have to build a living schedule—a schedule that could change at any given day based on how they were doing. In game development, these schedules are always malleable: they have to account for iteration, human error, and the fact that creativity can come and go in bursts. "On top of that," said Brennecke, "there is an expectation that we will get better and more efficient as we make more, and as the [development] tools get better."

The number of maps made a huge difference. Building 150 maps instead of 120 might mean several extra months of work, which would expand the schedule, which would cost Obsidian a lot of money. But Sawyer wouldn't give in. "I think, in retrospect, that's why our games are what they are," said Brennecke. "Making crazy decisions like that, where it's just, 'We can do it. Let's figure it out.'"

As Brennecke and Sawyer battled over *Project Eternity*'s scope, the art team was running into its own set of problems. For years, Obsidian's artists and animators had used a program called Softimage to create 3-D graphics, but by 2012 it felt obsolete, lacking pivotal features compared with its competitors. (By 2014 it would be discontinued.) To modernize, some of Obsidian's owners and Rob Nesler, the art director, decided to switch to

Maya, a more popular 3-D graphics tool that would work more smoothly with their game's engine, a modified version of Unity.*

Long term, Nesler knew this was the right choice, but there would be growing pains. It would take the art team weeks to learn how to properly use Maya, which meant that early production would move far more slowly. "People like to say, 'Oh, it's just another software package, you'll learn it,'" Nesler said. "But to really learn how to achieve mastery and competence, to be able to adequately schedule how long it'll take you to do something, you need to get to a level where you're able to problem-solve in these packages. . . . It takes time, months or years to become so good at something that when someone says, 'How long will it take you to do something?' you can say, 'It takes me this long.'"

Without the ability to estimate the length of basic art tasks, the producers couldn't put together an accurate schedule. Without an accurate schedule, they couldn't determine how much money the project would cost. Four million dollars wouldn't go very far if it took the team six months to build each map. If they were working with a publisher, they might have been able to renegotiate their contract to eke out more funding, but for *Eternity* that wasn't an option. "The budget was the budget," said Justin Bell, the audio director. "We couldn't go back to the backers and say, 'Give us more money.' It just wouldn't look good. So there was very little negotiation room."

Because of the switch to Maya—and the art team's lack of experience making isometric RPGs—it took a long time before *Eternity*'s early prototypes started looking right. For a while, it was too dark, too muddy, and too different from those old Infinity Engine

---

*   An engine, which we'll discuss more in chapter 6, is a collection of reusable code that helps developers create games. Unity is a third-party engine that's commonly licensed and used by independent studios.

games. After some heated arguments and long periods of iteration, the art team started to learn that there were certain aesthetic rules they needed to follow for a game like this. They shouldn't have tall grass, for example, because it would hide the selection circles that appeared under *Eternity*'s main characters. Short grass would allow the player to better keep track of his or her party. Another rule: floors had to be as flat as possible. Maps with different levels of elevation were particularly tricky. You'd usually start from the south or west section of a screen and move north or east, so each map had to escalate accordingly. If you walked into a room and there was a set of stairs going upwards to the south, it would feel disorienting, like you'd just walked into an M. C. Escher painting.

In the months following the Kickstarter, the ever-expanding *Project Eternity* team battled over dozens of these creative decisions, reducing the scope and cutting features as they tried to figure out the optimal way to build each area of the game. "For a game, especially with the 'fun factor,' you don't really get it until you start playing it and seeing it," said Brennecke. "You [think]: 'There's something that doesn't feel right. What doesn't feel right about this game?' That's where Josh and I come in and we sit down and we really analyze what is actually wrong with this."

After building a few technical prototypes, the team's first major goal was to hit "vertical slice"—a small chunk of the video game designed to resemble the final product in as many ways as possible. During traditional, publisher-funded development, it was important for a vertical slice to look impressive, because if the publisher didn't approve, the studio wouldn't get paid. "When you're focusing on a publisher, a lot of the times you'll just do things the wrong way [on purpose]," said Bobby Null, the lead level designer. "It's smoke and mirrors, hacking stuff in and trying to impress the publisher so they'll keep paying the bills." But with *Eternity*, the team didn't have to fool anyone. The checks were already deposited. They could approach their vertical slice in what they liked to call the "right" way, drawing models and designing areas using the same methods that they would then use to make the final game, which helped save time and money.

There was no big publisher demanding progress reports, but Obsidian did feel obligated to offer regular updates to the 74,000 Kickstarter backers who had funded *Eternity*. The upside of talking to fans was that they could be open and honest without worrying about a publisher's iron-tight PR strategy. The downside was that they had to be open and honest *all the time*.

Every week or two, the Obsidian team would put out a new update filled with details on what they'd been doing, sharing extravagant concept art and snappy chunks of sample dialogue. Some of these updates were incredibly in-depth, including photos of spreadsheets (spreadsheets!) and extensive explanations of systems like combat and character building. That meant getting instant feedback, which could be tough to handle. "You grow a thick skin pretty fast," said Kaz Aruga, a concept artist.

Eternity's developers, like most of the people who make games, were used to developing in isolation, getting feedback from the outside world only when they released a new trailer or wandered around a trade show. With the Kickstarter approach, they'd get criticism in real time, which could help make the game better in a way that just hadn't happened on previous projects. Josh Sawyer, who read the Kickstarter backer forums nearly every day, would constantly read and absorb fan feedback, to the point where he scrapped an entire system they'd planned after seeing a backer's compelling explanation for why it shouldn't be in the game. (That system, item durability, would've been tedious and boring, Sawyer said.)

Some backers were outspoken and demanding, even asking for refunds when they didn't like how *Eternity* was shaping up. Others were energetic, constructive, and supportive. A couple even sent packages to Obsidian full of treats. "It was actually really cool," said Darren Monahan, one of Obsidian's co-owners. "It felt like we had maybe three hundred or four hundred other people working on the game who weren't really working on the game."

Toward the middle of 2013, the *Eternity* team finished the vertical slice and shifted from preproduction to production, the phase in which they would build the bulk of the game. The artists had grown familiar with the tools and pipelines; Josh Sawyer and the other designers had laid out systems like spellcasting and crafting; and the programmers had finished up fundamental features like movement, combat, and inventory management. The level designers had built outlines and sketches for most of the areas. But the game was still very much behind schedule.

The biggest problem was *Project Eternity*'s story, which was coming together far more slowly than anyone on the team had expected. Sawyer and Brennecke had entrusted the main narrative to Eric Fenstermaker, a writer who had been at Obsidian since 2005. What made things complicated was that Fenstermaker was also the lead narrative designer on *South Park: The Stick of Truth*, a game that was going through a publisher change and its own development hurdles. *Eternity* was shipping later, so *South Park* became the priority.

Fenstermaker had come up with some high-level ideas for *Eternity*, and the team had already established a lot of the background lore, but it was clear they needed help to finish all of the story and dialogue. In November 2013 the team brought in Carrie Patel, a published novelist with no previous video game experience, to be *Eternity*'s first full-time writer. "Narrative being a little late to the party was [a challenge]," Patel said. "The way the story was assembled was: there were a bunch of treatments put together by different people in preproduction, and the result was trying to take the best of all of those and assemble them into a story. It created some challenges that we might not have had if we said, 'Let's just write the story and figure it out.'"

Patel found the transition to video games fascinating. Writing a video game was a totally different experience than writing a novel, in which a story moved in one linear direction. A game like *Eternity* would force writers to look at their stories less like roads and more like trees, where different players moved along different branches. Almost every conversation in *Eternity* allowed players to choose what to say, and the story had to account for each possibility. Late in the game, for example, the player had to decide which of the world's gods to support on their quest to track down the villainous priest Thaos. Patel and the rest of the writing team had to dream up dialogue for each deity's scenario, knowing that each player might see only one of them.

At the end of 2013, Obsidian decided to put out a teaser trailer to give the world a taste of what it had been building. Adam Brennecke sat down and started editing the trailer, while the concept artist Kaz Aruga was tasked with designing the logo. For Aruga, another industry newcomer who had worked on *Star Wars* cartoons before coming to *Eternity*, this was a terrifying prospect. He'd been working at Obsidian for less than a year, yet now he had to come up with one of the most important parts of the game, the image that would be plastered across *Eternity* and all of its marketing materials for years to come.

It was grueling. Every day, Aruga would get different bits of feedback from different department leads at Obsidian. Often these items of feedback would contradict one another, leaving Aruga wondering how he could possibly make everyone happy. "I was in the pressure cooker," he said. "That was a learning experience."

It took more than one hundred different sketches before Aruga finally came up with a logo that pleased the whole team.

On December 10, 2013, Brandon Adler, the production lead, posted an update on Kickstarter. "Through the hard work of the *Project Eternity* team we are proud to present our first in-game teaser trailer," he wrote. The trailer zipped between snippets of gameplay, to the accompaniment of epic choral chanting. Wizards flung flames at giant spiders. An ogre slammed his hammer down on a party of adventurers. A massive dragon spat fireballs. At the end, Aruga's logo appeared: towering onyx pillars flanking the project's official new name, *Pillars of Eternity*.

People were thrilled. This *Pillars of Eternity* game looked right out of the early 2000s, resembling *Baldur's Gate* and all those other old Infinity Engine games that people had missed so much over the past decade, but the graphics were sharper and prettier. "Oh my gosh!" wrote one backer. "The indoor scenes look absolutely amazing!" wrote another. "And, you know, the outdoor ones too."

Exhilarated at the positive reactions, the *Eternity* team entered 2014 feeling like the project had momentum, though the workload in front of them was intimidating. Brennecke's schedule had them on track for a November 2014 release, and there was still a great deal of game left to be finished. Even without a fancy 3-D world, *Pillars of Eternity* had grown humongous, thanks mostly to Josh Sawyer's edict that they ship with 150 maps.

On many games, once the schedule starts feeling too tight, the producers might look to cut features or areas that don't seem critical. But with *Pillars of Eternity*, Adam Brennecke had a unique problem: Obsidian had already promised many of those features to fans. During the Kickstarter, the developers had made a big show out of having a huge, fifteen-level optional dungeon that they now had to construct, no matter how many late nights it would take. And then there was that second big city.

Obsidian had already finished the first city, Defiance Bay, and it looked fantastic. It was complex, layered, and pivotal to the story. And now, after the developers had gone through the convoluted process of designing and modeling Defiance Bay's various districts, the thought of building a second city was making them all queasy. "Everybody said, 'I wish we hadn't done that,'" said Feargus Urquhart. "Ultimately it was not necessary."

"Even more districts of the one big city probably would've been easier," said Josh Sawyer. "And pacingwise, you go through all of Defiance Bay, then you do a bunch of wilderness areas and here's another city. It's like, 'Dude, this is act three, please get me the fuck out of here.'" Still, they'd made the commitment. The second city had to be there, and so they built Twin Elms, knowing that if they didn't deliver on every feature they'd promised in the Kickstarter, fans would feel betrayed.

In May 2014, Obsidian had to switch its focus again. It had struck a deal with the game publisher Paradox to help out with PR and marketing, and as part of that deal, the team had to go to E3, an annual video game trade show where developers converge to show off their hot new projects. Having a presence at gaming's annual mecca would be huge for *Pillars of Eternity*, but it also meant the team would have to spend weeks working on a demo that was functional and polished enough to pass for the final game.

The team's leaders decided to limit their E3 demo to closed-door sessions, with Obsidian's developers controlling the mouse, rather than put it on the show floor for everyone to play. This way, there'd be no risk of players running into bugs or crashes if they clicked on the wrong thing. Adam Brennecke also decided that the demo would comprise a chunk of the game that they needed to work on anyway. "My policy for E3 and for vertical slice is, it has to be something that's going to ship in the game, so the work is not wasted," said Brennecke. "I've been on a lot of projects where you do an E3 demo that has nothing to do with the game. [We think], 'Why are we doing this? It's such a waste of time.'"

Brennecke determined that they'd show off the first half hour of the game, in which the main character of *Pillars of Eternity* is traveling through a forest with a caravan of strangers. Enemies ambush the caravan, and the protagonist is sent fleeing through a nearby maze of caves, where he or she defeats monsters, darts through traps, and stumbles upon a group of cultists performing a disturbing ritual. The section had some story, some combat, and a cliffhanger ending—in other words, it was the perfect demo. "I [said], 'Let's just polish the shit out of it,'" Brennecke said. "None of this time is going to be wasted at all. It's the beginning of the game that needs the most polish, so let's polish the crap out of it.'"*

When E3 rolled around, Brennecke and crew spent three straight days in a small, hot booth, repeating a series of scripted talking points every half hour to groups of journalists. The monotony paid off with great press coverage. Reporters—especially those who had played and loved the likes of *Baldur's Gate*—were immediately sold on *Pillars of Eternity*'s potential. Wrote one previewer, on the website *PCWorld*, "I have no doubt this game will be great, provided Obsidian can avoid its typical pitfalls—bugs, terminated questlines, et cetera."

After E3 the *Pillars* team had to build yet another big public version of the game: the backer beta. Brennecke and Sawyer wanted to make *Pillars of Eternity* playable to the public at Gamescom, a German trade show where tens of thousands of

---

* "Polish," in video game parlance, generally refers to bug-fixing, fine-tuning, and all the other fiddly little acts that make games feel smooth and fun to play.

European gamers gathered every year. They thought it might be unfair to let Gamescom attendees play the game before the people who had funded it, so the *Pillars* team decided they'd give the demo to their Kickstarter backers at the same time. That meant they had a hard deadline: August 18, 2014.

The two months after E3 were a haze of long hours—crunch time—as the team spent evening after evening at the office, trying to finish up everything they needed for the backer beta. As August 18 drew closer, Adam Brennecke realized that the game wasn't in great shape, and sure enough, when Obsidian released the *Pillars* beta to Kickstarter backers, there was immediate criticism. "We got a lot of negative first impressions because it was so buggy, unfortunately," Brennecke said. "I think [the beta] needed another month to bake before we shipped it." Item descriptions were missing. Combat balance felt off. Character models would disappear when a player moved his party into a dungeon. Players were happy with the general themes and core mechanics, but the beta was so unstable, it left a sour first taste.

By September 2014, it had dawned on most of the *Pillars of Eternity* team that shipping that year would be difficult. It wasn't just the backer beta; the whole game needed more work. Obsidian needed to polish, to optimize, to spend more time zapping bugs and making sure that every area of the game felt both interesting and fun to play. "Everyone's looking at each other: 'No. We're not even near this. We're just not there yet,'" said Justin Bell, the audio director. "You have to be able to play from the beginning of the game all the way to the end and feel like it's a total experience, and that just was not even close to being the case."

Adam Brennecke and Josh Sawyer asked Feargus Urquhart for a meeting. Over lunch at the Cheesecake Factory, one of Urquhart's favorite haunts, Brennecke and Sawyer explained that trying to release the game in November would be a disaster. The team needed more time. Yes, they were out of Kickstarter money and would now have to dip into Obsidian's own funds, but for a game like *Pillars of Eternity*—Obsidian's most important game to date—the extra investment felt necessary. Urquhart argued against it, but Brennecke and Sawyer were persistent. In their minds, the choice was already made.

"Feargus sat Josh and me down," Brennecke said. "He said, 'If this game does not come out in March, you guys are both gone after this project.'"

Recalling the pressure, Brennecke could only laugh. "OK, we'll get it done."

One common theme in video game development is that everything tends to come together at the last minute. There's just something about those final hours. In the last months and weeks of a game's development, chaos reigns supreme as team members scramble to polish, playtest, and fit in all the last-minute features they can think to add. Then, suddenly, something clicks. It might be the visual effects, or the audio cues, or the optimization that gets a game's frame rate as stable as possible. Usually, it's all of the above: a single holy moment when a game's disparate parts coalesce into something that finally feels complete.

During that final stretch, the entire *Pillars of Eternity* team crunched nonstop to get the game out the door. Zapping bugs was particularly difficult thanks to the sheer size of the game. Obsidian's quality assurance testers had to play through all of *Pillars*, which could take upward of seventy or eighty hours, as they tried to break the game as much as possible. They knew it would be impossible to find and fix every bug. The programmers would have to do the best they could for now, then work overtime once the game had shipped and players started sending in their own reports.* Obsidian didn't need to worry about consoles—*Pillars of Eternity* was solely a computer game—but optimizing the game to run on as many different types of computers as possible became a big challenge. "We were having a lot of memory issues," said Brennecke. "The game would run out of memory a lot, so we had to figure out how to get the game stable and running on most machines." Delaying the game to March 2015 would ultimately gobble up an extra $1.5 million of the studio's money, according to Urquhart, but it was the right move. The extra time—combined with extended crunch for everyone on the *Pillars* team—led to a far more polished video game.

On March 26, 2015, Obsidian released *Pillars of Eternity*. Critics loved it. "It's the most captivating, rewarding RPG I've played on a PC in years," wrote one reviewer.† Outside of their Kickstarter backers, Obsidian sold over 700,000 copies of *Pillars* in the game's first year, exceeding most of their expectations and ensuring that a sequel would be possible right away. "The thing that was cool about this project is that it was a passion project for everyone," said Justin Bell. "And it was because of that history with *Stormlands*. It emerged out of the ashes of this really crappy event in Obsidian's history. And everyone was super, über-passionate about making something as special as they possibly could, through the sheer force of their own will."

Development on *Pillars of Eternity* didn't end once the game

---

* One particularly malicious and random bug, discovered in the days after *Pillars of Eternity* launched, would wipe an entire character's stats if a player double-clicked on an item before equipping it. Said Josh Sawyer: "Sometimes when a game ships, you see a bug and you go, 'How in the world did that possibly get through?'"

† Andy Kelly, "Pillars of Eternity Review," *PC Gamer,* March 26, 2015.

shipped, though. In the following months, the team would keep patching bugs and later release a two-part expansion, *The White March*. Sawyer kept working on balance patches for a year after launch, tweaking attributes and class abilities in response to fans' feedback. And the team kept interacting with backers on Kickstarter, keeping them up to date on patches and other projects Obsidian was working on. "Because eighty thousand people or so said they wanted this, and they gave us a new life, we were extremely respectful of that. It was really meaningful for them to give us this much money," said Rob Nesler. "That was sort of a purity in this whole thing that I really hope we can do again."

For just under $6 million, Obsidian had made one of 2015's best RPGs, a game that would go on to win several awards and help secure Obsidian's future as an independent studio. The company had staved off catastrophe. And it had built an intellectual property that was finally its own, with rights and royalties going to Obsidian itself rather than some big publisher. (Paradox, the publisher that helped with marketing, distribution, and localization, did not own any of the rights to *Pillars of Eternity*.) As the team passed around drinks during a lavish launch party at a Costa Mesa nightclub, Urquhart spoke to the crowd, telling them how proud and relieved he felt. Nearly three years ago to the day, he'd had to lay off dozens of employees, but now they could celebrate. Their gambles had paid off. They'd won. After years of uncertainty and dependence on other companies, Obsidian could finally stand on its own.

In the summer of 2016, when I visited Obsidian's offices for this book, its staff were preparing to launch a crowdfunding campaign for the sequel to *Pillars of Eternity*. At their offices, I watched an early version of the trailer, which showcased a giant god destroying the stronghold of Caed Nua, an area that fans of the first game knew well. I listened to Obsidian's developers argue and try to find common ground over the direction of the sequel and how they would approach a second campaign. Rather than Kickstarter, they'd decided to put this one on Fig, a crowdfunding site that Feargus Urquhart had helped create.

Obsidian wanted to return to crowdfunding not just to supplement the profits they'd made off the first *Pillars*, but also to maintain the spirit of an active community. As annoying as backers could be sometimes, *Pillars of Eternity*'s developers had enjoyed interacting with fans and getting instant feedback to their work. For *Pillars of Eternity II*, they wanted to take the same approach, even if they didn't anticipate getting the same kind of wild crowdfunding success. "While we can ask for money again," Urquhart told me, "we don't expect people to come out in the same levels."

Six months later, on January 26, 2017, Obsidian launched their Fig for *Pillars of Eternity II* with a goal of $1.1 million. They were funded in twenty-two hours and fifty-seven minutes. At the end of the campaign they'd raised $4,407,598, nearly half a million more than the first *Pillars*. This time, they didn't promise a second city.

Obsidian hadn't yet solved all its money issues. Not long after launching the Fig, the studio announced that its partnership with Mail.Ru had ended on the tank game *Armored Warfare* and it had to lay off some staff on that team. But for Feargus Urquhart and his team of developers, figuring out how to finance their very own video game was, somehow, no longer a problem.

2

■ ■ ■ ■ ■ ■ ■ ■ ■ ■ ■

UNCHARTED 4

Video games, like any works of art, are reflections of their creators. *The Legend of Zelda* spawned from Shigeru Miyamoto's memories of childhood spelunking. *Doom* came out of a *Dungeons & Dragons* campaign in which John Romero and John Carmack allowed their fictional world to become overrun by demons. And *Uncharted 4*, the final entry in the *Indiana Jones*–style action-adventure series starring the rogueish Nathan Drake, is the story of a man who spends way too much time at work.

Naughty Dog, the development studio behind *Uncharted*, shares more than a pair of initials with its stubbled protagonist. In game industry circles, Naughty Dog has two distinct reputations. One is that its staff are the best of the best, not just at telling top-notch stories, but also at making games so eye-poppingly gorgeous, competitors publicly wonder just what kind of dark magic the studio employs. The other is that they embrace crunch. To develop games like *Uncharted* and *The Last of Us*, Naughty Dog's employees worked endless hours, staying at the office as late as 2:00 or 3:00 a.m. during extended, hellish periods of overtime that popped up before each major development milestone. All game studios crunch, but few are as known for going all-out as Naughty Dog.

At the start of *Uncharted 4*, Nathan Drake has given up his life of high-octane treasure-hunting and settled into a mundane routine, spending his evenings eating noodles and playing video games with his wife, Elena. It's quickly made clear, through a memorable scene in which you, as Drake, shoot a toy pistol at targets in the attic, that he misses the adrenaline rush of his former career. When Drake's brother resurfaces after a many-years-long absence, it's only a matter of time before Drake is sucked into a new treasure hunt. Then he starts lying. And gambling with his life. As Drake grapples with the reality that he's addicted to the thrill of danger, he risks alienating Elena for good. *Uncharted 4* tells the story of a secret pirate society hidden out of history's view. But it also explores something more universal: How do you follow your dreams without destroying your relationships?

"Your life's passion sometimes isn't in line with your life's love," Neil Druckmann, the codirector of *Uncharted 4*, said. "And sometimes those things are in conflict. In games, especially, a lot of people enter the game industry because of how much they love this medium, and, for us, how much we feel like we could push it and dedicate our lives to it to a large degree. But at times, if you're not careful, it can become destructive to your personal life. So there was a lot of really personal experience to draw from."

You might think, after the accumulated lessons and experience of three other *Uncharted* games, that for Naughty Dog, *Uncharted 4* would have been a walk in the park. But between a director change, a major reboot, a compressed schedule, and months of crunch, making *Uncharted 4* felt more like a hike up Mount Kilimanjaro. Put another way: One of the series' running jokes is that whenever Nathan Drake jumps onto a roof or cliff, it's probably going to collapse. Toward the end of *Uncharted 4*'s development, everyone at Naughty Dog could relate.

The first *Uncharted* was an unusual move for Naughty Dog. Founded in 1984 by two childhood friends, Jason Rubin and Andy Gavin, the studio spent nearly two decades making plat-formers like *Crash Bandicoot* and *Jak & Daxter*, both of which turned into iconic franchises on Sony's PlayStation.* In 2001, Sony bought Naughty Dog, and a few years later it charged the studio with making a game for the new PlayStation 3. Under the veteran director Amy Hennig, Naughty Dog started a project completely different from anything it had done before: a pulp adventure game, inspired by the globe-trotting escapades of *Indiana Jones*. Players, controlling Nathan Drake, would hunt treasure and solve puzzles across the world.

It was an ambitious move. For game developers, making a new intellectual property is always more difficult than devel-oping a sequel, because there's no foundation to build on. And working on a brand-new platform—especially one like the PS3, with its unfamiliar "Cell" architecture—would make things even more complicated.† The studio had hired several talented new staff members who had Hollywood background but little experi-

---

* A platformer is a genre of game in which your primary action is jumping over obstacles. Think *Super Mario Bros.* Or *Super Plumber Adventure.*

† Thanks to the unusual way it handled data, the PlayStation 3's Cell processor was famously difficult for engineers to work with. Various developers criticized this architecture in the years following the PS3's launch, including Valve's CEO, Gabe Newell, who called it "a waste of everybody's time" in a 2007 interview with *Edge* magazine. (Three years later, perhaps as a mea culpa, Newell showed up at Sony's E3 press conference to announce that *Portal 2* was coming to PS3.)

ence developing games, which led to further hiccups as the rest of Naughty Dog tried to walk the newcomers through the nuances of making graphics run in real time.

During particularly rough days on *Uncharted*, Bruce Straley, the art director, would walk over to the design department and trade complaints with his colleagues there. Straley, who had been making games since the 1990s, was frustrated with *Uncharted*'s development and needed an outlet. Soon he was taking regular lunches with some of the designers, including an Israeli-born twentysomething named Neil Druckmann, who had started at Naughty Dog as a programming intern just a couple of years earlier. Druckmann, a rising star at the studio with dark hair and olive skin, had a stubborn streak and a head for storytelling. Although he was credited only as a designer on *Uncharted*, Druckmann wound up helping Hennig write the game's script as well.

Straley and Druckmann quickly became friends. They exchanged design ideas, commiserated about office politics, and analyzed the games they'd been playing, trying to figure out what made each level click. "We started playing games at home online, so we were still talking to each other and kicking around stuff even in multiplayer games," Straley said. "That's where the work relationship started forming."

Uncharted came out in 2007. Shortly afterward, Naughty Dog bumped Straley up to game director (alongside Amy Hennig, who was creative director), giving him more control over the design of *Uncharted 2*, which shipped in 2009. Then, as the bulk of Naughty Dog moved to *Uncharted 3*, Straley and Druckmann broke off from the *Uncharted* team to try something new. In November 2011, when *Uncharted 3* hit store shelves, work was under way on Straley and Druckmann's first project as codirectors, a postapocalyptic adventure called *The Last of Us*.

It was a wild departure from the *Uncharted* series. Where

Uncharted took after *Tintin*, *The Last of Us* would feel more like Cormac McCarthy's *The Road*. Where the *Uncharted* games were breezy and funny, *The Last of Us* would open with a soldier shooting and killing the main character's twelve-year-old daughter. But the goal wasn't just to make people cry. Straley and Druckmann watched movies like *No Country for Old Men* and wondered why so many video games had the subtlety of a sledgehammer. Why, they thought, couldn't their characters leave some thoughts unsaid? In *The Last of Us*, the disease-infected zombies and ruined roads of America would exist only to serve the story of their two main characters. Every scene and encounter would deepen the relationship between Joel, a grizzled mercenary, and Ellie, a teenage girl who becomes his proxy daughter as they travel. Where other games might have gone for the jugular—"Wow, Ellie, you sure do fill the emotional void left by my dead daughter!"—*The Last of Us* trusted players to fill in the blanks themselves.

Of course, it's easier to decide that you want to tell a subtle story than it is to—you know—tell a subtle story. For the second time in a decade, Bruce Straley and Neil Druckmann discovered that starting a new intellectual property from scratch could be an excruciating process. And up until the very end, they thought *The Last of Us* would be a disaster. It was "the hardest project that I'd ever worked on in my life," Straley said. He and Druckmann battled constantly as they tried to figure out how to balance poignant emotional beats with vicious zombie shoot-outs. They struggled with everything from the cover system to the story's finale. Focus testers would suggest that they add more video game–y elements— boss battles, ultrapowerful weapons, special enemy classes—but Straley and Druckmann stuck with their vision, even as early testers warned them that reviews might be mediocre.

Reviews were not mediocre. In June 2013, when *The Last of Us* came out, fans and critics wouldn't stop raving. It was the most successful game in Naughty Dog's history, turning Straley and Druckmann into game development rock stars and ensuring that they'd be project leads at Naughty Dog for as long as they wanted to be.

During those same years, from 2011 to 2014, Amy Hennig spent her days working with a small team on *Uncharted 4*. They had some ideas for how to switch things up. They wanted to add vehicles, for one. Maybe a grappling hook. And, most surprisingly, they wanted to have Nathan Drake go half the game without picking up a gun. Critics had called out previous *Uncharted* games for the dissonance between their stories, in which Drake is an amiable, fun-loving hero, and their gameplay, in which Drake can murder thousands of enemy soldiers without missing a beat. Hennig and her team thought it might be an interesting twist for Drake to stick to melee for a while, to show that the puckish adventurer could change his ways.

Uncharted 4, as Hennig envisioned it, would introduce the world to Nathan Drake's old partner, Sam. We hadn't seen Sam in previous *Uncharted* games, because for fifteen years Nathan had thought he was dead, left behind during a Panamanian prison escape gone awry. In Hennig's version of *Uncharted 4*, Sam would be one of the main villains, bitter toward Nathan for leaving him to die. Over the course of the story, as Nathan tried to pull away from his roots as a treasure hunter, the player would find out that he and Sam were actually brothers. Eventually they'd heal their relationship and unify against the game's real antagonist, a nasty thief named Rafe (voiced by the actor Alan Tudyk) who had served time with Sam in prison.

But *Uncharted 4* was struggling. Naughty Dog's vision of itself as a two-team studio, able to develop two different games simultaneously, turned out to be too idealistic. Throughout 2012 and 2013, the *Last of Us* team needed to dragoon more and more of *Uncharted 4*'s developers, leaving Hennig with just a skeleton staff. "We were hoping that we'd have two completely staffed teams," said Naughty Dog's copresident, Evan Wells. "They'd just sort of leapfrogged each other, and we just couldn't hire enough talent fast enough to keep up with the demands of the game's expansions in terms of expectations of scope. At best we maybe got to one and a half, or probably more like one and a quarter teams."

At the beginning of 2014, as Neil Druckmann and Bruce Straley finished up work on an expansion for *The Last of Us* called *Left Behind*, the studio went into emergency mode, calling several meetings in an attempt to diagnose the problems with *Uncharted 4*.

There are conflicting perspectives on what happened next. Some say the *Uncharted 4* team didn't get the staff and resources it needed to survive, because *The Last of Us* and *Left Behind* had vacuumed up so much of Naughty Dog's attention. Others say that Amy Hennig had trouble making decisions and that the nascent game wasn't shaping up very well. Some who were working on *Uncharted 4* wished that there was a more cohesive direction. Others thought it was perfectly understandable, considering how small the *Uncharted 4* staff was, that the game hadn't coalesced yet.

One part of the story is indisputable, however: in March 2014, after meeting with Naughty Dog's copresidents, Wells and Christophe Balestra, Amy Hennig exited the studio and didn't come back. Hennig's creative partner Justin Richmond left shortly afterward, as did a few other veterans who had worked closely with Hennig. "It's something that happens at different levels," said Wells. "It happened to happen at a fairly high level. But we have turnover for various reasons throughout the studio. And Amy's a friend of mine—I really miss her and I wish her well—but things weren't working out. So we went our separate ways, and we had to pick up the pieces."

The day after Hennig's departure, the gaming website *IGN*

reported, citing anonymous sources, that Neil Druckmann and Bruce Straley had pushed her out. In public comments afterward, Naughty Dog's leadership vehemently disputed that account, calling it "unprofessionally misreported." The studio didn't elaborate further, and Hennig remained quiet about what had gone down. "It was hurtful to get those rumors published out there, because we saw our employees' names being attached to that when they weren't involved in that process at all," Wells later told me.

But several people who have worked for Naughty Dog say Druckmann and Straley stopped seeing eye-to-eye with Hennig, and that they had fundamental disagreements on where to take the *Uncharted* series. When Hennig left, she signed a nondisparagement agreement with the studio that would prevent both her and Naughty Dog from making negative public comments about what had happened, according to people familiar with the arrangement. (Hennig declined to be interviewed for this book.)

Immediately after Hennig's departure, Evan Wells and Christophe Balestra called Neil Druckmann and Bruce Straley into a meeting to tell them that she was gone. Straley felt what he later described as "a sinking feeling in my gut" as he realized what they were about to say next. "I think I said, 'So what does this mean? Who's heading up *Uncharted 4*?'" Straley said. "And that's where [they said], kind of nervously, 'That's where you come in.'" After the massive critical and commercial success of *The Last of Us*, Druckmann and Straley were the studio's golden boys. And now they had to make a decision: Did they want to spend the next year of their lives with Nathan Drake?

It wasn't an easy question to answer. The directing pair had thought they were done with *Uncharted* for good. Both Druckmann and Straley wanted to work on other games—they'd been playing around with prototypes for a sequel to *The Last of Us*—and Straley in particular was feeling burned out. "I had just worked on one of the hardest projects—*the* hardest project that I'd ever worked on in my life with *The Last of Us*," Straley said. He wanted to spend the next few months relaxing, prototyping, and brainstorming without the stress of immutable deadlines. Moving immediately to *Uncharted 4*, which had been in production for over two years and was scheduled to ship just a year later, in 2015, would be like running a marathon and then hopping over to the Summer Olympics.

But what other choice did they have?

"*Uncharted 4* needed help," said Straley. "It was in a bad state in regards to the lines of communication, the pipeline, what people were doing. And it didn't feel like it was making the positive forward progress it needed. . . . So how did I feel? Not great? It's not a great position to be in, but I also believe in the Naughty Dog name. I believe in the team." In Straley's mind, he and Druckmann could maybe come on board for a few months, steer everyone toward a single direction, and then hop off to work on other projects, letting other design leads take the wheel once the ship was moving.

Druckmann and Straley said they'd do it on one condition: they needed full creative control. They weren't interested in finishing the story that Hennig had started, and while they'd try to salvage some of the characters (like Sam and Rafe) and environments (big areas in Scotland and Madagascar), they'd also have to throw out a lot of work that *Uncharted 4*'s team had done so far. They would need to scrap a great deal of cut scenes, voicework, and animation, which the studio had spent millions of dollars developing. They wanted to recast the major roles, which would mean ditching Alan Tudyk and other voice actors who had already recorded lines. Would Naughty Dog really be OK with that?

Yes, said Wells and Balestra. Do it.

Right away, Druckmann and Straley made a decision that they

thought might court controversy: *Uncharted 4* would be the last *Uncharted* game, or at least the last one starring Nathan Drake. The studio had been mulling this option under Hennig, but now it was official. "We looked at the previous games," said Druckmann. "We looked at the arcs, looked at where Nathan Drake was at, what kind of stories are still left to tell, and the only one that came to our mind was the final one—how do we take him out?"

It was a move that few other studios could pull off. What self-respecting video game publisher would put an end to a lucrative series just when it was at its peak? As it turned out, Sony would. Years of success had afforded Naughty Dog the cachet to do whatever it wanted to do, even if that meant saying goodbye to Nathan Drake for good. (Plus, Sony could always make more *Uncharted* games with other characters.)

Uncharted 4 had already been in development for roughly two years. But because Straley and Druckmann were changing so much of what Hennig had done, it felt to the two directors like they were starting from scratch. "It was daunting," said Straley. "We couldn't take what was there, because that was part of the problem. There was a breakdown both in the gameplay and the story side of things. Both sides needed a lot of work. It was red alert, all-systems-go, panic, freak-out, 'How the hell are we going to do this?' mode. After being burnt out on *The Last of Us*, and crunching there."

The directing pair talked often about "feeding the beast," a term they'd picked up from the Pixar book *Creativity, Inc.* that referred to a creative team's insatiable hunger for work. With *The Last of Us* done, there were now nearly two hundred people working on *Uncharted 4*, and they all needed things to do. As soon as Straley and Druckmann took over, they had to make fast decisions. Yes, they were keeping Scotland and Madagascar. Yes, there would still be a prison flashback. The directing pair met with the leads in each department—art, design, programming, and so forth—to ensure that their teams still had work to do every day, despite the turmoil.

"It was really stressful," said Druckmann. "Sometimes you feel like you don't have the proper time to consider choices, and you just have to make those choices and say, well if we get them eighty percent right, then we'll be better off than trying to take the time to get them one hundred percent right, because meanwhile the team is just sitting idly by, waiting for that section."

Many at Naughty Dog were frazzled by these sudden changes, especially those who had been working on *Uncharted 4* since the beginning. Although it helped to hear that Straley and Druckmann wanted to maintain as much of their work as possible, the thought of losing years' worth of progress was nauseating to some on the staff. "Each decision was sometimes a stab in the heart," said Jeremy Yates, a lead animator. "Awww, I can't believe we're cutting this thing that me or someone else had spent literally months working out. It was definitely a hard transition, but every time you do it, if you're honest and you look back at it, then you know what, that was the right decision. This is a better game because of it. It's more focused, more clear."

"The transition went relatively well [and] quickly," said Tate Mosesian, a lead environment artist. "They had a plan, a clear plan, and they expressed it to the team. It instilled confidence. As sad as it was to see the team that had such a long history with the franchise leaving, [we could] see the future and the light at the end of the tunnel."

Over the next few weeks, Straley and Druckmann sat in a conference room and stared at index cards, trying to craft a new version of *Uncharted 4*'s story. They'd decided to keep Nathan Drake's brother, Sam, but they wanted to make him less of a villain. Instead, he'd serve as a temptation, as the catalyst that got Nathan Drake out of domesticity and back to his treasure-hunting ways. They kept the antagonist Rafe, too, writing him as a rich, spoiled brat who was fueled by jealousy for Drake's success. During this process, Straley and Druckmann brought in a rotation of designers and cowriters, both to help plot the story and so they'd get a feel for who could replace them as directors when they eventually left the project.

For weeks, they'd meet in the same room, assembling index cards on a big board that became their *Uncharted 4* bible. Each index card contained a story beat or scene idea—one midgame sequence, for example, was just called "epic chase"—and taken together, they told the game's entire narrative. "One thing we've never done here is sat down and written down an entire script for the whole game start to front," said Josh Scherr, a writer who sat with Straley and Druckmann for many of these meetings. "That never happens. And the reason it doesn't happen is because game design is an iterative process, and if you do that you're just asking for heartbreak when things inevitably change because the gameplay doesn't work out the way you expected it to, or you have a better idea further down the line, or anything like that. You have to be able to be flexible."

Over the next few weeks, Druckmann and Straley put together a two-hour presentation that outlined their vision for *Uncharted 4*, then showed it to the rest of Naughty Dog. This was a story about addiction, they explained. At the beginning of the game, Nathan Drake would be working a standard day job and living peacefully with his longtime partner, Elena, although it would soon become clear that Drake felt unsatisfied. Sam would reemerge shortly afterward, dragging Drake into a convoluted adventure that would take them all across the world, through massive gunfights and deadly car escapes on their hunt for a treasure-filled pirate city. There would be quiet flashbacks as well as the big, explosive set pieces that fans would expect from an *Uncharted* game. We'd see Drake lying to Elena. We'd see Elena find out. And it would all end in Libertalia, the buried city, where Drake and crew would discover that what they thought was a pirate utopia was actually a haven of greed and paranoia.

This would be a large game, bigger than anything Naughty Dog had done to date. And they were still hoping to release it in the fall of 2015, a year and a half away. For the developers, it was helpful to see the road map for what *Uncharted 4* would ultimately look like, but the amount of work was scary. "Some people were pretty burnt out already," said Druckmann. "They were a little afraid of how ambitious this looked. And it took a while to reinspire them to this vision."

It helped that E3 was coming up soon. Some game studios saw trade shows as distractions, existing only for pomp, sizzle, and marketing copy, but Naughty Dog viewed E3 as a valuable milestone. They'd usually get a prime spot at Sony's annual press conference, and it was common for dozens of staffers to trek from Naughty Dog's Santa Monica offices to the Los Angeles Convention Center to attend the show. Every year, Naughty Dog developers would leave E3 feeling newly energized by the reactions to whatever slick new games they were showing.

E3 in June 2014 was no exception. At the end of the PlayStation press conference, when Sony's president, Andrew House, came out for one final teaser and the words "Naughty Dog" appeared on-screen, fans erupted. In the teaser, a wounded Nathan Drake staggered through the jungle, as a voice-over conversation with his longtime partner Sully made it clear that this was going to be their final adventure. Then came the title: *Uncharted 4: A Thief's End.* Druckmann and Straley knew they weren't going to kill Nathan Drake, but they sure wanted fans to think they would, which led to all sorts of fun buzzing. As Naughty Dog's developers prepared for what they all knew would be a grueling development cycle, they scoured sites like YouTube and NeoGAF for fans' reactions, drawing energy from the hype.

Then they got back to work. Sony's big new fan convention, PlayStation Experience (PSX), would take place in December 2014. To help kick off the inaugural PSX, the Naughty Dog team had agreed to put together an extensive gameplay demo for *Uncharted 4*, which meant they had just a few months to figure out what a slice of the final game would look like.

Naughty Dog, like many experienced studios, bought into the mentality that there was no way to know whether part of a game was fun until you played it. So, like other studios, they would build little "gray box" areas—self-contained spaces where all the 3-D models looked monochromatic and ugly because there was no proper art attached—and test out their design ideas to see which ones felt good to play. For designers, the upside of this prototype period is that they can experiment with new ideas without risking much time or money, though the downside is that very few of those ideas will make the cut.

During the Amy Hennig years, the team had tinkered with all sorts of gray-box prototypes for *Uncharted 4*. There was a slide mechanic that would allow Drake to propel forward, *Mega Man*–style. There were cliff walls that Drake could shoot and then scale, using the bullet holes as handholds to climb his way up. There was a scene in an Italian auction house in which the player could switch among multiple characters, hunting for clues as Drake and crew attempted to steal an artifact without drawing suspicion from the crowd.

At one point, during a gala in the auction house, Drake and Elena would have to dance across a fancy ballroom, maneuvering closer and closer to the artifact as the player pressed buttons along with the beat of the music, sort of like you would in a rhythm game (think *Dance Dance Revolution*, minus the jumping). In theory, this dancing mechanic might have been awesome, but in practice, it wasn't really working. "When you talk about, 'OK let's have this fun dancing gameplay,' it doesn't really fit with anything else, and it has to be deep enough and fun enough by itself to exist," said Emilia Schatz, a lead designer. "So it went by the wayside." The team considered salvaging the dance mechanic for an early scene in which Drake and Elena are eating dinner at home—a scene that's meant to display the state of their relationship after the past three *Uncharted* games—but watching them dance felt too awkward.

"It wasn't really fun," said Schatz. "A big goal of the level was try to make the player relate to these people, show their relationship. Not a whole lot of people dance in their living room like that." Later, someone had the idea that Drake and Elena should instead play a video game, and after some quick license negotiations, Naughty Dog snuck in a copy of the original *Crash Bandicoot*, which made for a nice moment as the couple traded barbs over a PlayStation 1.

Bruce Straley and Neil Druckmann knew that many of those early gray-box prototypes didn't mesh with their vision. Straley believed in designing around a set of "core mechanics," or basic actions that a player would perform throughout the game, and limiting those mechanics to what was essential. "That was the thing that I needed to do more than anything, was pin down what the core mechanics were going to be," Straley said. "Sifting through the prototypes and seeing what was going to work and what wasn't. What scales. What works with something else." For Straley, harmony was key. Prototypes that might have seemed cool in a vacuum—like ballroom dancing—wouldn't always work nicely with the vibe of the game. "There was a bunch of what I call 'theorycraft,'" Straley said. "There's a bunch of ideas that work on paper or when you're talking over lunch, 'wouldn't it be cool if' moments, but when you try to test them in the game, they fall apart quickly."

In addition to the basics of *Uncharted*—jumping, climbing, shooting—Straley and his team picked out two main prototypes for their deck of core mechanics. One was the drivable truck, which had been cut and re-added to *Uncharted 4* several times over the years. The second was the rope and grappling hook, which Drake could use to climb heights and swing across gaps. This rope went through dozens of iterations. At one point, the player would have to pull it out, wind it up, and aim it at a specific location on the map, which Straley found cumbersome, so he and the designers kept iterating until they'd transformed it into a single button press—one you could use only when you were within range of a hookable location.* "We made it more accessible, and faster, and more reliable," said Straley. "The grappling hook that was there wasn't going to be able to couple with combat, because it was so arduous in its implementation that you couldn't do it quickly. It wasn't responsive. When you're getting shot at, you need things to be instant, otherwise you hate the game."

They also wanted to add more sneaking, which had worked in *The Last of Us,* and which the team thought might be a good fit for *Uncharted 4.* It made more sense for Nathan Drake to creep around environments, scoping out enemies and taking them out one by one, than it did for him to go on a rampage with his machine gun out. But there were a lot of questions to answer. What would a typical level layout look like? How open

---

* In game design, even a question as simple as "How do you know when you can use the grappling hook?" can lead to all sorts of complicated discussions. Although Naughty Dog's designers were originally averse to putting an icon on the screen to indicate that you could use the rope—they hated user interface (UI) elements that felt too video gamey—they eventually relented. "People just start spamming the button everywhere if there's no icon," said Kurt Margenau, a lead designer. "Can I rope to that? Nope, can't rope to that."

would each area be? Would Drake be able to sneak up behind enemies and take them down? What sort of tools would he have for distracting or eliminating guards without getting caught? Many of the levels that the *Uncharted 4* team had already built were designed according to the early notion that Drake wouldn't be able to use guns, which Straley and Druckmann had abandoned. As the team prepared for PlayStation Experience, where they'd show off *Uncharted 4*'s gameplay for the first time, they needed to make a lot of big changes.

There was a more pressing question, though: Were Neil Druckmann and Bruce Straley going to direct the whole game? Moving directly from the grueling development of *The Last of Us* to production on *Uncharted 4* had felt, as Erick Pangilinan, one of the two art directors, described it, "like you just came from Afghanistan and then you've heard about Iraq." Both Druckmann and Straley were feeling drained. "Our initial idea was that we were going to come on and mentor people into game director and creative director positions, and we were going to back off," said Straley. "It wasn't going to be our project at all." Maybe then they'd take a long vacation, or spend their days on less stressful work, like the prototype experiments they'd wanted to make way back when *The Last of Us* shipped.

That never happened. As PSX 2014 drew closer and closer, it began dawning on Straley that they couldn't leave. The developers that he and Druckmann had eyed for leadership roles weren't stepping up, for various reasons, and Straley felt like he and Druckmann were the only ones in a position to fine-tune many of the game's core mechanics. Climbing, for example. Several designers had spent months developing an elaborate climbing system that involved a mixture of slippery and unstable handholds. On its own it was lifelike and fun to play with, but in the larger context of *Uncharted 4*, when you were trying to leap from cliff to cliff in the middle of an intense combat encounter, there was nothing more frustrating than slipping to your death because you pressed the wrong button. So Straley put it on hold, much to the dismay of the designers who had spent months scaling climbing walls and researching hard-core mountaineering techniques.

"That was probably a turning point for me," said Straley. "I had to make those kinds of decisions to craft a demo that would create hype and energy and create a section of the game that people [would] see the game for what it is. . . . That had to be that demo, and it had to be myself and Neil making those decisions. That was the turning point I think for me, which got me to say, 'OK, I've just gotta see this through.'"

By PSX, two things were clear. One was that *Uncharted 4* was not going to come out in 2015. Naughty Dog's bosses had hashed it out with Sony and agreed to a new ship date in March 2016. Even that date seemed dicey to some members of the team, but at least they'd have another full year to finish the game.

The second thing that became clear at the end of 2014 was that Neil Druckmann and Bruce Straley were stuck with Nathan Drake until the very end.

Most game projects have a single lead. Whether they call themselves "creative director" (à la Josh Sawyer on *Pillars of Eternity*) or "executive producer" (like *Dragon Age: Inquisition*'s Mark Darrah, whom we'll meet in chapter 6), the one thing they all have in common is that they always get the final call. In the case of creative conflicts and disagreements, the buck stops with that single guy or gal. (In the video game industry, sadly, the former has severely outnumbered the latter.)

Druckmann and Straley were an exception. On both *The Last of Us* and *Uncharted 4* they served as codirectors, which made for an unusual dynamic. They complemented each other well—Druckmann loved writing dialogue and working with actors, while Straley spent most of his days helping the team hone gameplay mechanics—but they still squabbled as much as you might expect from two ambitious, creative, alpha-type personalities. "It's like a real relationship, like a marriage," said Druckmann. "Like Drake and Elena. Who's Drake and who's Elena? I'm probably Elena."

Since their days swapping complaints over lunch during the first *Uncharted*, the directing pair had developed a unique rapport. "We try to work by just being as honest as we can with each other," Druckmann said. "When we don't like something, we let each other know right away. When a big decision is being made for the game, we make sure to loop each other in, so no one is surprised by something."

When they disagreed on something, they'd each rank how they felt about it, on a scale from one to ten. If Druckmann was at an eight but Straley said he was just a three, Druckmann would get his way. But if they were both in the nines or tens? "Then we have to go in one of the offices, close the door, and be like, 'OK, why do you feel so strongly about this?'" said Druckmann. "Sometimes those can become hours-long conversations, until we finally both get on the same page and say, 'OK, this is what it should be.' Where we end up might be not even those two choices that we started out with."

It was an unorthodox management style, which was something of a tradition at the studio behind *Uncharted*. Naughty Dog's staff liked to emphasize that, unlike other game studios, they didn't have producers. Nobody's job was simply to manage the schedule or coordinate people's work, the role a producer would fill at other companies. Instead, everyone at Naughty Dog was expected to manage him- or herself. At another studio, a programmer who had an idea for a feature might be expected to book a request with a producer before talking to his colleagues. At Naughty Dog, the programmer could just get up, walk across the room, and tell the designers what he thought.

This freedom could lead to chaos, like the time Druckmann and Straley each designed different versions of the same scene, costing themselves weeks of work because they hadn't talked for a few days. With dedicated producers, that might not have happened. But to Naughty Dog's management, this approach was best. "The amount of time you lose to those rare occasions is far surpassed by the amount of efficiency you get," said Evan Wells. "Rather than calling a meeting and discussing the validity of it and then getting approval and putting on a schedule. All that lost time is just not worth it."*

Perhaps because of this unusual structure, Naughty Dog took an abnormal approach to detail. If you look closely at any scene in *Uncharted 4*, you'll spot something extraordinary—the creases on Drake's shirt; the stitches on his buttons; the way he pulls the leather strap over his head when he equips a rifle. These details didn't pop up out of the ether. They emerged from a studio full of people obsessive enough to add them to the game, even if it meant staying at the office until 3:00 a.m. "We'll take it as far as we possibly can," said Phil Kovats, the audio lead. "We all wanted to make sure that, because this was the last Nathan Drake game we were making, it was going to go out with as much stuff as we possibly could."

---

* During the development of *Uncharted 4*, as Naughty Dog grew bigger than it had ever been, Christophe Balestra, one of the company's copresidents, designed a computer program called Tasker that helped the studio organize daily tasks and fixes. "When we were trying to finalize a level, there were these checklists that you need to fix every single one of these problems, and that ended up being crucial," said Anthony Newman, a lead designer.

Nowhere was this more evident than their E3 demo, which became the *Uncharted 4* team's biggest milestone as they entered 2015, following a successful showcase at PSX. This would be the "epic chase" from their index cards—a wild ride through the streets of a fictional city in Madagascar, showcasing the game's complicated new vehicles and explosions.

In the weeks leading up to E3, *Uncharted 4*'s artists and designers worked nonstop hours trying to make everything click. Once a week (and sometimes once a day) the whole E3 team would meet up in the theater to go over their progress. They'd review which mechanics weren't working, which effects required more polish, and which nonplayer character needed to be moved slightly to the left. "Basically everyone working on the sequence was in there, so the communication was very direct," said Anthony Newman, a lead designer. "Bruce and Neil would just play and [say], 'This is a problem, this is a problem, this is a problem.'"

The demo started off in a crowded marketplace, where Drake and Sully would get caught in a shoot-out, gun down a few mercenaries, and then flee from an armored tank. Climbing their way across buildings, they'd escape to a car they'd parked nearby. This would be an opportunity for Naughty Dog to dazzle fans with the new mechanics—*Hey look, an* Uncharted *game with driving in it!*—and as the demo progressed, Drake and Sully would skid frantically through a tangle of old streets, crashing through fences and fruit stands as they tried to shake off enemy vehicles. Then they'd find Sam, caught up in his own epic chase as the bad guys tried to run him off the road. Drake would tell Sully to take the wheel, then hurl up his rope and attach it to a passing truck, dangling next to the highway at sixty miles per hour.

Waylon Brinck, a technical art director, recalled spending hours and hours fashioning the grain sacks in the marketplace so that when mercenaries shot them, it'd look like they were deflating. Then the grain would start spraying out and forming neatly organized piles on the floor. It was the type of detail that some studios might see as an unnecessary waste of resources, but to Naughty Dog's artists, the extra hours were worth it. "That is a moment now that people remember, and it wasn't an accident," said Tate Mosesian, a lead environment artist. "From a gameplay standpoint, we try to hit these moments or these beats that help draw the player through, and oftentimes it's something as big as a collapsing building or as small as a grain sack deflating."

The demo looked incredible, and it turned out to be one of the most exciting parts of *Uncharted 4*, so in retrospect, maybe Naughty Dog shouldn't have shown so much of it at E3. But that's a question all developers have to ask: How do you convince fans that your game will be awesome without spoiling the best parts? "We were worried that we might be showing the coolest set piece in the game," said Druckmann. "But it felt like it was the one that was furthest along. . . . At the same time, you're trying to balance that with getting people excited and making sure you're going to sell this game."

That approach was effective, and Naughty Dog's staff were again inspired by the positive E3 buzz, which they'd need to get through the coming months. By July 2015, everyone on *Uncharted 4* was already feeling burned out. The weeks leading up to E3 had been a mess of late nights and weekends at the office, and everyone knew that the schedule wasn't going to get easier. Many of them had gone from crunching on *The Last of Us* to crunching on *Uncharted*, with few breaks or vacations in between. "I think everybody off of that demo was just [thinking]: Do whatever you can do to just show up every day and just get the job done," said Bruce Straley. "I know that there were feelings inside where I was [thinking], 'How do you muster the courage and the will just to keep going?' Because nobody else is. Everybody on the team, it felt like, was running on fumes."

Straley lived on the east side of Los Angeles, so it took him at least an hour to get to Naughty Dog's Santa Monica office. During *Uncharted 4*'s crunch, when he wanted to arrive at work first thing in the morning and stay until 2:00 or 3:00 a.m., he began worrying that the drive was excessively time consuming and maybe even kind of dangerous, so he rented a second apartment near the office. He'd stay there during the week, then go home on weekends. "It was close enough that I wasn't really a danger to my life, and I could come in early without traffic," he said.

And so Bruce Straley, who had once thought that he'd be on *Uncharted 4* for only a few months, now found himself living at a strange new apartment just to finish the game.

The word "crunch" calls to mind the gnashing of teeth, which is a fitting descriptor for the feeling of working endless hours on a big-budget video game. For decades, extended overtime has been a ubiquitous practice, seen as integral to game development as buttons or computers. It's also been controversial. Some argue that crunch represents failure of leadership and project management—that for employees to spend months working fourteen-hour days, usually for no extra money, is unconscionable. Others wonder how games can be made without it.

"We crunch on all of our games for sure," said Naughty Dog's copresident Evan Wells. "It's never mandated. We never say, 'OK, it's six days a week, OK, it's sixty hours a week.' We never [change] our forty-hour expectation or our core hours, which are ten thirty a.m. to six thirty p.m. . . . People put in a lot more hours, but it's based on their own fuel, how much they have in their tank." Of course, there was always a cascading effect: when one designer stayed late to finish a level, others would feel pressured to stay late, too. Every Naughty Dog employee knew that the company had certain standards of quality, and that hitting those standards would always mean putting in overtime. Besides, what self-respecting artist wouldn't want to milk every hour to make his or her work as good as possible?

"It's certainly a hot topic, and one that I don't want to dismiss as unimportant, but I feel that it's never going to go away," said Wells. "You can mitigate it, you can try to make it less impactful in the long term, make sure people have the chance to recuperate and recover from it, but I think it's the nature of an artistic endeavor, where there's no blueprint for making a game. You're constantly reinventing the product."

That was the biggest problem: reinventing the product. Even on the fourth entry in a series that Naughty Dog had been making for a decade, it was still impossible to plot out just how long everything would take. "The problem is, you couldn't task creativity," said Bruce Straley. "You can't task fun."

How could the designers know, without weeks of playtesting and iterating, whether the new stealth mechanics were worth keeping? How could the artists know, without weeks of optimization, whether those snazzy, beautiful environments would run at a proper frame rate? And how could the programmers know, until everything was finished, just how many bugs they'd have to mop up by the end of the game? At Naughty Dog, as at all game studios, the answer was always to estimate. And then, when those estimates invariably turned out to be too conservative, the answer was to crunch.

"To solve crunch, probably the best you could do is say: don't try to make Game of the Year," said Neil Druckmann. "Don't do that and you're good." Druckmann, like many veteran designers, viewed crunch as a complex issue. Naughty Dog was a studio full of perfectionists, he argued. Even if their managers tried to tell their employees to go home by 7:00 p.m., everyone on the team would fight to stay late and polish their game until the very last second. "With *Uncharted 4*, we tried even earlier than we'd ever done [to say] 'Here's the entire story, beginning to end, here are all the beats,'" Druckmann said. "And what we find is that instead of shrinking crunch, we just make a more ambitious game, and people work just as hard as the previous game. So we're still trying to figure out how to find that better work-life balance."

Erick Pangilinan's solution was to put in long hours every night—"I usually go home at two in the morning," he said—but never to work on weekends. "I'm very strict about that." Others sacrificed their health and well being for the sake of the project. One Naughty Dog designer later tweeted that he'd gained fifteen pounds during *Uncharted 4*'s final crunch. And some worried, during those last few months of 2015, that the game might never be finished. "The crunch at the end was probably the worst we've ever had," said Emilia Schatz. "It was honestly very unhealthy. We've done bad crunches before, but I never got the feeling we couldn't finish this project. Toward the end of *Uncharted 4*, you'd see other people in the hall and there'd be that look: 'I don't know how we're going to finish this. It just doesn't seem possible.'"

There was just so much work to do. They still had levels to finish, set pieces to tweak, art to polish. Catastrophes would occasionally impede their progress, like the time the studio's servers kept crashing because Naughty Dog was uploading hundreds of thousands of humongous asset files per day.* Even with the bulk of

---

* "It's not fun to debug those kinds of problems," said Christian Gyrling, a lead programmer. "At the center of all of our networking is the file server, and if you try to inspect what's going on, it's like taking a firehose to the face of information. And somewhere in that stream of information you have to deduce which machine is it that's causing things to go wrong."

the *Uncharted 4* team working extended hours for five days a week (if not six or seven), the finish line seemed miles away.

As more of the game came together, it became clearer which parts needed improvement, but it was difficult for team members to know what to prioritize. "There were a lot of leads meetings at the end where we were just reminding everybody, 'Perfect is the enemy of good,'" said the writer Josh Scherr. "You're polishing something that's at ninety-five percent while this thing over here at sixty percent needs a lot of love. So that was what made crunch hard, because [when] you'd get down into it, you'd have trouble seeing the forest for the trees."

In the last months of production, Neil Druckmann and Bruce Straley decided to cut one of the team's favorite set pieces, a sequence in Scotland during which Drake would climb a giant crane, then try to escape as it collapsed, fighting off enemies as he went. The designers had made an elaborate prototype for this crane sequence, and they all thought it'd be an exciting spectacle, but they just didn't have enough time to get it finished. "We had that all working in a prototype form," said Evan Wells. "But then just the sheer amount of polish it takes to take that prototype to completion . . . You hit FX, and sound, and animation. It hits every single department in so many ways, and it might take you a few days to put that prototype together, but it's going to take you a few months to really complete it."

Druckmann and Straley also started ramping up their focus tests. Participants in these tests—usually a diverse group of LA residents with varying amounts of gaming knowledge—would stroll into the office and assemble at a row of desks, each equipped with a pair of headphones and the latest build of *Uncharted 4*. As these testers played through multihour sessions of the game, faces glowing from the pale blue light of their monitors, Naughty Dog's designers could watch everything. They could gauge testers' physical reactions through a camera hooked up to the testing room, and see exactly what each tester was playing at any given time. Naughty Dog's designers could even annotate the footage, sticking in relevant notes like "died ten times here" or "face seemed bored."

During that final stretch, these focus tests became even more important to Druckmann and Straley. As *Uncharted 4* morphed from a collection of prototypes and gray-boxed levels into an actual game, the directing pair could start pinpointing big-picture problems like tone and pacing. After nearly two years with the game, Straley and Druckmann had lost all semblance of objectivity, which was why testers were so important. "They might not get certain mechanics," said Druckmann. "They might be lost for a while and lose all sense of pacing. They might be confused by the story and not pick up on certain nuances that you thought were pretty clear and wound up not being clear at all." Bits of individual feedback weren't that helpful—what if that bored tester was just having a bad day?—so instead, Naughty Dog's leads looked for trends. Were a lot of people getting stuck on the same encounter? Did everyone think one section of the game was too boring?

"The first few focus tests are really humbling," said Druckmann. "Bruce and I now get excited by them because it just puts everything into perspective. They're brutal and you feel defeated, and a lot of times the designers hate watching levels being played and they're pulling their hair out. 'No, turn around, the handhold is right there, what're you doing?' And you can't do anything."

By the end of 2015, *Uncharted 4*'s deadline looked terrifying. To hit its scheduled release date of March 18, 2016, Naughty Dog would have to submit its gold master in mid-February.* Fixing all

---

* A "gold master," or release-to-manufacturing build, is the version of a game that's sent to the publisher (in *Uncharted 4*'s case, Sony) to produce discs and distribute the game to store shelves.

the highest-priority bugs by February felt like it'd be an impossible task, and everyone at the studio was consumed by anxiety that the team might not get it done. "You always have that sinking feeling in your stomach, that you just don't know how it's going to pan out," said Evan Wells. "You just know, well, we've got three months. And you start looking back at old bug reports that you had in your last game. 'Three months out, how many bugs did we have? How many were [A-level bugs]?' How many were we fixing every day?' OK, we were fixing fifty a day, so we start running all those calculations like, 'All right, we're not totally screwed.'"

It helped that they were running focus tests every week. As they fixed more and more bugs, which ranged from major ("game crashes every time you shoot in the wrong place") to minor ("it's hard to tell that you should jump here"), the focus testers would give the game higher and higher ratings. And Naughty Dog's staff kept pushing themselves, working longer hours than they'd ever worked before to get *Uncharted 4* in shape. Problem was, they were running out of time.

"We started saying, 'OK, well, we're going to have to patch,'" said Wells, referring to the increasingly common practice of releasing a "day one" patch to fix bugs that have made it into the gold master. "When we put something on a disc, it's not going to be a completely polished, Naughty Dog experience, and we're going to use those three to four weeks between printing the discs and it landing on the shelves to put that polish in." In other words, anyone who bought *Uncharted 4* and played it without connecting

---

* When a game company is fixing bugs, the development team goes through a process called "triage" in which it labels each error based on how significant it is. The highest, "A" or "1" level bugs, are usually the ones that break a game entirely. If you find a bug in a video game, the developers have probably found it too—it's just a "C" level bug that nobody had the time (or inclination) to fix before launch.

to the Internet and downloading the patch would get an inferior version of the game. "We started trying to prepare Sony: 'OK, we're going to have a pretty big day-one patch,'" said Wells. "Things are not looking too smooth. We're going to come in pretty hot."

As Sony's engineers started preparing to expedite the patching process for Naughty Dog, word started getting around the company that *Uncharted 4* was on shaky ground. And eventually, the news reached the very top.

One night in December 2015, Wells was sitting in his office and playing through a build of *Uncharted 4* when he heard his cell phone buzzing and saw a San Francisco number he didn't recognize. It was Shawn Layden, the president of Sony Computer Entertainment America and the man in charge of all of Sony's development studios. Layden told Wells he had heard *Uncharted 4* needed more time. Then he dropped a megaton.

"[Layden said], 'So what if you guys had a ship date in April?'" said Wells. "And I [said], 'That would be so awesome.' So he said, 'You've got it. That'll be your new ship date.'"

Instead of hitting gold master by mid-February, they now had until March 18 to fine-tune, fix bugs, and ensure that *Uncharted 4* felt polished even without a day-one patch. It was, as Wells would later describe it to staff, a "Hanukkah miracle."

A little while later, a representative of Sony's Europe division came to Wells and asked if Naughty Dog could actually submit the gold master on March 15. Sony was overhauling some manufacturing plants in Europe, the representative said, and in order to print *Uncharted 4* on time, they'd need the game three days earlier.

"And we [said], 'Really?'" said Wells. "Those three days are huge for us. We really need that time." But Sony Europe had no flexibility. If Naughty Dog needed those extra three days, then they'd need to delay *Uncharted 4* again, this time to May. "It was so frustrating," said Wells, "because we were just [thinking], 'Oh my gosh, people are going to blame us again,' and it was not our fault this time. It was not our fault. But hopefully people have forgotten about that, and just remember the game."

Getting all that extra time was indeed a Hanukkah miracle for Naughty Dog, but every extra week of development meant an extra week of crunch. It was rough, said Bruce Straley, "especially when your brain and your body are saying, 'I've got just enough for one more week,' and you're like, 'Wait, I've got three more weeks?' That was really hard at the end." But they made it happen, thanks largely to Naughty Dog's collective experience and knowledge of when to stop working on a game. "It's the old phrase, 'Art is never finished, it's just abandoned,'" said Straley. "The game is just shipped. That's our motto in that last quarter of production; I walk around just saying, 'Ship it' to everything I see. 'Ship it. Ship that.'"

And on May 10, 2016, they shipped it. *Uncharted 4* sold 2.7 million copies in a week, received stellar reviews, and was, without a doubt, the most impressive-looking photorealistic game that had been made at that point. In the coming weeks and months, a number of burnt-out developers left Naughty Dog. Others took long vacations and started prototyping for their next two projects: the *Uncharted 4* expansion pack, which later morphed into a stand-alone game called *Uncharted: The Lost Legacy*; and a sequel to *The Last of Us*, officially titled *The Last of Us: Part II*.

For these projects, Naughty Dog would have proper preproduction time, and the team wouldn't have to jump right into the fire. "That's why you see everybody happy now," said Bruce Straley when I visited the studio in October 2016. "They're going home at decent hours, coming in at decent hours. They go surfing in the morning. They're going to the gym at lunch." But just a couple of months later, after Naughty Dog announced both games, news came out that Straley wasn't returning to codirect *The Last of Us:*

Part II. The official word at the studio was that he was taking a long sabbatical.

At the end of *Uncharted 4*, after nearly losing their lives in Libertalia but somehow escaping, Nathan and Elena realize that maybe they need a little bit of adventure after all. Maybe there is a way to find a balance between their work and their personal lives. Elena explains that she's just purchased the salvage company where Nathan works, and that she wants the two of them to go on journeys together—minus the near-death experiences. From now on, they'll be hunting for artifacts in a far more legal capacity. "It's not going to be easy, you know," says Nathan. Elena stares at him for half a second before responding. "Nothing worthwhile is."

3

STARDEW VALLEY

Amber Hageman was selling pretzels when she first met Eric Barone. She was about to finish high school, he had just started college, and they both worked at the Auburn Supermall, just south of Seattle. Barone was handsome, with dark eyes and a shy smile, and Hageman was drawn to his passion for making things—little games, musical albums, drawings. Soon, the two started dating. They discovered that they both loved *Harvest Moon*, a series of serene Japanese games that put players in charge of restoring and maintaining their own farms. During dates, Hageman and Barone would sit side by side and play *Harvest Moon: Back to Nature* on PlayStation, passing the controller back and forth as they befriended villagers and planted cabbages for profit.

By 2011 the couple had grown serious and started living together at Barone's parents' house. Barone, who had just earned a degree in computer science from the University of Washington Tacoma, was struggling to find an entry-level programming job. "I was just kind of nervous and awkward," Barone said. "I didn't do well at the interviews." As he scuffled around the house, applying for any job he could find, Barone started thinking, *Why not make a video game?* It'd be a good way to improve his programming skills, build some confidence, and maybe help him land a decent job. He'd tinkered with a few big projects before, like a Web-based clone of the action game *Bomberman*, but he hadn't completed any of them. This time, he told himself, he would finish whatever he started. He told Hageman he'd be done in six months or so, just in time for a new wave of job openings.

Barone's vision was well defined, if unglamorous: he wanted to make his own version of *Harvest Moon*. The original series had grown less popular thanks to a trademark dispute and a sharp decline in quality, and it was tough to find a modern game that evoked the tranquility of the original farm simulators.* "I just wanted to play another game that was exactly like the first two *Harvest Moon*s, but just with different people and a different map," he said. "I could've played that forever, different iterations of that same thing. But it didn't exist. So I just figured, why hasn't anyone made this? I'm sure there's a lot of people out there who want to play this kind of game."

He also wanted to do it solo. Most video games are built by teams of dozens of people, each of whom specializes in fields like art, programming, design, or music. Some games, like *Uncharted 4*, employ staffs in the hundreds and use work from outsourced artists across the world. Even small independent developers usually rely on contractors and third-party game engines. Eric Barone, a self-proclaimed introvert, had a different plan. He wanted

---

* The publisher Natsume had owned and distributed the *Harvest Moon* games since the franchise first started, but in 2014, the series' longtime developer, Marvelous, decided to split off from Natsume and publish its own games. Natsume still owned the *Harvest Moon* name, so Marvelous released its farming games under the title *Story of Seasons*. Meanwhile, Natsume developed its own line of new *Harvest Moon* games. Yes, it's all very confusing.

to write every line of dialogue, draw every piece of art, and compose every song on the soundtrack by himself. He even planned to program the game from scratch, eschewing established engines, because he wanted to see if he could. Without collaborators, he wouldn't have to talk through ideas or wait for approval to get things done. He could make decisions based on what he—and only he—thought was best.

Barone planned to put his little *Harvest Moon* clone on the Xbox Live Indie Games (XBLIG) marketplace, a popular storefront for independent developers. Unlike other digital distributors in 2011, XBLIG had few restrictions and would feature games from any developer—even a college graduate with no experience. "My idea at the time was it would take a few months, maybe five, six months, and then I would put it on XBLIG, and sell it for a couple bucks, and maybe make a thousand dollars off it or something," Barone said. "And it would be a good experience and then I would move on."

Using a rudimentary set of tools called Microsoft XNA, Barone started writing basic code that would let his characters move around on two-dimensional screens. Then he ripped some sprites from Super Nintendo (SNES) games and taught himself how to animate them, manually drawing different frames to create the illusion that the images were moving.* "There was no methodology at all," Barone said. "It was just completely haphazard and scrappy and random."

By the end of 2011, Barone had given up on finding a day job. He'd become obsessed with this new project, which he called *Sprout Valley* (later retitled *Stardew Valley*), and he wanted to finish it before joining the grind of full-time employment. The

---

* In video game parlance, a sprite is a two-dimensional image representing a character or object on the screen.

premise of *Stardew Valley* was simple. You'd create a character and customize his or her appearance, from hair to pants color. At the beginning of the game, your hero would quit his menial office job at a giant corporation to go live in an idyllic village called Pelican Town, where he'd inherited an old, disheveled farm from his grandfather. As this hero, you'd be tasked with growing crops, cultivating relationships with the villagers, and restoring Pelican Town to its former glory. Barone wanted to make it feel satisfying to do mundane chores like planting seeds and clearing debris in *Stardew Valley*, just as it was in *Harvest Moon*. You'd even be able to team up in online multiplayer with your friends.

Barone's daily habits rarely changed: every morning he'd wake up, make coffee, and stumble over to his computer, where he'd spend anywhere between eight and fifteen hours plugging away at the game. When Hageman got home, they'd eat dinner and go for a walk, where they would talk about *Stardew Valley* and mull over important questions like "Which characters should you be able to marry?" and "Which characters should you be able to kiss?"

Living rent free helped Barone get away with this pattern for a few months, but soon the couple wanted to move out on their own. They'd saved some money while living at Barone's parents' house, which helped, but it couldn't pay for everything, especially if they wanted to live in downtown Seattle. Barone's video game project brought in a whopping zero dollars a month, so Hageman, who was finishing up her undergraduate degree, had to support them both. Once they found a place, she started juggling two jobs, working as a coffee shop barista on the weekends and a caretaker after school. "We just kind of lived a humble life and it worked for us," Hageman said. As the months went by, they settled into this routine: Barone worked on his video game; Hageman paid for food, expenses, and rent on their tiny studio apartment.

A less patient girlfriend might not have tolerated this arrangement, but Hageman didn't seem to mind it. "When we were living at home it wasn't as hard, and then when we moved out to Seattle, the reality of having to support him became more real, but it really wasn't a problem ever," she said. "He was working so much that it was impossible to be frustrated."

It was true: Barone was working a lot—but he wasn't working very efficiently. Because he was making *Stardew Valley* by himself, there was nobody to hold him accountable or force him to stick to a schedule. He had no employees or expenses. No producers were hovering behind his computer chair, telling him to stop overscoping and just ship the damn game. Any time Barone thought of a cool feature or an interesting character for players to befriend, he'd add it. Every week, the game grew exponentially bigger.

Of course, it's not very hard to distinguish between a game made by hundreds of people and a game made by one. The more realistic a video game looks—the higher the graphic fidelity, the more polygons in each 3-D model—the more likely it's the product of a humongous, expertly trained staff that can handle highly technical aspects of art and engineering. Games like *Uncharted 4* demanded massive teams (and tens of millions of dollars) because they needed to make people's eyes pop.

For Barone, sitting alone in his studio apartment, game development meant something else entirely. His game didn't have high-end 3-D graphics or a fully orchestral soundtrack. *Stardew Valley* used hand-drawn two-dimensional sprites and music that Barone composed himself with an inexpensive audio production program called Reason. Although Barone had little experience making games, he did know how to write music from years of playing in bands. (In high school, he'd wanted to be a professional musician.) He'd learned how to program in college, and he was gradually teaching himself how to draw the simplistic backgrounds and sprites that would make up *Stardew Valley*. By reading pixel art theory and watching guides on YouTube, Barone figured out how to compose each sprite by drawing individual pixels. He knew nothing about complicated video game lighting techniques, but he learned how to fake them, drawing semitransparent white circles that he'd place behind torches and candles to evoke the illusion that they were brightening rooms.

Where he really could've used help was scheduling. Some game developers set their project milestones based on what they think will take them the longest to make, while others build schedules around the demos they'll have to create for public events like E3. Eric Barone had a different approach: he made whatever he felt like making. One morning he might have been in the mood to compose the theme song, and then in the afternoon maybe he'd draw character portraits or obsess over fishing mechanics. On any given day, Barone might look at his 2-D sprites—which by now had graduated from SNES rip-offs to original pixel art—and decide they were all terrible and that he had to start over.

Hageman and other family members started regularly asking Barone when *Stardew Valley* would be done. *In a month or two*, he'd say. Two months later, they'd ask again. *Just another few months*, he'd say. As time went on, Barone kept extending the window. *Three more months. Six more months.* "Part of making a game by yourself, when you have no money and you have a girlfriend who wants to have a life together, is that you just have to get people to accept that you're going to do this, and not try to dissuade you from it," said Barone. "I had to convince everyone that they should believe in me. Part of that is, if I had just from the beginning said, 'Oh it's going to take five years,' I don't think anyone would've accepted that. I wasn't even really conscious of this, because it sounds really manipulative, but thinking back, I feel like maybe subconsciously I knew that I had to give it to them in little bits at a time. 'Oh, it'll take six months. It'll take a year. OK, two years.'"

In mid-2012, after nearly a year of working daily on *Stardew Valley*, Barone launched a website and started posting about the game on *Harvest Moon* fan forums, where there were plenty of people sharing his belief that the series had gone downhill. Those same people were instantly drawn to *Stardew Valley*. The game looked lively and colorful, like an undiscovered Super Nintendo game that someone had dug up after two decades and covered with a fresh coat of paint. The sprites were primitive, sure, but it was hard not to be charmed when you saw *Stardew Valley*'s jolly farmer pull a little white turnip out of the ground.

Fueled by the positive feedback, Barone started thinking about how he would get *Stardew Valley* into people's hands. He'd already ditched the Xbox in favor of the PC, which had a significantly bigger audience but was dominated by a single storefront: Steam, a massive network operated by the game publisher Valve. Indie game developers couldn't just slap their games on Steam and call it a day, though: they needed to get Valve's explicit approval.

This was a problem. Barone didn't know anyone at Valve. He didn't have any publishing contacts. He didn't even know anyone else who made video games.

Worried that nobody would even be able to discover the game he'd spent a year making, Barone searched the Internet and stumbled upon a new program that seemed promising: Steam Greenlight. With Greenlight, Valve crowdsourced its approval process, allowing fans to vote on the games they'd want to play. Games that hit a certain number of votes (a number that the famously secretive Valve kept quiet) would automatically get a spot in the store.

In September 2012, Barone put *Stardew Valley* on Steam Greenlight. "I thought that the game was basically done," Barone said. "I thought, 'Yeah, I could have a game ready within six months.'"

Shortly afterward, a British developer named Finn Brice approached Barone with a proposition. Brice, who ran a company called Chucklefish, was curious to see what *Stardew Valley* was all about. "Anyone could see the potential early on," Brice said. "A PC-platform *Harvest Moon* that was looking really good was immediately appealing." Barone e-mailed Brice a build of the game, and soon enough the whole Chucklefish office was gathering around Brice's desk to watch him play it. Parts of *Stardew Valley* were unfinished, and it would crash occasionally, but it charmed them all.

Finn Brice made Barone an offer: in exchange for 10 percent of profits, Chucklefish would serve as a de facto publisher for *Stardew Valley*. Chucklefish didn't have the scale and reach of big publishers like Electronic Arts (EA) and Activision, but it did have lawyers, PR people, and other staff who could help Barone with the more tedious aspects of game development. (You don't really know boredom until you've tried to read through a stack of trademark documents.)

Barone loved the thought of being associated with Chucklefish's space adventure game, *Starbound*, which had raised hundreds of thousands of dollars in preorders. He also learned that a bigger publisher would demand a much larger slice of the *Stardew Valley* revenue pie—probably closer to 50 or 60 percent—which made 10 percent seem like a solid deal. "So of course I decided to take that opportunity," Barone said.

On May 17, 2013, *Stardew Valley* earned enough votes to win approval on Steam Greenlight. Thrilled, Barone went to his website to send out an update to his ever-growing base of fans. "I will do my scientific best to get this game into your hands as soon as possible," he wrote, "without skimping on making it as fun and feature-rich as I can (within a reasonable time frame). I still can't give an exact release date, it is very hard to predict and I don't want to make an empty promise. However, you can be certain that I am working hard every day and making continual progress!"

A few more months. *Just a few more months.* As development continued, Barone kept repeating that mantra, even though his mind was wandering into dark places. He had started waking up in the mornings with the gnawing feeling that his game wasn't good enough. "I realized that it was crap," Barone said. "And I needed to do something better. Like, this wasn't going to be a big hit or anything." He started hacking *Stardew Valley* apart like an overzealous woodcarver, throwing out the features and code he'd spent months writing. "I thought at some point that I was almost done with the game," Barone said, "but then my mind changed and I thought, 'OK, this isn't ready. I'm not happy with this, I don't want to put my name on it.'"

In the following months, Barone remade all the sprites. He redrew the characters' portraits. He scrapped core features, like the procedurally generated section of the game's underground mine, and he rewrote large pieces of code to make *Stardew Valley* run more smoothly. After nearly two years spent working on the game, Barone felt like he had improved all his game development skills. He was now a better pixel artist than he had been when he started, he was a better programmer, he was better at visual effects, and he was better at designing audio. Why not take the time to improve all those parts of the game?

"He redid the portraits probably fifteen times or some crazy amount like that," said Amber Hageman. "Of course now in retrospect I can see that his art was improving a lot and it was totally worth it. . . . But at the time, he would be sitting and fiddling and changing one person for days and days and days, and I was like,

'Come on, it looks great, you don't have to worry about it.' He's kind of a perfectionist, and if he didn't get the right feeling about it, he would want to keep doing it."

Money was becoming tighter for the couple. They had eaten into most of their savings, and Hageman was still only working part time as she prepared to graduate from college. To help with the bills, Barone considered putting *Stardew Valley* on Early Access, a service that let Steam users pay for unfinished versions of games before their final release dates, but he got anxious at the thought of taking other people's money before his game was done. It'd be too much pressure. Instead he found a part-time job as an usher for the Paramount Theatre in downtown Seattle, working there a few extra hours every week so they wouldn't go broke.

Once a month, Barone would post an update on the *Stardew Valley* website, outlining new features (Fruit trees! Cows! Fertilizer!) and putting on an optimistic face for fans. By the end of 2013, Barone had hundreds of followers watching and leaving friendly comments on each of his blog posts. Yet his morale had tanked. For two years Barone had been in front of a computer every day by himself, developing and playtesting the same game over and over again. Seeds of anxiety had been germinating inside him, and they would sprout at the worst possible times.

"There were points when I was depressed and just thinking, 'What am I doing?'" Barone said. "I have a degree in computer science and I'm working a minimum-wage job as an usher at the theater. People would ask me, 'Do you do anything else?' And I [said], 'I'm making a video game.' I just felt embarrassed about it. They must have thought, 'Oh, this guy is a loser.'"

Some days Barone didn't work at all. He'd get up, put on some coffee, kiss his girlfriend goodbye, and then binge on eight-hour sessions of *Civilization* or old *Final Fantasy* games. When Hageman got home, Barone would click back to *Stardew Valley* so she wouldn't know he was goofing off. "I went through periods of extreme unproductivity," Barone said. "I would just be alt-tabbing and browsing Reddit and just not working." Maybe it was Barone's body trying to get him to take it easy—he hadn't taken off a weekend in two years.

"There were certainly points where he was super frustrated and hated the game," said Hageman. "But he never got to the point where he actually stopped working on it. He would hate the game for a day and work on it to try to make it better, and then the next week he'd be ecstatic about the game. That was just kind of his style."

Really, Barone needed a proper break. At the beginning of 2014, he saw Hageman playing with her brand-new tablet and got an idea. He'd put *Stardew Valley* on pause for a while and make a mobile game: something small and easy, that he could finish within a few weeks. For the next month Barone ignored *Stardew Valley* and started hacking together an Android game about a surfboarding purple pear. Players would have to use the touchscreen to guide the pear through obstacles and compete for the highest score. On March 6, 2014, Barone released *Air Pear* to little fanfare. "It made me realize that I don't want to be a mobile developer," Barone said. "I actually hate it."

Even if making the next *Candy Crush* wasn't Barone's ultimate destiny, the hiatus helped him zoom out a little bit. All those seven-day workweeks had been smothering him. He started taking more breaks from *Stardew Valley*, writing on his website (where fans had speculated that, because he hadn't updated in two months, he might be dead) that he was spending fewer marathon sessions on the project, "not only to enjoy life but also to make my time developing *Stardew* more productive (so that when I do sit down to work I am more focused)."

After she graduated from college, Amber Hageman started

working full time as a lab technician, which helped with their cash problems. (Later in 2015 she would start attending graduate school, where she would receive a regular stipend for her studies in plant biology.) Hageman didn't mind being the only breadwinner, but as she came home every day and saw how good *Stardew Valley* looked, she started pushing Barone to let go. "I would be frustrated," Hageman said. "Well, you know, you're sick of it—why don't you just release it?" By the end of the year, Barone's fans were asking the same thing. Where was *Stardew Valley*? Why couldn't they play it yet?

Writing on his blog in April 2015, Barone yet again addressed the question. "As soon as I know when the game is to be released, I'll announce it," he wrote. "I don't have any intention of being deceptive or secretive." He added that he didn't want to write down a date just to have to delay it, and he didn't want to build more hype for *Stardew Valley* until the game was ready.* "I've been working on *Stardew* for years and I want it to be released as much as anyone," Barone wrote. "However, I'm not willing to do that until the game is not only complete, but also in a state I'm happy with. It simply could not be released in its current form. . . . It's not a finished game yet. It's tantalizingly close to being a finished game, but it's also a huge project and I'm just one guy."

Being a solo developer came with two major challenges. The first was that everything took a very long time. Because he didn't

---

* When I first met Eric Barone in September 2016, we'd just seen the launch of one of the most hyped indie games in history, *No Man's Sky*. Slurping down pho noodles at a shop near his house, we had a long conversation about how that game had failed to deliver on its developers' promises. "You can make a bunch of money by creating hype based off just saying stuff, and it works," Barone said. "But it's just not my style. I don't even like hype at all. I don't want any hype. I would much rather create a great game, and I really truly believe that if you create the right game, and it's a really good game, it'll hype itself. It'll market itself."

have a strict schedule, Barone had a tendency to build 90 percent of a feature, get bored, and move on to something else. Although he'd been working on *Stardew Valley* for nearly four years, he still hadn't finished many of the game's core mechanics, like childbirth and marriage. And it sure was hard to get excited about coding an options menu. "I think that gave me a false impression that it was close, because when you just boot up the game and play it from the first day, it seems like you can do everything," Barone said. "But then if you actually look into it, everything needs a little more work." It would take months to revisit these incomplete features and finish them all.

The second major challenge was loneliness. For four years now, Barone had sat by himself at a computer, rarely talking to anyone but Amber Hageman. He had no coworkers with whom to bounce around ideas, nobody to meet for lunch and a kvetch session about the latest game industry trends. In exchange for complete creative control, he had to embrace solitude. "I think to be a solo developer you have to be someone who's OK with being by yourself a lot," Barone said. "And I'm that kind of person. I'm OK with it. But it's lonely, I have to admit. It's part of why I got that usher job, just so I could go out and interact with some other people sometimes."

Staring at the mountains and trees of *Stardew Valley*, Barone found himself again unable to tell whether his game was any good. It resembled *Harvest Moon*, sure. You could harvest crops and go on dates and hang out with cute people at the annual egg festival. But Barone had worked on the game for so long now, he found it impossible to judge the squishier parts. Was the writing good? The music? Were the portraits pretty enough, or should he redo them yet again? "That's another issue with being a solo developer," Barone said. "You lose all objectivity about your game. I had no idea when the game was fun. In fact I thought the game was garbage even up until a few days before release, I was like, 'This game sucks.'"

Others disagreed. In September 2015, a group of Chucklefish staffers went on Twitch and streamed themselves playing an hour of *Stardew Valley*. The game still wasn't finished, but it was close enough. They could show off the basics, guiding along their main character as she cleared debris off her farm and met the friendly residents of Pelican Town. Fans thought it looked great. "Looks and sounds awesome," wrote one commenter. "You really are a one-man army."

"It was becoming increasingly clear the closer we got that this was going to be a big deal," said Finn Brice. "Even with our faith in the project, it far surpassed what we were hoping for. And what we were hoping for was already several orders of magnitude higher than what Eric expected."

At the beginning of 2015, Barone had decided he wasn't going to add anything new to *Stardew Valley*. Instead, he said, he'd spend the rest of the year fixing bugs and tweaking small things to make the game feel more fun. It didn't take him very long to violate that rule. By November he'd added crops, crafting recipes, private bedrooms (that you could visit if you befriended their owners), a quest log, a traveling merchant, and a horse (that you wouldn't need to feed or care for, so as to keep things "stress free," Barone told fans).

Despite those late additions, the game was almost done—except for one key part. Barone had originally promised that *Stardew Valley* would come with both single-and multiplayer modes, but hooking up the multiplayer was taking far longer than he'd anticipated. As 2015 dwindled and winter started approaching in Seattle—where he and Hageman had ditched the cramped studio in favor of a modest house that they now shared with two other friends—it became clear that releasing the "complete" version of *Stardew Valley* might take another year.

Barone spent weeks trying to make a decision. It would feel crummy to release an incomplete game. But fans had been asking him for years when *Stardew Valley* would come out. Wasn't it time? Without multiplayer, the game might not sell as well, but he'd been working nonstop for four years. Like *Stardew Valley*'s silent protagonist, Barone had grown tired of the daily grind. "I was so sick of working on *Stardew Valley* that I just had to release it," Barone said. "I just reached this point where all of a sudden I [thought], 'OK, it's pretty much ready. I'm super sick of working on it. I don't want to work on it anymore.'"

On January 29, 2016, Barone announced the news: *Stardew Valley* would be out on February 26. It would cost $15. Barone had no idea how to launch a marketing campaign, but hey, that was why he'd agreed to give 10 percent of his profits to Chucklefish, whose PR people sent codes for *Stardew Valley* to journalists and Twitch streamers. Barone had been skeptical about streaming—"I was afraid that people would see it on Twitch before launch and then they'd feel like they'd already seen the game and they weren't going to buy it," he said—but early streams and videos generated more buzz for *Stardew Valley* than any press outlet. That month, it was one of the most popular games on Twitch, appearing on the streaming website's front page nearly every day.

During those final February weeks, Barone gave up all pretense of taking days off. He spent every waking hour sitting at his computer (or standing, thanks to a makeshift standing desk he'd created by putting his monitor on top of an empty Wii U box) and fixing bugs. Other than his roommates and a couple of friends he'd asked to check out the game, he had no testers. There was no QA team. He had to catch, document, and fix every bug on his own. "That was hellish," Barone said. "I didn't sleep for days." Early in the morning before his game was due to come out, while trying to fix a pesky last-minute localization error, Barone fell asleep standing at his desk.

On February 26, 2016, a drained Eric Barone launched *Stardew Valley*. His girlfriend and housemates, Jared and Rosie, had taken off work for the occasion, and they sat upstairs with Barone while the game went live. As they all cheered and celebrated, Barone stared at his Steam developer account. When he clicked over to the live chart, he could watch the numbers move in real time as people bought and began to play *Stardew Valley*. As soon as he opened the chart, he'd know whether or not his game was an immediate success.

At this point, Eric Barone had no idea what to expect. He'd felt burned out for a long time now, and even with his friends telling him the game was great, there was no predicting how the world would react to his little *Harvest Moon* clone. Would people buy it? Would they actually like it? What if nobody cared?

He opened the chart.

Six months later, on a warm Thursday afternoon in Seattle, Eric Barone hopped down the front steps of his apartment, carrying a box full of video game plushies and wondering how much he could fit in his car. Friday was the start of Penny Arcade Expo, or PAX, a gathering of geeks from across the globe. Tens of thousands would be crowding the show floor, hunting for cool new games to play, and Barone had booked a small booth to demonstrate *Stardew Valley*. It was his first convention ever, which was causing him some anxiety. He'd never even met another game developer, let alone potential fans of his work. What if they were awful?

Alongside two of his housemates (and me, visiting from New

York), Barone started packing his trunk with essentials: two small computer monitors, a homemade banner, a bag full of water bottles, some cheap pins, and stuffed toys from *Stardew Valley*. When we'd finished packing, Barone opened the front passenger's door and climbed to the driver's seat. The door had been broken for months, he said. The car, a hand-me-down, had belonged to his family for nearly twenty years. I asked if he planned to get the door fixed. He said he hadn't really thought about it.

It was a familiar, almost hackneyed scene: Independent game developer scores coveted spot at big conference, recruits housemates to help man the booth. If the developer is lucky, the weekend's press and exposure will lead to a few hundred new fans. For indies, that's a huge opportunity. Great word of mouth during shows like PAX can transform a small game into a huge success.

But Eric Barone didn't need any help. On that Thursday in Seattle, as he climbed across the front passenger's seat, *Stardew Valley* had already sold 1.5 million copies. Since he'd launched the game, it had grossed close to $21 million. Eric Barone, who was twenty-eight years old and couldn't open the front door of his car, had over $12 million in his bank account. And he still drove around town in a broken Toyota Camry. "People are asking me: When are you buying that sports car?" Barone said. "I don't need it. I don't know when that's going to change, you know? At some point I guess I'll probably buy a house, but I'm not in a rush. I don't really need luxuries. I know that doesn't make you happy."

For the next few days, standing in a cramped booth on the sixth floor of the Washington State Convention Center, Barone shook hands and signed autographs for the first time in his life, feeling like a genuine rock star. Fans came dressed up as *Stardew Valley* characters like the purple-haired Abigail and the suave

Gunther. Some people brought him art and homemade presents. Others shared personal stories about how playing *Stardew Valley* had gotten them through tough times. "I heard a lot of people thanking Eric in just these really sweet, heartfelt ways, and that was really nice for me to see," said Amber Hageman, who helped run things at the booth. "That was basically what I wanted. I wanted Eric's work to be appreciated and for other people to experience his music, writing, all these things I'd always admired and thought he was really good at. Getting to hear other people appreciate that and let him know, that was really cool to see."

The past year had been a blur for Eric Barone and Amber Hageman. After *Stardew Valley* launched, Barone watched it leap to the top of Steam's best-seller lists, selling tens of thousands of copies a day. He had thought the game might do well, but the final numbers were beyond expectations, which was simultaneously gratifying and terrifying for Barone. With success came pressure to keep making the game better. Now that more than five people had gotten their hands on the game, Barone had to spend all of his free time zapping the bugs that kept popping up. "It would be right as we were trying to go to sleep," said Hageman, "and he'd be freaking out like, 'OK, I just have to stay up and fix this,' and he'd be up the whole night."

It became a vicious cycle. Fans would submit bug reports, and Barone would release patches to fix those bugs, only to inadvertently trigger *more* bugs. Then he'd pull all-nighters trying to fix the new ones. This pattern went on for weeks. "I think success like that on your hands can be quite a shock," said Chucklefish's Finn Brice. "Suddenly you feel as if you owe a lot of people a lot of things."

What this success also meant—and what was still tough to internalize, six months later—was that Eric Barone was now a multimillionaire. You might not have guessed it from the modest house he shared with his girlfriend and housemates, or from the broken Toyota he drove around Seattle, but in half a year he had already made more money than most game developers see in their careers. Barone's previous life—working as an usher, relying on Hageman for income—felt like it had existed in another dimension. "Before the game came out, we had to budget for food and stuff," he said when I asked if he had done anything with his new-found riches. "Now I'll get a bottle of wine if I want it, or whatever. I don't worry about that." He paused to think for a few seconds. "I also bought health insurance, which I didn't have before."

Later, Barone would tell me that he bought a new computer.

"It was really just surreal, is how it felt at first," said Amber Hageman. "It's really abstract. Yeah, we have a lot of money suddenly, but it's all just numbers on a computer screen. . . . We've talked about how eventually we'll be able to get a house, which is cool. And the Sunday newspaper that always comes with a really fancy house magazine in it, we flip through that just for fun, because that's actually somehow possible now. We're not actually going to do that. It's just fun to look at."

In 2014, the *New Yorker* writer Simon Parkin published an article titled "The Guilt of the Video-Game Millionaires," examining the complicated emotions triggered by indie developers' financial successes. In the article, game makers like Rami Ismail, the designer of *Nuclear Throne*, and Davey Wreden, the creator of *The Stanley Parable*, described the litany of feelings that came with newfound wealth: depression, anxiety, guilt, creative paralysis, and so on. "The money has made relationships complicated," Edmund McMillen, the designer of the platformer *Super Meat*

Boy, told Parkin. "I'm just a guy who makes games. I'm an artist who likes to be alone. This success has artificially elevated me; it's caused jealousy, even hatred."

Eric Barone was caught in a similar emotional vortex. In the months after launching *Stardew Valley*, he felt overwhelmed with intense and sometimes paradoxical feelings. At first, as the numbers started climbing and he started getting calls from big companies like Sony and Valve, Barone started letting it get to his head. "I thought I was some kind of hotshot," he said. Microsoft took him out to fancy dinners. Nintendo invited him to tour its swanky headquarters in Redmond (a place so secretive that, to get in, you had to sign an NDA, a nondisclosure agreement, promising not to take any photos). "Everyone wanted something from me," Barone said. "Nintendo wants me to port the game to their consoles, and I think what they really want is an exclusive deal, but I'm not doing that."[*]

Yet insecurity kept creeping in. Barone felt like a tourist in a foreign country, trying to absorb decades' worth of gaming knowledge as publishers wined and dined him. He had always liked video games, but until now, he didn't know much about the culture surrounding them. "I was thrown into this crazy world all of a sudden," he said. "I went from being an absolute nobody to suddenly being thrust into this scene, which I felt like a total outsider from. . . . I'm just a guy who got lucky, and happened to make the right game at the right time."

Barone sunk deeper into his work, sacrificing sleep to keep cranking out patches for *Stardew Valley*. Then he started looking at his massive list of tasks, a list that included not just several patches full of new content, but the multiplayer mode he'd

---

[*] Barone would later announce ports of *Stardew Valley* for the PlayStation 4, the Xbox One, and the Nintendo Switch.

promised for years before the game launched. What bummed Barone out the most was that programming the multiplayer wouldn't offer any creative challenges. It was simply a matter of writing lines and lines of networking code, which he dreaded.

One morning, halfway through 2016, Eric Barone suddenly stopped working. He just couldn't do it anymore. After four and a half years of nonstop work, the thought of dedicating months of his life to *Stardew Valley*'s multiplayer mode was nauseating him. "I just felt completely burned out," he said. "I was doing so many interviews, and talking on the phone with people every single day and doing business deals, merchandise. It just got to me at some point." He called up Chucklefish and said he needed a break, and the publisher offered to put one of its own programmers on multiplayer, which Barone happily accepted.

It's normal, in game development, for staff at big companies to take long sabbaticals after shipping their games. When the crunch is over and they've made it out of the hellfire, game developers are generally entitled to take a month or two off to recharge. Barone hadn't done that in February when the game had launched, but over the summer, he decided it was time for a long break. He spent hours playing PC games and zoning out in front of the computer. He drank a lot. He smoked a lot of pot. He had started taking an herb called ashwagandha, which helped relieve stress and keep him energized, but even that couldn't get him motivated to spend much more time on *Stardew Valley*.

On August 6, 2016, Eric Barone wrote a new post on the *Stardew Valley* website. He wanted to update fans on the progress of his newest patch, 1.1, which was supposed to add new features and content to the game. "To be entirely honest," he wrote, "the main reason the update is taking so long is that I was feeling very burnt out for a while recently, and my productivity went way down. *Stardew Valley* has consumed nearly every waking moment of my life for almost five years now, and I think my brain demanded some time away from it."

Barone added that he'd spent the summer doing very little, and feeling awfully guilty about it. "In truth, I've always had ups and downs, periods of intense productivity and energy followed by periods of low motivation," he wrote. "I've been this way for as long as I can remember. This time around did seem a little worse than usual, but I reminded myself that with the success of *Stardew Valley*, my life got very weird very suddenly. It's probably normal to need some time to adjust. I'm not even sure if this recent funk was due to the sudden success, to my own volatile brain chemistry or simply a result of working too hard for too long without a break. Sometimes I forget that I am actually a human with the need to relax and have a little fun."

There wasn't much more time for relaxation, though. After PAX, Chucklefish told Barone that to hit the deadlines for the PS4 and Xbox One versions of *Stardew Valley*, he'd have to finish the 1.1 patch by the end of September. Barone again went into manic work mode, crunching for weeks to hit that deadline. Once he got there, burnout snuck up on him yet again, and the cycle continued.

In November 2016, as he kept working intermittently on *Stardew Valley*, Barone got an e-mail from a representative of the publisher NIS America asking if he'd like to meet a man named Yasuhiro Wada. Of course, Barone said. It would be crazy to pass up that kind of opportunity. Wada, a Japanese designer who'd been making games since the 1980s, was in Seattle promoting his new simulation game, *Birthdays the Beginning*. Before that, however, Wada had been best known for designing and directing a game about running your very own farm. He'd called it *Harvest Moon*.

Anxious and intimidated, Barone drove to the office space that NIS America had rented in downtown Seattle, knowing he was about to meet the man whose work had inspired him the most. "I was quite nervous about meeting him," Barone said. "But I figured I have to do this, because it makes for a great story if nothing else."

Barone and Wada shook hands and exchanged pleasantries, speaking to one another through Wada's Japanese-English translator. Barone said he'd brought his Super Nintendo cartridge of the original *Harvest Moon*, which Wada signed with a smile. They had dinner, drank beers, and played each other's games. "It was so surreal," Barone said. "Just to talk to this guy who made *Harvest Moon*. He was thirty when the original *Harvest Moon* came out and I was just a little kid playing it. And now I'm meeting the guy and talking to him about his development on that game, and he knows *Stardew Valley*."

Wada told Barone that he enjoyed playing *Stardew Valley*, and that he was thrilled to see how Barone had iterated on the genre he'd pioneered all those years ago. "He kind of got addicted to cleaning up his farm," said Barone. "He spent most of the time just chopping the grass with a scythe and chopping down trees."

Five years earlier, Barone had been living with his parents, flunking job interviews and trying to figure out what to do with his life. Now the creator of *Harvest Moon* was chopping trees in his best-selling video game. "Surreal" may have been an understatement.

In December 2016, nearly a year after *Stardew Valley* had launched, I called Barone to see how he was doing. We spoke about his meeting with Wada, about his manic work cycles, and about the glitches that he and Chucklefish had been running into with their console ports. He told me he was again sick of *Stardew Valley*, and that he was ready for something new.

I asked if he'd started planning his next game.

Yes, Barone said. He was thinking he might make a game about catching bugs.

I asked how long he thought it might take.

"I'm trying to be a little more realistic this time around," Barone said. "I'm hoping it takes two years."

4

DIABLO III

On May 15, 2012, hundreds of thousands of people across the world loaded up the Battle.net Internet client and slammed the launch button for *Diablo III*, a game that the developers at Blizzard had been making for nearly ten years. Fans had waited patiently for this moment, counting down the days until they could again click-click-click their way through demons in a hellish hodgepodge of gothic fantasy. But at 12:00 a.m. Pacific time on May 15, when *Diablo III* went live, anyone who tried to load the game found themselves greeted with a vague, frustrating message:

The servers are busy at this time. Please try again later. (Error 37)

After a decade of turbulent development, *Diablo III* had finally gone live, but nobody could play it. Some people gave up and went to bed. Others kept trying. An hour later:

The servers are busy at this time. Please try again later. (Error 37)

"Error 37" turned into a meme, mushrooming across Internet forums as fans vented their frustration. *Diablo* players had already been skeptical about Blizzard's decision to make *Diablo III* online only—a decision that cynics assumed was driven by fear of piracy—and these server issues nourished the belief that it had been a bad idea. It immediately occurred to fans that if they could play *Diablo III* offline, they would be fighting their way through New Tristram right now, not trying to figure out what Error 37 meant.

Over at Blizzard's campus in Irvine, California, a group of engineers and live-ops producers sat in their self-proclaimed "war room," stressing. *Diablo III* had outsold their wildest expectations, but their servers couldn't handle the flood of players trying to log into the game. Around 1:00 a.m. Pacific time Blizzard posted a brief message: "*Please note that due to a high volume of traffic, login and character creation may be slower than normal. . . . We hope to resolve these issues as soon as possible and appreciate your patience.*"

A few miles away, at the Irvine Spectrum outdoor mall, the rest of the *Diablo III* team had no idea that people couldn't play their game. They were busy partying. Hundreds of hard-core fans, dressed in spiky armor and carrying giant foam battle-axes, had come out for the official *Diablo III* launch event. As Blizzard's developers signed autographs and passed out swag to the crowd, they started to hear whispers about overloaded servers. Soon it became clear that this wasn't a standard launch hiccup.

"It really caught everybody by surprise," said Blizzard's Josh Mosqueira. "It's kind of funny to say. You have such an anticipated game—how can it catch anybody by surprise? But I remember being in the meetings leading up to that, people saying, 'Are we really ready for this? OK, let's double the predictions, let's triple the predictions.' And even those ended up being super conservative."

Later that day, as fans tried again to load *Diablo III*, they found another vague message: *Unable to connect to the service or the connection was interrupted. (Error 3003)*. Error 3003 didn't grow as popular as its younger, catchier brother, although it did make one wonder how the other 2,966 errors had been averted. The next day, Error 37 reemerged, along with a host of other server issues that continued plaguing *Diablo III* players for days after the game launched. Blizzard's war room was active 24/7 as tired engineers gathered around computers, sipping on coffee and trying to figure out how to bolster their network.

Within forty-eight hours they'd managed to stabilize the servers. Errors would still pop up sporadically, but for the most part, people could now play the game without interruption. On May 17, once things had settled, Blizzard sent out a statement of apology. "We've been humbled by your enthusiasm," they wrote. "We sincerely regret that your crusade to bring down the Lord of Terror was thwarted not by mobs of demons, but by mortal infrastructure."

Finally, the world could play *Diablo III*. Like its predecessors, the third *Diablo* would let you build up a character and hack your way through landscapes full of demons, collecting fistfuls of shiny loot along the way. You'd unlock abilities based on the class you'd selected (wizard, demon hunter, etc.), switching between a large array of spells and skills. And you'd power through dungeon after dungeon, all of which were procedurally generated so that no two playthroughs would be the same. It appeared, at first, to be the game that fans had been waiting for.

In the weeks to come, however, players would discover that *Diablo III* had some fundamental flaws. It was satisfying to rip through hordes of monsters, but the difficulty ramped up way too fast. Legendary items dropped too infrequently. The endgame was too challenging. And, perhaps most frustrating of all, the loot system seemed to revolve around the in-game auction house, where *Diablo III* players could use real-life money to buy and sell powerful equipment. This controversial system made

Diablo III feel like a dreaded "pay-to-win" game, in which the best way to beef up your character wasn't to play the game and make fun decisions, but to type your credit card number into a form on Blizzard's website.

Since Blizzard's founding in 1991, the studio had developed a reputation for making fantastic games, including the cultural touchstones *Warcraft* and *StarCraft*. When you saw the jagged blue Blizzard logo attached to a game, you knew you were getting something unparalleled. With *Diablo II* in 2000, Blizzard had developed the definitive action-RPG, a game that inspired countless all-nighters and LAN sessions as millions of teenagers gathered to battle disfigured demons and hunt for elusive Stones of Jordan. *Diablo II* was widely considered one of the best games ever made. Now, in May 2012, the rocky launch of *Diablo III* had associated the Blizzard logo with something that the company had never experienced: public failure. And even after Error 37, the problems were just getting started.

Josh Mosqueira had always hated winters in Montreal. A Mexican-Canadian with a thick blended accent who had served as a Black Watch infantryman in the Canadian army, Mosqueira spent his early career years writing role-playing games for the publisher White Wolf while trying to break into the video game industry. After working on a few games and spending a seven-year stint at Relic Entertainment in Vancouver, Mosqueira moved across Canada to work on *Far Cry 3* at Ubisoft's massive office in Montreal, where winter temperatures tended to drop a few degrees lower than they should in any human-inhabited city.

On one particularly snowy day in February 2011, more than a year before Error 37, Mosqueira got a call from Jay Wilson, an old friend from his Relic days. Wilson was now working at Blizzard

Entertainment in Irvine, California, and they were looking for a new lead designer on *Diablo III*, the game he was directing. Someone from Ubisoft had applied, so Wilson wanted to know what the culture was like over there. Would this prospective new designer fit in? The two friends got to talking, and then Wilson offered up another option: What if Mosqueira took the job?

Mosqueira said he'd have to think about it. He looked out his window, watching the snow fall, and realized there wasn't much to think about. "Fast forward two and a half months, and I find myself walking into these halls as the lead designer for the console version of [*Diablo III*]," Mosqueira said. His job was to direct a very small team—three, at first, including him—that would adapt *Diablo III* for the Xbox and PlayStation. This was a surprising initiative for Blizzard, which for years had resisted releasing games on consoles, instead choosing to put out massive hits like *World of Warcraft* and *StarCraft II* only on PC and Mac. With *Diablo III*, Blizzard's brain trust finally saw an opportunity to explore the giant world of console gaming.

Mosqueira and his team settled into a section of the office and started playing around with prototypes, trying to figure out how to get *Diablo III* feeling good on a controller. Blizzard had given Mosqueira's team liberty to overhaul everything for the console version, and they took advantage of that freedom, changing the skills of every class to account for their new control scheme. "A lot of the timing of skills on console felt off, because instead of focusing on your cursor, your eye, you're focusing on your character," Mosqueira said. "So we essentially went in and tweaked every skill in the game."

Toward the end of 2011, as the *Diablo III* PC team started crunching for the spring release, Mosqueira and his colleagues put the console project on pause so they could help finish the game. "The three of us—and at that time we were about eight—

eight of us were all new to Blizzard, so we sort of felt like we have to," Mosqueira said. "We want to be part of this. It's going to be really exciting. It's going to be a big moment in Blizzard history, and we're just happy to be part."

Then came *Diablo III*'s launch, and Error 37, and manic days at Blizzard in May 2012 as they tried to stabilize the servers. While Mosqueira and his crew went back to work on the console version, *Diablo III*'s other designers began trying to solve the game's deeper problems. Players clearly weren't happy with the loot system, for example, but what precisely was wrong with it? How could Blizzard make the endgame as addictive as it had been in *Diablo II*, where players spent hours and hours fighting through demons and hunting for gear even after they'd already finished the story?

The biggest problem, the developers realized, was the game's difficulty. Blizzard's designers had originally built *Diablo III*'s difficulty system to mirror *Diablo II*. You'd play through the full game once on Normal mode, then play it a second time on the challenging Nightmare mode, and crank through a third time on Hell mode. *Diablo III* repeated that structure and introduced a fourth difficulty option, Inferno. Designed for players who had already hit the level cap, Inferno was blisteringly tough, to the point where you couldn't beat it without the game's best gear. But *Diablo III*'s best gear dropped only when you played on Inferno mode, creating a nasty, demonic version of the chicken-and-egg dilemma. How could you get Inferno gear if your gear wasn't good enough to get through Inferno in the first place?

There was one option: the auction house. If you didn't want to bash your head against the wall in Inferno mode, you could dish out real money for better gear, which was the exact opposite of what most players wanted to do. As a result, some crafty players found ways to abuse the system. Thanks to *Diablo III*'s random number generator, the chances of getting loot from a powerful enemy weren't much better than the chances of getting loot from smashing a stationary pot. Once players realized this, they'd spend marathon sessions doing nothing but breaking pottery. It wasn't particularly fun, but hey, it beat giving away real money.

What became apparent to Blizzard in the coming months was that people were more interested in gaming *Diablo III* than they were in playing it, a problem that would take serious investment to fix. From May 15 through the end of August, the *Diablo III* team released roughly eighteen free patches and hotfixes that fixed bugs, tweaked character skills, and addressed various player complaints. The largest of these patches, on August 21, 2012, added a system called Paragon levels that would let players get stronger once they'd hit the level cap (60). It also made Inferno mode less difficult and added a bunch of unique effects to legendary gear, so getting a sleek new weapon would make you feel like a devastating war machine.

But Blizzard knew these patches were just bandages—temporary solutions to get players to do more than smash pots. There was still a leaking wound in *Diablo III*'s side. And it would take a great deal of time to stitch it up.

In the center of Blizzard's sprawling Irvine campus is a giant statue of a *Warcraft* orc. Surrounding that statue is a ring of plaques, each with a different message that's meant to be a mantra for Blizzard employees. Some of them seem like they've been ripped from parody motivational posters—"Think Globally"; "Commit to Quality"—but one resonated strongly with the *Diablo III* team throughout 2012: "Every Voice Matters." Players were frustrated, and Blizzard's developers felt compelled to listen to them. *Diablo III*'s producers and designers took to as many Internet hangouts as possible, from Reddit to the Blizzard forums, to collect and collate feedback on how to make the game better. In blog posts and letters throughout the summer and fall, Blizzard promised players that they had a long-term plan to fix the auction house, improve the loot system, and make *Diablo III*'s endgame more fun.

This sort of commitment was atypical. Usually, a developer would release a game and then move on, maybe leaving behind a skeleton team to fix any lingering critical bugs before the studio dove into its next project. But Blizzard had built its reputation as a premier developer by sticking to games for the long haul. Blizzard would update all its games with free patches for years and years after they launched, believing that the support would lead to goodwill from fans, which in turn would lead to better sales.[*]

By the end of July 2012, *Diablo III* had sold an astounding ten million copies. Blizzard's developers felt like they'd made a fun game, but they also knew it could be so much better. "It was a diamond in the rough," said Wyatt Cheng, a senior technical designer. "We knew we needed to polish it a little bit more. It just needed that extra little bit." It helped that Blizzard's CEO, Mike Morhaime, had told the *Diablo III* team to keep working on updates and releasing free patches for the indefinite future. "There are few other companies where (a) we could sell millions of copies and still feel like we could've done better," said Cheng, "and (b) given some of the initial launch problems, [we'd be] given this long runway to work on the game and make it better."

That was one way of looking at the situation. The other was that the people who worked on *Diablo III*—some of whom had been on the game for nearly a decade—wouldn't get a break. Any-

---

* *Diablo II*, released in 2000, was still receiving new patches in 2016. *StarCraft*, released in 1998, got a new patch in 2017. No other company has maintained and updated its old games for so long.

one who's spent a great deal of time on a single project knows how relieving it feels to finish—and how when it's done, you never want to look at it again. "I was listening to a podcast," said Cheng, who had started on *Diablo III* in the early days. "There's a person who's been making the tours promoting her book"—the psychologist Angela Duckworth—"and she used to write about grit. She said grit is this quality that a lot of successful people have. And it's this persistence, to push forward with something. Anything worth doing, it's not necessarily day-to-day fun sometimes. Sometimes it is. Great when it is. But grit usually means that somebody sees the long-term goal and they see the long-term vision and they push through any obstacles that they have on a day-to-day basis, with the end in mind."

The "end," or at least the next big milestone, was *Diablo III*'s expansion. Traditionally, Blizzard would produce meaty expansion packs for every game the company released, and *Diablo III*'s developers knew theirs would be the best opportunity to overhaul the game. Toward the end of 2012, they started putting together a giant Google document full of problems that they needed to fix and features they wanted to add, like an item revamp and a new set of goals for the endgame.

But they needed a new leader. *Diablo III*'s longtime director, Jay Wilson, had told the team that he planned to step down, citing burnout after nearly a decade spent working on the same game.[*] Blizzard needed a new director, not just to lead development on the expansion, but also to shape the future of *Diablo III*. And there was one newcomer who might make the perfect fit.

When he first saw the opening on Blizzard's internal website, Josh Mosqueira wasn't going to apply. He'd been enjoying the

---

[*] Oddly, Blizzard would not give Jay Wilson permission to be interviewed for this book.

challenges of porting *Diablo III* to consoles, and he liked oversee-
ing a small team. Although his squad had expanded from three
to around twenty-five, it was still a drastic departure from his
days at Ubisoft, where he'd had to help coordinate a team of four
hundred–something people. Even when Wilson and other leaders at Blizzard encouraged him to apply for the director position,
Mosqueira was reluctant. "I was just really happy being a lead and
having a console project to look after," he said. "Just getting my
hands dirty actually working on the game and not just Power-
Points."

But Mosqueira also loved the culture of *Diablo III*'s development team, and soon enough he was persuaded to file an ap-
plication. After a gantlet of interviews, not only with Blizzard's
management but also with all his coworkers, Mosqueira was
called into the office of Blizzard's cofounder Frank Pearce for the
news. He'd gotten the job. Mosqueira hadn't been on the *Diablo
III* team for very long, but people respected him as a designer and
leader, and Blizzard wanted him to drive the future of the game.
"When they told me, it was a pretty amazing moment," Mosqueira
said. "Quickly followed by a lot of panic, when you realize that
Diablo's one of the big franchises, not just at Blizzard but in the
industry, and to be given that responsibility was intense."

After becoming director, one of Mosqueira's first moves was
to sit down with the rest of the staff on *Diablo III*, who had all once
been his colleagues but now reported to him. He asked how they
were feeling. What did they like about the game? Where did they
see *Diablo III* going in the years to come? Usually, video game
expansions were additive—they'd provide new content, new areas, new loot—but for *Diablo III*, Blizzard wanted to make something transformative. "It quickly became apparent that they really
wanted to use the expansion to not just adjust and pivot from the
launch, but really create this platform that will take *Diablo* into

the future," Mosqueira said. "That's the kind of pressure that the team put on themselves. And they were thinking really big."

What had also become clear to Mosqueira, and what he tried to convey to the rest of his team, was that they didn't really know what *Diablo III* was yet. Mosqueira liked to point out that when gamers got wistful about *Diablo II*, they weren't remembering the game's original incarnation—they were thinking about what it became in 2001, after the developers reacted to fans' feedback and released the expansion *Lord of Destruction*. That was the game people remembered. It was the result of millions of players giving Blizzard feedback, and Blizzard reacting directly to that feedback.

"What makes it really hard is you can build a game, you can test a game, and you can think you know the game—until you release it," said Mosqueira. "Within the first day, probably more people have spent more hours playing the game collectively than [in] the entire development up to that point. So you're going to see things you never intended. You're going to see players reacting to things. . . . They're playing with it, they're engaging with it, they're interacting with it. And really, what makes it hard is learning the discipline and the rigor to know how to react to that."

As the *Diablo III* team looked ahead to the expansion, which they were calling *Reaper of Souls*, they saw it as a chance to make amends—not just for Error 37, but for all of *Diablo III*'s early faults. This was the team's chance to make their own *Lord of Destruction* and reach the heights that *Diablo II* had set all those years ago. "We took it as, this is our one opportunity to win back the fans," said Rob Foote, a senior producer. "Let's do it."

It might have seemed odd, to an outside observer, that a game ten years in the making would launch with so many problems. Mosqueira's theory was this: *Diablo III*'s issues were a direct result of a development team haunted by the beloved *Diablo II*. As he said in a 2015 talk: "The specter of *Diablo II* loomed large over the team. The pressure of trying to live up to the legacy of this incredible game weighed heavily on the team and impacted so many of the decisions."

Where BioWare's *Dragon Age: Inquisition* team was bedeviled by negative reactions to *Dragon Age 2* (see chapter 6), Blizzard had the opposite problem: *Diablo III* had to surpass *Diablo II*'s massive success. The designers of *Diablo III* had been willing to make big innovations in some areas, like the flexible skill system, generally considered a highlight of the game. But, in Mosqueira's view, they were too rigid about other series traditions.

As a newcomer, Mosqueira was willing to challenge everyone's conceptions of what made *Diablo* feel like *Diablo*, even if it meant picking fights with some of Blizzard's veterans. For the console version, which was still in development alongside *Reaper of Souls*, Mosqueira had fought hard for an "evade" feature that would allow players to use a joystick to roll around on the ground, dodging enemies' attacks. This was controversial. "Evade was extremely contentious on the team," Mosqueira said. "Extremely, extremely contentious. I would get into very heated discussions with some of the other designers about why we needed it on console."

Mosqueira argued that players would get bored walking around for hours at a time without having some method of switching up their movement, like the beloved jump button in *World of Warcraft*. Other designers pointed out that offering an evade feature would diminish the impact of items that boosted players' movement speed—a concept from *Diablo II*—therefore making the game less rewarding in the long term. "Both are really strong arguments," said Mosqueira. "Both are right arguments. At the end of the day, you have to say, 'OK, I'm willing to sacrifice some of that long-term reward for the short-term visceral feeling.' . . . I understand I'm giving away the power reward, but for this to feel like a console game, my thumbs need to do something at regular intervals, and it just feels good. It's a console thing to do." (Mosqueira eventually won this battle, and the evade feature made it into the game.)

By experimenting on consoles, where there was less pressure to adhere to the formula of *Diablo II*, Mosqueira and his team could take steps that seemed radical to the rest of the team. "I think that was one of the most liberating things," he said. "The PC team, for all the right intentions, because of all the pressure, the expectation, some of their initial design was very conservative. But on console, it was a bit of the Wild West. And in some ways, looking back at it . . . there's a level of being very naive. We've been mucking around with this game for about six months, not knowing all the history behind all the decisions leading up to this moment, just walking in like kids and pushing buttons."

For a game that had been in development for so many years, a fresh perspective could be useful, especially when Blizzard began reexamining core parts of *Diablo III*, like the loot system. In the PC version of *Diablo III*, enemies would spawn fountains of loot when they died, offering that familiar dopamine rush for players as they picked up cool new weapons and accessories. But without a mouse and keyboard, sorting through all those glittering rings and amulets could be a chore. As the *Diablo III* console team playtested the game, Mosqueira found that this loot overload was impeding people's progress, forcing them to stop every few seconds just to organize their inventories.

That's when they tweaked the formula. "We said, 'OK, every time a gray or a white item's going to drop, seventy percent of the time it's going to just drop gold,'" said Mosqueira. The change might have seemed drastic to *Diablo II* devotees, but it wound up forming the foundation for what the team called Loot 2.0, a system that would improve *Diablo III* on both PC and consoles. "We started realizing that maybe we can be dropping less," said Mosqueira, "and if you're dropping less, well, we need to drop better."

With Loot 2.0, Mosqueira and his team hoped to address every criticism players had about gear in *Diablo III*. Fans complained that it took way too long to get the top-tier "legendary" items, so Loot 2.0 guaranteed that each major boss would drop legendary gear. Fans pointed out that, when they did finally get legendary items, the game would generate those items' stats randomly, making it likely that a player would spot a shiny orange weapon and get excited, only to find that the weapon was useless for his class.[*] So Loot 2.0 introduced a weighting system, skewing the random number generator to increase the chances that when a player picked up a legendary item, it would be something they needed.

As Blizzard's developers met throughout 2013 to talk about what they wanted to do with *Reaper of Souls*, "randomness" became a driving conversation topic. After all, random numbers had always been the pulsing heart of *Diablo*. Since the first game in 1996, which sent players battling through procedurally generated dungeons under the decrepit city of Tristram, *Diablo* games had relied on a random number generator for just about everything. Dungeon layouts were random. Treasure chests were random.

---

[*]   Randomly generated items didn't quite mesh with *Diablo III*'s stat system. Whereas in *Diablo II* every stat was useful to every character, no matter what class you played, *Diablo III* took a more focused approach. In *Diablo III*, an axe of strength would be useful only to a barbarian, so it'd really suck to get one if you were playing a demon hunter. And an arrow quiver that boosted intelligence—the primary stat for wizards—was useless to just about everyone. Wizards couldn't use arrows.

Most magical items were random, too; the game would piece them together from a large table of prefixes and suffixes, with each item's attributes tied to its name. (A "Lucky" belt would boost the amount of gold you received from monsters. A sword "of the Leech" would offer health every time you attacked.)

This randomness was what gave *Diablo* its mass appeal. Playing a *Diablo* game was sort of like campaigning in *Dungeons & Dragons*: every time you played, you'd have a different experience. There was something naturally addicting about finding a new item and hitting "identify," knowing you could wind up with pretty much anything. *Diablo* appealed to that same instinct that makes us want to feed all our cash into slot machines and lottery tickets. It would have fit in nicely next to the craps tables at a sparkly Vegas casino.

It took a long time before the designers realized that their obsession with random numbers was hurting *Diablo III*. "I started to worship at the throne of randomness," said Kevin Martens, a lead designer. "And when I could make something more random, I would, missing the point that randomness is a tool to get replayability. . . . When people ask me, 'What's the major difference between *Reaper of Souls* and *Diablo III*?' my shortest possible answer is: We shaved the rough edges off randomness. We made randomness work for the player instead of against them."

That was where *Diablo III* diverged from Las Vegas—Blizzard didn't want the house to always win. Josh Mosqueira and his team realized that the way to keep players happy was to give *them* the edge. "When *Diablo III* shipped, whether you got a legendary [item] or not was just a whole bunch of die rolls," said Mosqueira. "Sometimes you'd get lucky; sometimes you wouldn't get lucky. . . . In *Reaper*, we just said, OK, we don't want to cheat. We don't want the player to feel that we're making it easier for them or anything like that, but we just need to raise the floor, so it doesn't take me 104 hours to find a legendary."*

They also needed to do something about the difficulty. Back when they'd developed the original version of *Diablo III*, Blizzard's designers had believed that players wanted a game more challenging than any *Diablo* before it. "We had this video, '*Diablo*'s going to brutalize you,'" said Martens. "We had people on our team talking about how hard it was and how even though they're experienced developers, they still get murdered. The truth is—now we're on Hindsight Mountain looking back—that some people want it really hard and some people want a little bit easier. And everything in between."

It wasn't just that Inferno mode was too tough. Players had lost their appetite for playing through the same campaign multiple times, with nothing changing but monsters' strength. The structure that had felt rewarding in 2001 was, for several reasons, a slog in 2012. Video game design had made drastic leaps in the past decade. Dozens of *Diablo* clones had emerged over the years, and some of them had even improved *Diablo II*'s structure (though none were quite as successful). When *Diablo III* came out, people expected a less repetitive rhythm.

Reaper of Souls was the opportunity to solve these problems. Blizzard's short-term solution for *Diablo III* had been to make Inferno mode less challenging via postgame patches, but with *Reaper*, they could take things further. "It was probably late November of 2012 when I started to think maybe we should completely redo the difficulty system," said Martens. That was a tough

---

* One of Mosqueira's favorite anecdotes was that when he played *Diablo III* for the first time, as an axe-wielding barbarian, it did take him 104 hours to find a legendary item. (He checked.) When he finally saw that shiny orange item hit the floor, he was elated—until he saw that it was an arrow quiver. Barbarians couldn't use arrows.

prospect, though. "The whole game is built for these four difficulties. Every monster has their numbers tuned for each of these four difficulties."

Kevin Martens zoomed out. What if, instead of treating difficulty levels as stages, the Blizzard team overhauled *Diablo III*'s structure entirely, making it so monsters would scale with the player's power over the course of the game? And then what if they added a new modifier system, so that anyone who wanted more of a challenge could switch to Hard or Expert modes to boost enemies' health and damage? If you wanted to make things a little easier, you could simply flip back to Normal. To solve Inferno mode's chicken and egg problem, Blizzard would kill both the chickens and the eggs.

To an outside observer this might have seemed like an obvious method—most other games use difficulty modes this way—but for a *Diablo* game it was revolutionary. "Initially it seemed like this impossible mountain to climb," Martens said. "You knew you needed to change this major thing, [but] you never thought about the game in that terms, in automatic difficulty before. We'd never considered it in that manner."

They'd never considered it because of *Diablo II*. It had never occurred to the team that they should change the difficulty structure because that was just always how *Diablo* games had done things. Playing through the game on Normal, then again on Nightmare, and then a third time on Hell was part of what made *Diablo Diablo*, wasn't it? Blizzard had taken flack during *Diablo III*'s early development just for the minor act of making health orbs drop from enemies, which some fans saw as breaking series tradition, so it had been tough to even think about a move as drastic as upending *Diablo*'s entire structure. But what if they did? And what if they found a better replacement for it?

In the months after launch, several *Diablo III* players had complained about not being able to teleport back and forth between the game's four acts, and Blizzard had been looking to find a way to address that feedback. "We worked with the engineers and they said, 'Oh yeah, we can figure out a way to do that," said Rob Foote. "And actually, I think it was an engineer who said, 'But couldn't we do something better?'"

Again, they all went into brainstorming mode. What if, instead of solely letting players teleport between areas, *Diablo III* gave them a whole new mode that changed everything? And what if that mode became the focal point for *Diablo III*'s new endgame?

They would call this new feature Adventure Mode. Once you'd finished *Reaper of Souls*, you could open up this new Adventure Mode and jump into any area of the game, from the deserts of Caldeum to the frozen peaks of Arreat. Each of the game's five acts would give you a series of randomized bounties like "kill a boss" or "clear a dungeon," and the more bounties you completed, the more loot you'd snag. Adventure Mode would also add special events and what the game called "Nephalem Rifts," multitiered dungeons that shuffled areas and monsters from all throughout *Diablo III* like some sort of gothic mixtape. As Blizzard envisioned it, Adventure Mode would entertain players for hours and hours once they'd finished the game. It sure beat smashing pottery.

In August 2013, at the Gamescom trade show in Germany, Blizzard prepared to announce *Reaper of Souls* to a packed room full of reporters and fans. This expansion would center on the demonic archangel Malthael. It would come with a new class, the crusader. And it would introduce all sorts of features, starting with Loot 2.0, in a free patch that Blizzard hoped would signal that the developers of *Diablo III* were listening to the complaints.

"Right before we were going to do the announcement, the energy in the room was tense," said Josh Mosqueira. "I could feel that everybody was [thinking], 'Mmm, this better be good.' You could feel that they almost were expecting to be disappointed." Then Blizzard put on the announcement video: a four-minute opening cinematic for *Reaper of Souls*, introducing the world to Malthael. Holding a nasty scythe in each hand, the archangel sliced his way through a group of Horadrim mages and attacked his former brother, the angel Tyrael. "The Nephalem will stop you," Tyrael said. Responded Malthael: "No one can stop death."

Gamescom's audience erupted in applause. "It's almost like this wave of excitement," said Mosqueira. "You could feel it. I said, 'OK, I think people are willing to give us another chance. Let's not fuck it up.'"

Originally, Blizzard had planned to put out *Reaper of Souls* later in 2013, but the *Diablo III* team realized they needed more time, delaying it to the first quarter of 2014. This was a surprise to just about nobody. Blizzard had a reputation for taking its sweet time with games—*Diablo III* had taken ten years, after all—and you'd be hard-pressed to find a Blizzard game that hadn't missed at least one deadline.

One quote, delivered by the director of *StarCraft II*, Dustin Browder, has always stuck out as a telling description of how Blizzard makes video games. In June 2012, over a year after Blizzard had hoped to ship *StarCraft II*'s first expansion, *Heart of the Swarm*, Browder spoke to me about the game's progress. "We are ninety-nine percent done," he said, "but that last one percent's a bitch." *Heart of the Swarm* wouldn't come out until March 2013. That last one percent took nearly a year.

"The thing that makes scheduling challenging is iteration," said Rob Foote. "You have to allow for iteration if you want to make a great product." Iteration time was the last one percent. Blizzard's producers tried to leave blank slates at the end of their schedules so that their development teams could push, tug, and polish every aspect of their game until they felt like they had something perfect. "And it's challenging too," said Foote, "because people say, 'What's in that, it's a lot of time, what are they actually doing?' They're iterating. We don't know what they're going to do, but they're going to be doing something."

Even with the extra time for *Reaper of Souls*, Josh Mosqueira and his crew had to cut some features. In conjunction with Adventure Mode, the *Diablo III* team had devised a system called Devil's Hand that would place fifty-two high-powered enemies throughout the game's world. Players would be able to kill them all for collectible items in hopes of eventually getting all fifty-two. The *Diablo III* team didn't have enough time to get Devil's Hand's collection system in shape, though, so Mosqueira decided to cut it. "We figured, we have extra time, but we can't get both of these right," he said. "And the really important one is Adventure Mode, because that really changes the way people play the game. So we had to put Devil's Hand off to the side."*

As the months went by, everyone at Blizzard felt ecstatic about the progress they were making. Since Error 37, they'd changed *Diablo III*'s formula, overhauled the loot system, and thought they could win back millions of players with *Reaper of Souls*. But Mosqueira still felt like the game had a critical flaw that they had yet to address, something that seemed at odds with how they wanted people to play the game: the auction house.

When Blizzard first announced *Diablo III*'s real-money auction house, cynics saw it as a cash grab. After all, Blizzard got to take a healthy cut every time a player sold an item. Blizzard's developers argued that they had more noble motives, insisting

---

* Ideas from Devil's Hand would later reemerge in Kanai's Cube, a versatile magic box that would, among other things, let *Diablo III* players absorb and collect powers from their legendary gear.

that they'd built the auction house to improve the experience of trading items for players. Back in 2002, *Diablo II: Lord of Destruction* had become infested with third-party gray markets, in which people would trade real money for powerful items on sketchy, insecure websites. Blizzard's goal was, as Kevin Martens put it, to provide "a world-class experience" for those players, one that was safe and secure.

Not long after *Diablo III*'s launch, however, it became apparent to Blizzard that the auction house was hurting the game. Some players enjoyed trading, sure—especially the ones who were farming loot and selling it for a healthy profit—but for many, the auction house made *Diablo III* a significantly worse experience. It reduced the thrill of hunting for gear. What was the fun in getting a great roll on a cool new piece of armor if you could just hop on the market and buy a better one?

One group of players, who called themselves the Ironborn (after *Game of Thrones*' House Greyjoy), made a point of refusing to use the auction house. They even sent petitions to Blizzard asking if the developers would consider adding an Ironborn mode to *Diablo III*. "This was a community of players who were saying, 'Hey guys, *Diablo III* is the exact same game, but I'm having this whole new experience choosing to play it without the auction house,'" said Wyatt Cheng. "You can look at *Diablo* through that lens and say, you know what, we've got this really amazing game, but the auction house is having this distorting effect on how some people might perceive it."

One day in September 2013, as *Reaper of Souls* was in full production, Josh Mosqueira sat in a meeting, doodling in a notebook. It was one of Blizzard's routine monthly strategy meetings, at which CEO Mike Morhaime would get together with company executives and project leads to talk about the business, and much of the technical finance talk was bouncing off Mosqueira. Then the conversation turned to *Diablo III*, and suddenly they were talking about the auction house.

"[Mike] said, 'Well what do you think?'" said Mosqueira. "If I was anywhere else, I probably would've said, 'You know what, I think we still need to figure things out,' or 'I'm not quite sure.' But looking at those guys, and knowing how important having our players have faith in us was, I said, 'You know what, guys? Maybe we should just kill it.'"

After some brief discussions about how the logistics might work—How would they communicate it to players? What would they do with current auctions? How long would they need to wait?—the decision crystallized. It was time for *Diablo III*'s auction house to die. "I was [thinking], 'Wow, this is happening,'" said Mosqueira. "I think to Mike's credit, Mike's a huge gamer. He loves the games. He loves players more than anything else. And he's just willing to make those decisions, and say, 'You know, this is going to hurt. But it's the right thing to do.'"

On September 17, 2013, Blizzard announced that it would shut down the auction house in March 2014. Fans were, for the most part, thrilled by the news. Now you'd be able to go hunt for loot in *Diablo III* without the nagging feeling that you could just pay money for something better. Wrote one *Kotaku* commenter: "Good job Blizzard, you've actually restored some faith in me. I may actually play this again."

"*Diablo* is best experienced when, as a result of slaying monsters, you get better items that allow you to make your character more powerful," said Wyatt Cheng. "And if the activity that I do to make my character more powerful does not include killing monsters . . . then that's not a good place to be."

Now it felt like they'd found the perfect formula for *Reaper of Souls*. In addition to the new area (Westmarch), and boss (Malthael), the expansion would come with Loot 2.0 (free to all players via patch), Adventure Mode, and an overhauled difficulty system. The week before *Reaper of Souls* released, Blizzard would remove the auction house. As they finalized the development of the expansion and prepared for launch, Mosqueira and his team felt like this was the big moment. They were going to win people back.

When *Reaper of Souls* launched on March 25, 2014, there was no Error 37. Blizzard had bolstered its infrastructure this time around. Plus, the company had decided to improve the error messaging system so that even if something went awry, the warning wouldn't be so vague. "I think one of the other lessons that we learned is if you were there, anxious, and you logged in, and you got Error 37, you [thought], 'What is Error 37? I have no idea what this is,'" said Josh Mosqueira. "Now, all the error messages are more descriptive. They say, 'This is the problem we're having. Here's a time frame where you can expect this problem to be fixed.'"

As they watched the reactions pour in, Blizzard's staff collectively breathed a sigh of relief. So did *Diablo* players. "*Diablo III* has finally rediscovered the moment-to-moment gameplay that made the series great," wrote a reviewer for *Ars Technica*, "and fixed—or removed—almost everything that got in the way of that greatness. *Reaper of Souls* is the redemption of *Diablo III*."

Two years after launch, people were finally falling in love with *Diablo III*. "When you went to the forums, or when you started getting feedback directly from fans, the issues they were complaining about were more specific and less broad," said Kevin Martens. "That was when I really thought, 'OK we're finally getting there.'" As Martens and other designers browsed through Reddit or Battle.net, they were encouraged to see players complaining about underpowered items or asking Blizzard to buff specific builds. No longer were people offering the three words of feedback that serve as a death warrant for any game: "This isn't fun."

What was most gratifying for Josh Mosqueira was that people especially loved the console version of *Diablo III*, which launched on PS3 and Xbox 360 in September 2013 and on the newer consoles (PS4 and Xbox One) in August 2014. After decades of clicking, many gamers almost felt sacrilegious saying so, but playing *Diablo III* was more fun with a PlayStation 4 controller than it ever had been with a mouse and keyboard.

In the coming months and years, Blizzard would go on to release more patches and features for *Diablo III*. Some were free, like a dungeon called Greyhollow Island and a revamped version of the cathedral from the first *Diablo* game. Others cost money, like the necromancer character class. Although fans lamented the absence of another big expansion pack (which, as of early 2017, hadn't happened), it was clear that Blizzard had committed to supporting *Diablo III* for years after its release. Other developers might not have bothered—especially after the launch day catastrophe. "Mike Morhaime, the president of the company, said to us, 'We want to win and earn the love and trust of our players,'" said Wyatt Cheng. "We had all this work we had done in this game. We believed in the game. We knew it was great, and it would've been so tragic, I think, if we were at a company that said, 'Oh, Error 37, pull the plug.'"

Josh Mosqueira, on the other hand, was done with *Diablo III*. In the summer of 2016, Mosqueira left Blizzard, joining Rob Pardo, a veteran Blizzard executive and the lead designer of *World of Warcraft*, to form a new studio called Bonfire. "Leaving this team and this company was the hardest non–life threatening decision I've ever had to make," Mosqueira said. "I felt that I wanted to take a chance and try to do something totally different."

At least he'd left Blizzard with something great. *Diablo III* was one of the best-selling video games in history, having sold thirty million copies as of August 2015. It also proved a point that would influence numerous game developers in the years to come, including but not limited to the makers of *The Division* and *Destiny* (whom we'll meet in chapter 8): every game can be fixed.

Often, the developers of a video game hit their stride toward the end of a project, when they learn what their game really feels like to play. For *Diablo III* and games like it, launching was just the beginning of the development process. "Even with a game that has a really strong vision, a really strong identity like *Diablo*," said Mosqueira, "I think one of the challenges is that at the beginning of a project . . . before a game comes out, everybody has a slightly different version of the game in their head. One of the hardest things to do is get it out. But once it's out, there's less discussion about that because you can now [see] what it is. Game development's really hard, but it's a different type of hard before it's released. It's more existential before it's released."

Diablo III was proof that, even for one of the most accomplished and talented game studios in the world, with near-limitless resources to make a game, years can pass before that game properly coalesces. That even for the third game in a franchise, there are still an impossible number of variables that can throw everyone off. That even a game that launches with crippling issues can, with enough time, commitment, and money, turn into something great. In 2012, when Error 37 spread across the Internet, gamers had thought *Diablo III* was doomed. And then it wasn't.

5

■■■■■■■■■■

HALO WARS

In the summer of 2004, Ensemble Studios' management team flew to Chicago for an off-site retreat that felt unusually somber. They were having what some would call an identity crisis. Ensemble had spent years working on prototypes for video games that just weren't making any of them happy, and they needed to get away for a few days and talk things through. "We said we should be doing what we're passionate about," said Chris Rippy, an Ensemble producer who was at the retreat. "Get back on track."

The question was, what would that look like? Ensemble, based in Dallas, Texas, had been making the same type of video game for nearly ten years. They'd built their reputation on *Age of Empires*, a cerebral game series in which you'd start off with a handful of villagers and gradually build an entire civilization. Like Blizzard's *Warcraft* and Westwood's *Command & Conquer*, *Age of Empires* was a real-time strategy game, or RTS, in which the action unfolded without turns or pauses. You'd progress through different technological "eras" (Stone Age, Bronze Age) as you harvested resources, constructed buildings, and trained armies to conquer your opponents.

To finish the first *Age of Empires*, Ensemble's staff went through what Dave Pottinger, a lead designer, described as "a terrible death march which could never be repeated today," working one-hundred-hour weeks for nearly a year. When it finally came out in 1997, *Age of Empires* was an immediate hit, selling millions for Ensemble and its publisher, Microsoft. This was followed by a glut of profitable *Age* sequels, expansions, and spin-offs, eventually leading Microsoft to buy Ensemble. By 2004, the studio was working on yet another game in the series, *Age of Empires III*, which was due to come out at the end of 2005.

What had always been unorthodox about Ensemble—and what ensured that people rarely left the studio—was that they saw themselves as a family. Since Ensemble's founding in 1995, the company had been made up mostly of young, single men who spent nights and weekends together. "On any given Saturday night, a good chunk of the team was at someone's apartment," wrote Ian Fischer, a lead designer, in a magazine retrospective.* "Friday after work there'd be a dozen people in the play-test area playing *Quake* (then *Quake 2*, then *Half-Life*) until 3am.... If you didn't actually share an apartment with the guy you sat next to, you were probably going to be having a beer at his place later that night."

Even through the early 2000s, as Ensemble's cofounders grew up and started real families, they shared what they saw as an uncommon amount of chemistry. Every prospective employee had to go through a rigorous interview process that, for a while, in-

---

* Ian Fischer, "Blast from the Past: Ensemble Figures Out How to Go from Empires to Kings," *Gamesauce*, Spring 2010, www.gamesauce.biz/2010/09/05/ensemble-figures-out-how-to-go-from-empires-to-kings.

cluded meetings with all twenty-something people at the studio. If just one person said no, the prospective employee was out. "It was really like a family," said Rich Geldreich, a graphics engineer. "It was a combination family slash a little bit of a frat house."

During that summer of 2004, with *Age of Empires III* in the works, many of Ensemble's veterans grumbled that they were sick of making *Age* games. Some were tired of RTS games in general. They'd tried several times to get a second development team off the ground, one that would experiment with other genres, but that team always seemed to fail.

Ensemble would fall into the same pattern every time. The second team would play around with prototypes and early concepts for a while, then the main *Age* team would invariably run into some sort of catastrophe, such as when they had to redo *Age of Empires II*'s entire design after a year because it wasn't fun to play. Ensemble's management would then ask the second team to put their own project on hold and come help with the latest *Age* game. Every time this happened, the second project would lose momentum and peter out, like a steam engine that stopped getting coal.

"The pattern we fell into, starting with *Age II*, was that we so overbid and underfinished the games that even though we tried to do other things, we ended up having to pull everybody in just to get the [*Age*] game finished," said Dave Pottinger. In previous years, Ensemble's second team had prototyped an RPG, a platformer, and several other experiments, all of which were discarded. Canceling prototypes wasn't an unusual practice for a game studio, but the pattern was becoming rough for Ensemble's staff, who wanted to show the world that they could expand beyond *Age of Empires*. That was why the management team was sitting in Chicago during the summer of 2004, trying to figure out their next move.

Chris Rippy, Dave Pottinger, and the rest of Ensemble's managers evaluated their options. They had two projects in development: there was *Age of Empires III*, their next flagship game, and then there was a car action game called *Wrench* that no one was particularly excited about. For two days, they sat and debated. Did they really want to keep working on *Wrench*? Why were they still doing it? Inertia? Tons of other ideas kept resurfacing. What if they made a *Diablo* clone? What if they built a massively multiplayer online game (MMO)? And what if they developed a real-time strategy game for consoles?

For decades, the accepted wisdom had been that real-time strategy games would work only on a computer. Because of the genre's speed and complexity, the RTS was best suited to a mouse and keyboard, so a player could zoom around the map with one hand and type in orders on the other. Consoles didn't have mice and keyboards; they had controllers, whose joysticks and limited buttons proved ineffectual for fast-paced multitasking. For as long as RTS games had existed, nobody had been able to solve this problem. Zealots of PC gaming would point to *StarCraft 64* (2000), a subpar port of Blizzard's *StarCraft* that didn't capture the nuances of its PC counterpart, as evidence that an RTS simply couldn't work on a console.

Angelo Laudon, a veteran programmer and member of the Ensemble management team, had always believed otherwise. Like most engineers, Laudon relished the act of solving impossible problems, and he thought a console RTS made for one hell of a challenge. "Angelo was fired up about it," said Chris Rippy. "We had some loose ideas on how to make it work." During the meetings in Chicago, both Laudon and Rippy pushed hard for a console RTS, arguing that it was the perfect opportunity for Ensemble. They had talent and experience. Gamers respected them as RTS developers. And their parent company, Microsoft, was months away from launching the much-anticipated Xbox 360, a powerful new machine that could be home to the first great RTS on consoles.

This plan would also allow Dave Pottinger and others on the team who were sick of making RTS games to work on other projects. For years, Ensemble's CEO, Tony Goodman, had wanted to make an MMO along the lines of Blizzard's *World of Warcraft*, which was due to come out a few months later, in November 2004. (Nearly everyone at Ensemble was playing the beta.) The thought of developing a big multiplayer game was polarizing at the studio, but Goodman and some of the other veterans, like Ian Fischer, had always wanted to make it happen.

By the end of the Chicago trip, Ensemble's management had green-lit three new projects. First was the console RTS, which they gave the code name *Phoenix*. Second was the MMO, code-named *Titan*. The third game, code-named *Nova*, would be a sci-fi action-RPG and *Diablo* clone led by Pottinger, once he and his team had finished work on *Age of Empires III*. If Blizzard could juggle *StarCraft*, *World of Warcraft*, and *Diablo*, the managers thought, why couldn't Ensemble do something comparable?

When the management team got back to Dallas, they announced that they were canceling *Wrench* and starting these other, more exciting projects. On *Phoenix*, Angelo Laudon would be the lead programmer. Chris Rippy would be the producer. And to figure out what the game would feel like to play, they brought in one of their most experienced developers—a designer named Graeme Devine.

Devine, a Scottish expatriate with long hair and a high-pitched laugh, had one of the most eclectic résumés in gaming. As a teenager in the 1980s, he'd done programming work for Atari, Lucasfilm Games, and Activision. Before he'd turned thirty, Devine had founded his own company, Trilobyte, and designed a smash hit called *The 7th Guest* that blended tricky puzzles with cinematic storytelling. After falling out with his Trilobyte cofounder and watching the studio collapse, Devine went to id Software to work alongside one of his old friends, the legendary programmer John Carmack. He spent four years helping develop games like *Quake III* and *Doom 3* before leaving for Ensemble in 2003, where he was put in charge of coding pathing algorithms—the mathematical formulas that told units how to move—for *Age of Empires III*.

In hindsight, this felt like an odd choice to the management team. Devine had a legendary brain for game design and storytelling—why did they have him teaching *Age of Empires* units how to walk around? Recalled Devine: "Dave Pottinger called me up and said, 'Hey, we're not really using you properly at Ensemble. We'd really like to try to break this RTS on a console thing—how'd you like to head up a team to try to get RTS on a console?'"

Sure, Devine told Pottinger. When would they start?

The *Phoenix* team was now Graeme Devine, Angelo Laudon, and Chris Rippy, as well as a few other artists and programmers. It was a small, close-knit group whose members were excited to work on something that wasn't *Age of Empires*. "Our team of misfits," Devine liked to say. It didn't take long before they had a basic concept in place. *Phoenix* would be a sci-fi game in which humans battled against aliens, sort of like *StarCraft*. Playing as the humans would feel drastically different from playing as the alien race, which Devine called the Sway. The goal was to evoke *War of the Worlds*, pitting hulking alien war machines against the scrappy armies of mankind.

The ideas were the easy part. Far harder, Devine knew, would be figuring out the controls. Most video games, when they first enter development, already have a set of controller conventions they can follow. You know that if you pick up a first-person shooter, the right trigger is going to fire shots and the left trigger is going to aim. The left joystick will always control the character's movement while the right joystick rotates the camera. Designers working on big series like *Call of Duty* or *Assassin's Creed* might make small tweaks to the core formula, but they don't have to rethink the controls every time they start developing a new game.

Phoenix didn't have that luxury. The main reason real-time strategy games had never done well on consoles was that there had never been a great control scheme. Right away Devine and the team had to start asking fundamental questions that most games would have already solved. How would you move around the screen? Would you control a cursor, as you would in *Age of Empires*, and use that to select units and give them actions? Or would you control units directly? Would you be able to select multiple units at once? How would you construct buildings?

Answering these questions would be impossible without testing all the possibilities, so Devine and his team spent months experimenting. "We were burning through tons and tons of prototypes," said Colt McAnlis, who had been hired as a graphics engineer for *Phoenix*. "How to move the camera; how that works, moving the camera and grabbing units; how not to make people nauseous in the process. It was a lot of groundbreaking R and D."

They cranked through hundreds of different control schemes. They played games like *Pikmin* and *Aliens versus Predator: Extinction*, both console games with RTS elements, and tried to pinpoint what worked. "We started incorporating all of their ideas, and skipping the stuff we didn't care for," said Chris Rippy. "All of these games did something really smart and really cool, and we just kind of put them all together into one package."

Every week—usually every day—they'd hold mandatory playtesting sessions, where the small *Phoenix* team would sit down and play through the prototypes they'd developed that week. It was a rigorous, focused process that led them to throw out a whole lot of work. "The feedback system at Ensemble was brutal, it was honest, but it forged a good game," said Devine. From there, they came up with a few control schemes that seemed to feel satisfying, like an "area select" option that would let you take command of a group of units by holding down the A button.

Now they just needed corporate approval. Although Microsoft gave Ensemble the freedom to pursue prototypes like *Phoenix* and the other "second team" games they'd canceled over the years, those games couldn't move forward until they got an OK from Ensemble's parent company. Until the bosses in Redmond gave the green light to *Phoenix*, it would remain in purgatory, unable to enter full production or hire new staff.

When Xbox executives came down to visit, the *Phoenix* team showed them their prototypes. Microsoft seemed happy with what they saw, telling Ensemble to keep up the good work. Toward the end of 2005, as the rest of the studio prepared to ship *Age of Empires III*, the *Phoenix* team kept plugging away, buoyed by the fact that they'd finally made a non-*Age* game that Microsoft cared about.

Members of the *Age of Empires III* team, busy working late nights to finish their game, were far less thrilled. "This was an interesting period for Ensemble because it was the first 'second game' that Microsoft got excited about," said Dave Pottinger, who was the lead programmer on *Age of Empires III*. "And unfortunately for us, it was an RTS. Because we had tried for so long not to make an RTS. We didn't want to get pigeonholed into just the RTS company. But of course that's exactly what Microsoft wanted. That's what we were good at, that's why they had bought us, and that's what they wanted us to do."

Microsoft hadn't green-lit any of Ensemble's previous prototypes, but its representatives had *really* liked *Phoenix*. Executives on the Xbox team, who were laser focused on beating Sony's Play-Station 3 in the so-called console war, loved the idea of getting one of their flagship studios on the new Xbox 360. What they didn't love was that this was a new IP. In Microsoft's eyes, this sort of brand-new franchise would be hard to market properly. Real-time strategy games were a tough enough sell in the first place, often performing far worse in the market than the first-person shooters Microsoft loved making. Without some sort of established brand attached to *Phoenix*, Microsoft's executives feared that the game wouldn't move enough copies to justify their investment.

For Ensemble, getting a game green-lit meant progressing through a series of meetings with Xbox executives like Phil Spencer and Peter Moore, which is what the *Phoenix* team had to do. During the first meeting, things went smoothly. But when Graeme Devine and his team met with Microsoft for the second green light meeting, Microsoft gave them a new mandate: Make it a *Halo* game.

"*Halo* was incredibly hot at the time," said Peter Moore. The first two games had sold millions of copies, and *Halo 3*, coming in 2007, was one of the most anticipated games ever. "We felt that [*Halo*] was IP that lent itself well to a real-time strategy game, given the way that the universe was constructed. Good guys versus bad guys. All the stuff you needed in an RTS. And I think that probably the data and the evidence lent towards a lower-risk opportunity in *Halo* than in new IP."

This sort of move isn't uncommon in the video game industry, where publishers tend to be conservative and risk averse, leaning toward established franchises and sequels whenever possible. Even the most ambitious game studios sometimes rejigger their games to incorporate familiar franchises. Yet for Devine and his development team, who had spent nearly a year working on this project, telling them to change it to a more marketable IP was like telling a new mother to go swap her infant for a better-looking one.

Over lengthy, heated discussions, Microsoft's executives explained that if Ensemble wanted to make its console RTS, it would have to be based on *Halo*. End of story. "It was basically put as, either you make this *Halo*," Devine said, "or you're all going to get laid off."

Devine was shattered. He'd spent months creating and cultivating *Phoenix*'s world and characters, and he thought they were just as important to the game as anything else they'd done. It wasn't just "the console RTS"—it was his own unique creation. "When you're knee deep in making your own IP, you love it," Devine said. "You really do, you love it. It's yours and it's fantastic."

He also realized that substituting *Phoenix*'s lore for *Halo* characters would have all sorts of logistical consequences. They'd have to scrap most of the work they'd done so far. "When you're presented with making *Halo*, you try to explain it's not just a matter of calling these aliens the 'Covenant' and these humans the 'UNSC,' it's actually a huge change," Devine said. "That I don't think came across very loud and clear. I think Microsoft felt that it was just a color change, a graphical change."

"I don't remember being one hundred percent surprised," said Chris Rippy. "I'm sure it was way more painful for Graeme, because he put blood, sweat, and tears into that design and he's a passionate guy too, so I know it was more painful for him."

Heartbroken, Devine considered quitting Ensemble. He sat at his computer and started up Google. What was this whole *Halo* thing about, anyway? It was huge, sure. But why did people care about it? Were they just into shooting aliens' heads off? Or was there some sort of hidden depth that Devine didn't know about? As he read more and more about *Halo* lore, from the superpowered hero Master Chief to the complex alien empire known as the Covenant, Devine started to realize it might be the latter. "My view of [*Halo*] Friday night was that it was a bunch of purple aliens that moved really fast in front of you and you shot them," Devine said. "My view Monday morning was, 'Boy, they put a lot of thought into this across a lot of years. Maybe there is something more to it than I thought.'"

With that, Devine and crew made their decision: *Phoenix* would become *Halo Wars*. Goodbye, Sway; hello, Master Chief. Except they weren't allowed to use Master Chief. Bungie, the studio behind *Halo*, didn't want this team of strangers in Texas messing around with their iconic lead character. Bungie and Ensemble were sister studios, but Bungie was the older, more popular sister—the one who got all of mom and dad's attention. *Age of Empires* was big, but compared with *Halo* it had the cultural impact of a brunch photo on Instagram. In 2005, Bungie's first-person shooter series was one of the biggest things on the planet.

A few days later, the *Phoenix* leads flew up to Seattle to visit Bungie. First they met with the studio's top leaders. They sat down with Joe Staten, the longtime writer of *Halo*, to talk about the lore and story. They geeked out about control schemes with Jaime Griesemer, *Halo*'s design lead. Later they addressed the rest of Bungie's staff in a conference room. As Chris Rippy and Graeme Devine stood in front of the makers of *Halo* and talked about their exciting new project, they were greeted by nothing but blank stares.

"We told them that we were going to be making a *Halo* RTS, and I don't think any of them had any idea or any warning that this meeting was going to happen," said Rippy. "And if you know the Bungie guys, they are very protective of their stuff. So I think we shocked them. I wouldn't say it was hostile, but the reception was cold. And it's not their fault. If somebody had come to us and said, 'Hey we're making this *Age of Empires* action game,' we'd probably have the same reaction if we didn't know what was going on."

To mitigate the tension, Devine and Rippy did what they did best: they played video games. Just a few minutes after telling Bungie's staff about *Halo Wars*, Devine set them all up with an early build of *Phoenix*, to prove that they'd made a console RTS that felt good to play. "By the time [Bungie] had processed a little of the shock, they were already in front of the game playing it," said Rippy. "That helped a lot." It also helped that Devine was eager to absorb as much *Halo* lore as humanly possible. Everything Joe Staten said, Devine gobbled up, no matter how esoteric or granular it got. By the end of the visit, Devine wanted to be able to explain, in detail, the difference between a San'Shyuum and a Sangheili. (The San'Shyuum, of course, are the prophetic leaders of the Covenant, while the Sangheili are a race of saurian warriors.)

When the *Halo Wars* team landed back in Dallas, they scrapped just about everything they'd done. They kept the control scheme and the user interface, but all the other ideas they'd put into the *Phoenix* project would be useless for a *Halo* game. The team began drawing up new design ideas, story beats, and concept art for *Halo Wars*, knowing that they were essentially starting from scratch.

Because Bungie maintained ownership over all things *Halo*, Ensemble would have to get Bungie's approval on even the most basic story ideas, which could be a bureaucratic process. Ensemble decided that they wanted the game to revolve around a group of United Nations Space Command (UNSC) soldiers on a ship called the *Spirit of Fire*, and that the bulk of combat would take place on the planet Arcadia, which the team had invented just for *Halo Wars*. All these decisions had to go through Bungie.

Recognizing that it might help to be charming, Graeme Devine designed a fictional travel pamphlet for Arcadia and showed it to Joe Staten, who was responsible for the series' lore at Bungie. "I said, 'I'm adding a new planet. Please, can I add this? Here's a travel brochure for it,'" Devine said. Staten was amused by Devine's quirky pitches, and in the coming months, Devine would fly up to Seattle every few weeks to collaborate with Bungie on *Halo Wars*' story. "I think in the beginning they were really worried," said Devine, "but after a while they started to really trust me."

Yet the *Halo Wars* team always felt like they were a couple of steps behind. It was difficult to tell a story in the *Halo* universe when the *Halo* universe existed mostly in the heads of a bunch of people who lived two thousand miles away. And besides, Bungie had its own project to deal with—the secretive *Halo 3*. "We ran into problems of what they were willing to show us and tell us on *Halo 3*, which made things difficult," said Chris Rippy. "They were looking after their story and what they were doing. They were being pretty protective, so that led to some gaps in our knowledge that we would have to work around."

The truth was, a large chunk of Bungie's leadership was never really happy about *Halo Wars*, according to several people who used to work at both companies. Bungie tolerated Ensemble's questions as cordially as they could. They got a kick out of the whimsical Graeme Devine, and Joe Staten was always classy. But in private, Bungie's staffers would gripe that they didn't want another studio touching *Halo*. When Ensemble sent over questions or asked for permission to use certain parts of the lore, Bungie would sometimes stonewall them. In a 2012 interview with the website *GamesIndustry.biz*, Ensemble's boss, Tony Goodman, went public about their strained relationship. "Bungie was kind of sore about the idea," he told the site. "What they called it was 'the whoring out of our franchise' or something."

Tension between the two studios only exacerbated Ensemble's other problems. Development on *Halo Wars* was not going smoothly, and by some estimates, the switch to *Halo* had set the team's progress back months. They were happy with their control scheme—designers at Ensemble were convinced they'd finally cracked the "console RTS" code—but conceptualizing and building the world of *Halo Wars* took far more time than they thought it would.

By the middle of 2006, Microsoft had officially green-lit *Halo Wars*, which meant that Ensemble's management could staff up the project and start producing the art and code they'd need to get it out the door. Now they'd have to confront the problem that had popped up a few months earlier: outside of Graeme Devine, Chris Rippy, Angelo Laudon, and the rest of their small team, nobody else at Ensemble really wanted to work on *Halo Wars*. After a decade of nothing but *Age of Empires* and its spin-offs, the studio's veterans were sick of RTS games. Given the choice, many of them had flocked to the nascent MMO project in hopes of channeling their *World of Warcraft* obsessions into a big hit of their own. Others had moved to Dave Pottinger's "sci-fi *Diablo*," *Nova*.

Nobody at Ensemble could agree on what to do next, so they all just did different things. Employees would joke that their studio's name had become an ironic punchline; these days, they didn't feel like much of a family at all. Theoretically, most of their resources should have been funneled into *Halo Wars*, because their parents at Microsoft hadn't green-lit any of the other prototypes, but the studio had become fractured and cliquish. The *Age of Empires III* team didn't want to move to *Halo Wars*, and, even as the *Halo Wars* team needed to staff up, some of them didn't want the *Age* guys on their turf either.

"We were fine with it," said Colt McAnlis, the *Halo Wars* engineer. "It was a lot of politics internal to Ensemble. We were like, 'Fine, you guys move there and leave us alone.'" The *Halo Wars* team, which mostly consisted of younger, less experienced Ensemble staff, saw the veterans as arrogant and difficult to work with. "When they made a decision, they would put the hammer down," said McAnlis. "There wasn't a discussion. There wasn't an evaluation. It was just like, 'No, we're doing it this way. If you don't like it, get out.'"

Elsewhere at Ensemble, there was a perception that *Halo Wars* was just something they had to do to please Microsoft, like when a Hollywood actor shoots a superhero movie so he has the leverage to film his passion project about climate change. Most of Ensemble's veterans wanted to make other games.

At one point, the studio's leadership decided that the big MMO wouldn't take place in a brand new sci-fi world, as had been originally planned. During an all-hands meeting, Ensemble's management announced that actually, they were going to make it a *Halo* MMO. "[The designer] Ian Fischer got on stage and said, 'We've chosen an IP and it's going to be *Halo*,'" said Graeme Devine. What raised some eyebrows—and what portended bad news for Ensemble—was that they hadn't gotten official approval from Microsoft to make this decision. "We realized that Microsoft wouldn't plunk that kind of money down on an unproven IP," said Dave Pottinger. "The idea to use the Halo IP was created as a way to get the game made. So, yeah, we didn't exactly ask permission, though they knew. We knew it was going to be a risky choice."

From the outside, this all might have seemed insane. Fewer than one hundred people worked at Ensemble, yet the studio was simultaneously trying to develop three different games including an MMO, which itself would require a staff in the dozens. (*World of Warcraft*, which set the bar that Ensemble aspired to reach, had a team of fifty to sixty when it launched in 2004, according to a Blizzard spokesperson.) The studio couldn't expand without getting approval from Microsoft, and Microsoft seemed to have no interest in green-lighting any of Ensemble's other prototypes, including the *Halo* MMO. But Ensemble kept working on all three games nonetheless. "At one point we had a sci-fi RTS on a console, we had a sci-fi MMO, and we had a sci-fi *Diablo*, all three of which were different," said Dave Pottinger. "In the most negative view it was a testament to how much we weren't getting along at that point."

As a result, the *Halo Wars* team remained understaffed. "For the longest time," said Rich Geldreich, "I would wonder why we only had roughly twenty-five-ish people total on the project, when it's our next big major game, and there were all these prototypes going on." What *Halo Wars* really needed was more programmers, especially ones who knew how to handle the trickier aspects of RTS development, like simulating artificial intelligence. In a real-time strategy game, the computer must make thousands of tiny decisions every second, quietly calculating when to construct buildings and move phalanxes of units around the map. For inexperienced programmers, this was a difficult task to handle.

"Imagine you've got a game world consisting of hundreds of entities, and they all have to pathfind and make decisions in real time, or seemingly in real time," said Geldreich. "There's AI involved with that. When you give them commands, they're really high-level commands like 'go here' or 'attack here' or 'stop' or something. They have to figure out how to pathfind from A to B, and that can be very complex. Imagine if, as a unit is pathfinding from A to B, a building blows up, or a new route is created because a bunch of trees are cut down. It's a very dynamic problem." Add online multiplayer to the equation—where a laggy connection could desync two computers and throw all the simulations off—and you've got all sorts of potential for a broken video game. It didn't help that, instead of using the technology they'd developed for the *Age* games, the *Halo Wars* team had started from scratch with a brand-new engine that could take advantage of the Xbox 360's unique computing power. "Pathfinding was always a difficult problem in an RTS, but we had invested probably close to twenty man-years in pathing at that point," said Dave Pottinger. "The *Halo Wars* team threw it all away and started over."

Despite these hiccups, Microsoft was gung-ho about Ensemble's game. On September 27, 2006, the publisher revealed *Halo Wars* to the world, showcasing the game with an intense CGI trailer that depicted a war between the human Spartans and their alien opponents. At one point, Ensemble had scheduled the game to be finished by the end of 2007, and perhaps that's what Microsoft was expecting then, though scrutiny of the studio might have made it clear that wasn't going to happen.

Graeme Devine and his "team of misfits" were enjoying themselves, but the *Halo Wars* team was shorthanded, and too far behind in key areas. One day, frustrated that the art team wasn't properly capturing the *Halo* aesthetic, Rich Geldreich printed out four hundred full-color screenshots from *Halo* games to hang on all the walls. "I plastered them everywhere in the studio," he said. "In the bathrooms, in the kitchen . . . the hallways, the meeting rooms. Because I was pissed off that this game didn't look like a *Halo* game."

Other teams weren't faring much better. After nearly a year's worth of work, Dave Pottinger's *Diablo* prototype, *Nova*, got canceled. Microsoft chose to instead green-light a promising action-RPG from a different studio called *Too Human.** For a few

---

* This may have been the wrong call. *Too Human*, released by the developer Silicon Knights in 2008, was poorly received by fans and critics. In 2012, fol-

months Pottinger and a small team worked on another proto-type—a "spy Zelda" game called *Agent*—but he couldn't get the headcount he needed to finish it, and soon enough he had moved to *Halo Wars*. Pottinger's team split up. Many of the artists went to the MMO, while the programmers joined him on *Halo Wars*, which desperately needed the coding help.

In early 2007, Graeme Devine and his crew started working on a *Halo Wars* demo for E3, where they hoped to quash fans' skepticism that *Halo* would never work as a real-time strategy game. By the time the show came around, they'd created a slick ten-minute video, narrated by Devine, that demonstrated a series of battles between UNSC marines and the nasty alien Covenant. In the demo, the player built two Warthogs—*Halo*'s iconic armored pickup trucks—and had them leap over a crevasse near his base. "Warthogs can gain strategic control of areas of the map that other vehicles can't get to," Devine explained in the video.

Fans were hyped, which energized the developers at Ensemble. "That was a really sexy demo and we came away from E3 that year really excited about the game," said Dave Pottinger. "The reception was good. Graeme was the perfect showman and said all the right things about loving the IP. And he really did love the IP. We got people excited that somebody who was good at making RTSs and cared about *Halo* was going to go make the perfect marriage between the two."

But as work on the project continued, it remained clear that *Halo Wars* was in trouble. In the months following E3 2007, two major problems emerged. One was that the *Halo Wars* team

---

lowing a long legal battle, a jury ruled that Silicon Knights had breached its licensing agreement with the maker of the Unreal Engine, Epic Games, while working on games like *Too Human*. In addition to paying hefty damages, Silicon Knights had to recall unsold copies of *Too Human* and even pull the game from the Xbox 360's digital store.

remained understaffed. Many of Ensemble's veterans were still working on the *Halo* MMO, which still hadn't been green-lit but was taking up a great deal of the studio's resources. The second problem was that the design was constantly changing. As a result of Ensemble's various prototype cancellations and internal politics, there were several experienced lead designers on the *Halo Wars* team by the end of 2007, including both Graeme Devine and Dave Pottinger. Devine, who had been leading design since the *Phoenix* days back in 2005, had a specific vision in mind for the game, while Pottinger, the senior *Age* designer who had just joined the project a few months earlier, had other ideas in mind.

But an orchestra needs only one conductor, and the *Halo Wars* team spent a great deal of time getting into fights. "Not yelling fights, but loud fights," Devine said. "It's funny, it's always around game things. Should the economy be cheaper or should the economy be more expensive? Should bases be freestanding or bases all be connected together? It's all good stuff—it's not, 'Oh my gosh your T-shirt is terrible.' It's all just awesome stuff that makes a game much better. But at the time it's highly stressful."

One of the biggest fights centered on what Devine called the "rule of eight," a guideline that the *Halo Wars* team had been following since back in the *Phoenix* days. What that meant was that the player could select only eight units at once, to ensure that the gameplay didn't feel too clunky and complicated on a controller. Some of the designers began to question this rule, arguing that it was making *Halo Wars* too simple. Devine pushed back. "When you playtest every single day, you get very good at the controls," Devine said. "And you forget that you had to learn them at one point. And so all of a sudden you think, well ten of these would be perfectly easy. Sixteen, even."

It's a common dilemma in game development: when you're working on the same game for years, you'll inevitably get bored.

It's tempting to make changes just for the sake of making changes, to spice things up because you're sick of using the same simple control scheme when you get into work every day. For *Halo Wars*, that became a constant point of tension. Devine and his team had intentionally made this game simpler than its RTS counterparts on the PC because the console controls would be so unfamiliar to people. And now some people were trying to make it more complicated? "We were trying to avoid layers of thinking," said Chris Rippy. "One of the biggest problems with long game development is, when you playtest the game for too long, you invent problems and you add layers to the game that don't need to be added."

Although they had impressed fans with that Devine-narrated demo at E3 2007, the *Halo Wars* team was in a sad state. They'd scripted the demo entirely by hand, with code that wouldn't work in the final game. Sure, the graphics were running in real time, but the artificial intelligence wasn't properly hooked up, and playing an actual match of *Halo Wars* wasn't nearly as satisfying as the demo made it look.

In Dave Pottinger's eyes, *Halo Wars* needed to go in a totally new direction. "We didn't have a game that was fun," said Pottinger. "It didn't work. The E3 demo was a pretty kick-ass demo but not something that was representative of the gameplay. It was just entirely built for E3." In the months that followed, the *Halo Wars* team continued to argue over the game's basic features. Were the units on the screen too small? Why was base building so complicated? Should they have "control groups" that would allow players to assign hotkeys to different squads of units, as in *Star-Craft* and other RTS games?

After all the squabbling, something had to give. That something turned out to be Graeme Devine. "When lead designers are fighting, it's not good," Devine said. "So we had one meeting where I said, 'Dave, you take the lead design position. I'm hav-

ing a lot of fun on the story. I'm just going to stick to the story.'"
Devine remained the face of the game, showing it off at Microsoft
marketing meetings and press events. And Dave Pottinger, who
for years had resisted working on another RTS game, became the
lead designer of *Halo Wars*.

Right away, Pottinger made big changes to the core mechanics of *Halo Wars*. "We basically threw the design out and started
over," Pottinger said. He altered almost all the units, including
the leaping Warthogs they'd shown at E3, which weren't quite
working out. (Warthogs would remain in *Halo Wars*, but they
would no longer have the ability to jump gaps.) He ditched the
sprawling base-building system, replacing it with "prefabricated"
bases that each held a finite number of slots. He overhauled the
resource system, reducing the amount of time players would have
to spend managing their economy. And he added a "select all"
button, which the team had resisted for a long time. With *Halo
Wars* scheduled for release in just a few months, Pottinger threw
out nearly all of Devine's design work. "I took over the design,"
Pottinger said, "and Graeme kept doing the story stuff which was
a full-time job, and he did a great job at that."

At the same time, Ensemble's other team was also dealing
with turmoil. For years now, a large chunk of the studio had
been working on their dream project, the *Halo* MMO. The MMO
wasn't exactly a secret—Microsoft knew that Ensemble wanted
to make its own version of *World of Warcraft*—but Microsoft
still hadn't given it the green light, either. To some on the Xbox
team, it was a surprise to find out that Ensemble had dedicated
so many staff to the *Halo* MMO when the studio should have
ostensibly been focusing on *Halo Wars*. "It was very common for
people [from Microsoft] to show up and go, 'What the fuck is this,
why are you working on that?'" said Colt McAnlis. "I remember
there were some key meetings I was in where people were like, 'We

didn't know you guys were putting resources on this. We thought these resources were over there.'" (Others dispute this, saying that Microsoft's management was well aware of how many people Ensemble had on the MMO.)

Soon enough, the ax came down. Microsoft made it clear to Ensemble's leadership that it had no interest in spending tens of millions on an MMO, and the project was unceremoniously canceled. "We made trade-offs," said Dave Pottinger. "Part of why we did *Halo Wars* was to give us a chance to do the MMO. . . . I think unfortunately the MMO was going to be a huge thing, and Microsoft decided that it wasn't going to be something they wanted us to do." Some members of the MMO team split off and worked on new prototypes for a while—including a potential *Age of Empires 4*—while others moved over to *Halo Wars*.

All of this drama was undoubtedly raising eyebrows at Microsoft. Ever since the original *Age of Empires* in 1997, there had been bouts of tension between Ensemble and its publisher. As long as Ensemble was shipping games—and generating profits—those tensions would ultimately fizzle. But Ensemble hadn't released a new game since *Age of Empires III* over two years earlier, in 2005. All this talk about an MMO had frustrated Microsoft's executives, who were scaling back on PC gaming in favor of the red-hot Xbox 360. (The *Halo* MMO, unlike *Halo Wars*, was designed for PCs.) Keeping Ensemble's hundred-plus staff on the payroll was starting to seem like a bad investment.

"Contrary to popular belief, headcount's not completely free at Microsoft," said Shane Kim, who was a vice president in the Xbox division. "The fact of the matter was it was sort of zero-sum, a lot of headcount. They're very expensive. And we decided we needed to deploy that in other areas."

■ ■ ■

Unlike most game developers, Colt McAnlis enjoyed getting to work at 6:00 a.m. His coworkers wouldn't typically arrive for another four or five hours, and he felt most productive when he was coding by himself, with nobody around to distract him. McAnlis was responsible for some of the most complicated engineering work on *Halo Wars*: art tools, light shaders, multicore threading processes. Solitude helped.

One Monday in September 2008, McAnlis arrived at the office at his usual time. It didn't take long for him to realize that something was off. Instead of empty desks, he found dozens of his coworkers mulling around. "I [thought], 'Wait, what the hell was going on?'" he said. "What are you all doing here?" Nobody would give him a straight answer until a few hours later, when a coworker mentioned that a bunch of Microsoft bigwigs were coming to visit.

Word got around that everyone at Ensemble needed to go to the auditorium for an all-hands meeting. As they filed in, they started seeing scores of Microsoft employees: HR people, vice presidents, executives. When the whole company had gotten settled, Ensemble's CEO, Tony Goodman, stood up front and dropped a nuclear bomb.

"Tony gets onstage and says, 'We have some news,'" said Graeme Devine. "'Ensemble is going to be closing after *Halo Wars*.'"

After fourteen years and a dozen games, Ensemble's time was coming to an end. The good news, Goodman said, was that Microsoft wanted them to finish *Halo Wars*. Everyone at Ensemble would keep his or her job for another four months or so, which would give people a fair amount of time to look for new gigs. "Microsoft wanted to talk to us about keeping us all on through the end of *Halo Wars*," said Devine, "and [Tony] hands it over to Microsoft to explain exactly how they were going to do that, because we'd all just gotten the news that we have no jobs after we ship this game."

For two hours, Microsoft's representatives, including VP Shane Kim, stood in front of the room and answered questions from hurt Ensemble employees. "They're going, 'Why us?'" said Kim. "'You've got Rare, you've got Lionhead [two other game studios]. . . . Surely there must be other places you can cut instead of us.' Unfortunately, it's one of the darker sides of the job." Kim tried to be diplomatic, adding that Microsoft would be giving solid severance packages to those Ensemble staff who stayed until *Halo Wars* was out the door.

Some people started crying. Others got angry. "I flipped the fuck out," said Colt McAnlis. "My wife and I had just gotten pregnant for the very first time. And our baby was due at the end of January, which was supposed to be the exact date the company was supposed to close. We had a newborn that was supposed to be delivered the day I was no longer supposed to have a job." Two people—the brothers Paul and David Bettner—immediately quit Ensemble and started their own studio, Newtoy, which went on to make the popular *Scrabble* clone *Words with Friends*. One might say their move worked out nicely: in 2010, Zynga purchased Newtoy for $53.3 million.

Rich Geldreich, the graphics engineer, also left the studio shortly after hearing about the shutdown. "My brain had cracked in two," he said. "I went crazy. I just couldn't handle the fact that Ensemble imploded. It was such an awesome company. I had five years invested in that company, and all that technology and coding and everything and it just was gone. And everybody was cracking around me. We were all going crazy. It was ridiculous." (Soon afterward, Geldreich took a job at Valve.)

Those who remained at Ensemble found themselves in another uncomfortable situation. It wasn't that they'd be out of jobs in a few months—it was that some of them *wouldn't* be out of jobs.

Tony Goodman informed everyone that he'd negotiated a contract with Microsoft as part of the closure. With this deal, he told the team, he'd be able to start an independent new studio, which he was calling Robot Entertainment. The Microsoft contract would allow them to make an online version of *Age of Empires* as they tried to get their business going.

The problem was, Goodman had secured only enough money to hire less than half of Ensemble's current staff. And only a few people knew exactly who had made the cut. "People all of a sudden were jockeying for new jobs," said Colt McAnlis. "It was madness for a while because none of us really knew what was going on. There was always this watercooler chat: 'Hey did they talk to you? No they didn't talk to you? Well, if they offered you a job would you accept it?'"

Those who were invited to join Robot found out quickly, but to those who weren't getting spots, the following days were miserable. At one point, to clear the air, a manager tacked a piece of paper to the wall with a full list of Ensemble employees who would be going to Robot. Dozens of people came crowding around to see who'd made the cut. "It was like that scene in all the movies when the teacher comes out," said McAnlis. "'Here's who's been accepted into the cheerleading squad,' and everybody rushes to the board."

To many at Ensemble, this new layer of politics was making a bad situation even worse. "In our view we saved half the jobs," said Dave Pottinger. "[To] whoever wasn't offered a spot at Robot, we screwed half the company over. . . . I think we tried to do our best. We made mistakes." Other than Rich Geldreich and the Bettner brothers, everyone remained at Ensemble, despite the chaos. (The severance packages helped.) And over the next few months, Ensemble tried to put aside politics—and the fact that their studio would be shutting down—to finish *Halo Wars*.

"The motivation was to go out on as good a note as we could," said Dave Pottinger. Ensemble's staff wound up crunching for months, sleeping at their desks up until the very last minute to finish *Halo Wars* by the end of January, when they knew they'd all have to leave. "The thing I'm most proud of at the end was, when we announced the closure, the next day [three people left]," said Pottinger. "Every single other person stayed to finish the game."

"[We were] dead men walking," said Graeme Devine. "It was pretty crazy." In early 2009, Microsoft flew Devine around the world on a press tour. Traveling alongside the polarizing British designer Peter Molyneux, who was about to release the RPG *Fable 2*, Devine conducted interviews and showed off demos of *Halo Wars*. When journalists asked him about Ensemble's closure, he dodged their questions. "I remember pieces of paper being put in front of me by Microsoft [telling me] 'This is what you can say,'" Devine said.

For those surreal final months, Ensemble's staff tried to put their internal politics aside, coming together in hopes of releasing something they could all take pride in having made. Even though they all knew the studio was closing, they kept coming into work every day. They kept crunching. And they kept doing everything they could to make *Halo Wars* as good as possible. "There were great days like nothing had ever happened and nothing was happening, and then there were depressing days," said Chris Rippy. "But it was a prideful group and everybody wanted to do a great job, and everybody knew this was kind of the studio's legacy, and wanted to do something to represent the studio properly."

On February 26, 2009, *Halo Wars* came out. It was received fairly well, getting solid reviews from gaming sites like *Eurogamer* and *IGN*. When they look back, those who were on the *Halo Wars* team say they're proud to have released even a half-decent game after what they went through. Microsoft even hired a new developer—Creative Assembly—to make a sequel, *Halo Wars 2*, which came out in February 2017.

A few studios rose from the ashes of Ensemble. There was Robot Entertainment, which went on to make *Age of Empires Online* and then a popular tower-defense series called *Orcs Must Die!* A different faction of ex-Ensemble developers started a company called Bonfire, which was also purchased by Zynga, then shut down in 2013.* Those developers later founded yet another studio, Boss Fight Entertainment. Nearly a decade after Ensemble's closure, many of its former employees are still working together. They were a family, after all. "We hated each other, but we loved each other too," said Pottinger. "Ensemble lost very few people over its run compared to any other studio. . . . You don't have a turnover rate of—it was less than four percent or something like that—you don't have that if you don't make people happy."

Back at E3 2008, just a few months before Ensemble closed its doors for good, the *Halo Wars* team put out a cinematic trailer that may have, in retrospect, been a subconscious cry for help. "Five years. Five long years," the trailer's narrator said, as a group of marines fought off the invading Covenant alien forces. "At first it was going well."

A group of Covenant forces descended from the sky, taking out marine after marine in what quickly became a bloody massacre. The narrator continued: "Then setback after setback, loss after loss, made what was going to be a quick and decisive win into five years of hell."

---

* Not to be confused with the other video game studio named Bonfire, which Blizzard's Josh Mosqueira cofounded in 2016.

6

■■■■■■■■■ ■

DRAGON AGE: INQUISITION

The website *Consumerist* once held an annual poll for "Worst Company in America," asking readers to select the country's most reviled corporation through a March Madness–style elimination tournament. In 2008, as the US economy collapsed, the insurance salesmen at AIG took top honors. In 2011 the award went to BP, whose oil rigs had just spilled 210 million gallons of crude in the Gulf Coast. But in 2012 and 2013, a different type of company won the award, beating out the likes of Comcast and Bank of America, as over 250,000 voters flocked to declare that the United States' worst company was in fact the video game publisher Electronic Arts (EA).

There were many reasons for this ignominious victory, including the rise of optional "microtransaction"* payments in EA games and the spectacular disaster of the publisher's online-only

---

* Microtransactions, which rose to popularity in the mid-2000s thanks to publishers like EA, are in-game items (like weapons or costumes) that players can buy with real money. Few things inspire more anger from video game fans.

SimCity reboot.* What may have rankled gamers most, however, was what they believed EA had done to BioWare.

BioWare, a development studio founded in 1995 by three medical doctors who thought making games might be a cool hobby, leaped into fame in 1998 with the *Dungeons & Dragons*–based role-playing game *Baldur's Gate* (a game so influential that it would play a major role in the stories of two other games in this book, *Pillars of Eternity* and *The Witcher 3*). In the following years, BioWare became renowned for a string of top-tier RPGs like *Neverwinter Nights*, *Star Wars: Knights of the Old Republic*, and a space opera called *Mass Effect* that appealed not just to people who liked to shoot aliens, but also to people who liked to smooch them.

In 2007, Electronic Arts bought BioWare, and in recent years, it had seemed to fans that the studio was in a funk. BioWare's two new flagship franchises, *Mass Effect* and the Tolkien-ish *Dragon Age*, were beloved but stalling. *Dragon Age 2*, released in 2011, was panned for feeling incomplete. And 2012's *Mass Effect 3*, which put a bow on the spacefaring trilogy, angered hard-core fans with a controversial ending in which the player's choices didn't seem to matter.†

---

* Thanks to network issues, *SimCity* was essentially unplayable for days after it launched in March 2013. Even when the servers settled down and the game started working, players discovered flaws in the simulation: for example, cars would always take the shortest routes between destinations, even if those routes were full of traffic. Cops wouldn't cross intersections. Trading didn't function properly. At *Kotaku*, we created a special tag for the occasion: "SimCity Disaster Watch."

† BioWare later released free downloadable content that expanded and added more choices to *Mass Effect 3*'s ending. EA's labels president, Frank Gibeau, endorsed the decision. Recalled BioWare studio head Aaryn Flynn: "Frank once said to [*Mass Effect 3* lead] Casey [Hudson] and I, 'Are you sure you guys even want to do this? Are you just going to feed the trolls up there?' We're like, 'No, we want to do this, we really want to get this right, do this thing.' He said, 'OK if you want to.'"

Surely, fans thought, these missteps were EA's fault. The problems started when EA purchased the studio, didn't they? All you had to do was look at the long list of iconic studios that EA had acquired and then shut down—a list that included Bullfrog (*Dungeon Keeper*), Westwood (*Command & Conquer*), and Origin (*Ultima*)—to fear that BioWare might be next. Fans went to *Consumerist* to send a message, even if that meant declaring a video game publisher more heinous than a predatory mortgage lender.

Amid these theatrics, BioWare's studio head, Aaryn Flynn, was staring down a far more relevant challenge: *Dragon Age: Inquisition*, the third game in the fantasy series. *Inquisition* was going to be the most ambitious game that BioWare had ever made. It was a game with a lot to prove—that BioWare could return to form; that EA wasn't crippling the studio; that BioWare could make an "open-world" RPG, in which the player could move freely through massive environments. But, as Flynn knew, *Dragon Age: Inquisition* was already behind schedule thanks to unfamiliar new technology. Their new game engine, Frostbite, was requiring more work than anyone at the studio had expected.

"The discovery of what's possible on a new engine is both exhilarating and humbling," Flynn wrote on BioWare's blog in September 2012, just after announcing *Dragon Age: Inquisition*. Perhaps if he had taken a few shots of vodka beforehand—or if he didn't have to worry about what Electronic Arts' PR staff would think—he might have added what BioWare staffers were really thinking: *What's possible is that the new engine is a technical disaster.*

BioWare's main headquarters are nestled in a small office complex near downtown Edmonton, a city best known for its enormous shopping mall and for temperatures that regularly plummet into the obscene. It's no wonder the studio came up with *Dragon Age*. If you want to dream up a fantasy world inhabited by fire-breathing mythical creatures, few cities are more suitable for the act than Edmonton.

Dragon Age, which BioWare hoped would become the *Lord of the Rings* of video games, first entered development in 2002. After a hellish seven-year slog, BioWare released the series' first game, *Dragon Age: Origins*, in November 2009. It was appealing to all types of gamers. Hard-core RPG fans dug the strategic combat and consequential choices, while the more romantically inclined loved that they could seduce their dreamy party members, like the snarky knight Alistair and the sultry wizard Morrigan. *Dragon Age: Origins* became a massive success, selling millions of copies and, most important, inspiring hundreds of thousands of lines of fan fiction.

Leading the *Dragon Age* development team was Mark Darrah, a well-liked BioWare veteran who had been at the company since the late 1990s. Darrah had a dry sense of humor and a bushy beard that had been bright red in 2013, when I first met him, but three years later was invaded by blotches of gray. "Mark is very good at the business of game development," said Cameron Lee, a producer at BioWare. "Internally, we call the *Dragon Age* team the pirate ship. It'll get where it needs to go, but it's going to go all over the place. Sail over here. Drink some rum. Go over here. Do something else. That's how Mark likes to run his team." (An alternative take, from someone else who worked on the game: "*Dragon Age* was referred to as the pirate ship because it was chaotic and the loudest voice in the room usually set the direction. I think they smartly adopted the name and morphed it into something better.")

After shipping *Dragon Age: Origins* in 2009, Darrah and his crew of pirates already had some ideas for their next big game. Whereas in *Origins* you played a fanatical Grey Warden whose life was dedicated to thwarting demons, the next *Dragon Age* game would be about larger-scale political conflict. Darrah envisioned a game about an Inquisition—in *Dragon Age* lore, an autonomous organization that solves conflicts across the globe—with the player as leader and Inquisitor.

Then, plans changed. Progress had stalled on one of BioWare's other games, the MMO *Star Wars: The Old Republic*. Developed at BioWare's studio in Austin, Texas, *The Old Republic* kept missing release dates, gradually slipping from 2009 to 2010 to 2011. Frustrated EA executives wanted a new product from BioWare to bolster their quarterly sales targets, and they decided that the *Dragon Age* team would have to fill the gap. After some lengthy discussions, Mark Darrah and Aaryn Flynn agreed to deliver *Dragon Age 2* in March 2011, just sixteen months after the release of *Dragon Age: Origins*.

"*The Old Republic* moved, and there was a hole," said Darrah. "Basically, *Dragon Age 2* exists to fill that hole. That was the inception. It was always intended to be a game made to fit in that." Darrah wanted to call it *Dragon Age: Exodus* ("Which I wish we'd stuck with") but EA's marketing executives insisted that they call it *Dragon Age 2*, no matter what that name implied.

The first *Dragon Age* had taken seven years to make. Now BioWare would have just over a year to build a sequel. For any big game, that would be difficult; for a role-playing game, it was near impossible. There were just so many variables. *Dragon Age: Origins* had contained four giant areas, each with its own factions, monsters, and quests. Decisions the player made at the beginning of *Origins*—like how the character's "origin" story unfolded—had a significant impact on the rest of the story, which meant that BioWare's writers and designers had to build different scenes to account for every possibility. If you played as a dwarf noble who had been exiled from the labyrinthine city of Orzammar, the other dwarves would have to react accordingly upon your return. If you were a human, they wouldn't care nearly as much.

None of this was achievable in a year. Even if BioWare forced everyone to work nonstop overtime on *Dragon Age 2*, they just wouldn't have the bandwidth to make a sequel as ambitious as fans expected. To solve this problem, Mark Darrah and crew shelved the old Inquisition idea and made a risky call: instead of taking you through multiple areas of their fantasy world, *Dragon Age 2* would unfold within a single city, Kirkwall, over the course of a decade. That way, the *Dragon Age* team could recycle locations for many of the game's encounters, shaving months off their development time. They also axed features that had been in *Dragon Age: Origins*, like the ability to customize your party members' equipment. "It didn't pan out perfectly, but had we not made those decisions it would've been significantly more troubled," said Mike Laidlaw, the creative director of *Dragon Age*.* "So we made the best calls we could on a fairly tight time line."

When *Dragon Age 2* came out in March 2011, players reacted poorly. They were loud about their anger, hammering the game for its tedious side quests and reused environments.† Wrote one blogger, "The drop in overall quality is staggering on a cosmic level, and there's no way I'd ever recommend anyone buying this game under any circumstances." The game didn't sell as well as *Dragon Age: Origins*—although "in certain dark accounting corners of

---

* At most video game studios, the title "creative director" refers to the lead of a project, but EA used different nomenclature.

† Some fans have warmed to *Dragon Age 2* in the years since it was released, and many at BioWare say they're still very proud of the game. "*Dragon Age 2* is a project where I think everybody who worked on it, we were all in this together, we all grew closer," said John Epler, a cinematic designer.

EA, it's considered a wild success," Darrah said—and by the summer of 2011, BioWare had decided to cancel *Dragon Age 2*'s expansion pack, *Exalted March*, in favor of a totally new game. They needed to get away from the stigma of *Dragon Age 2*.

Really, they needed to reboot the franchise. "There was something to be proven, I think, from the *Dragon Age* team coming off *Dragon Age 2*, that this was a team that could make 'triple-A quality' good games," Darrah said. "There was a bit of a tone, not within the studio but around the industry, that there were essentially two tiers of BioWare: there was the *Mass Effect* team and then there was everyone else. And I think there was a lot of desire to fight back against that. The *Dragon Age* team is a scrappy bunch."

There are certain things in role-playing games we've grown to take for granted. Rare is the gamer who comes home from the store with the latest *Final Fantasy*, pops it into their PlayStation, and goes on Facebook to talk about what a beautiful save system it has. You won't find many reviews raving about the new *Fallout*'s ability to properly toggle between combat and noncombat game states. *Skyrim* didn't sell millions because it knows how to keep track of your inventory. These systems are necessary but unglamorous, and certainly not fun to make, which is one of the reasons most video games use engines.

The word "engine" calls to mind the guts of a car, but in game development, an engine is more like a car factory. Every time you build a new car, you'll need many of the same components: tires, axles, plush leather seats. Similarly, just about every video game needs the same core features: a physics system, a graphics renderer, a main menu. Coding new versions of those features for every game would be like designing new wheels every time you wanted to manufacture a sedan. Engines, like factories, allow their users to recycle features and avoid unnecessary work.

Even before finishing *Dragon Age 2*, Aaryn Flynn and Mark Darrah were looking for a new engine for their fantasy franchise. Their in-house game engine, Eclipse, felt creaky and obsolete for the type of gorgeous high-end games they hoped to make. Basic cinematic effects, like lens flares, were impossible for Eclipse to handle. "Graphically, it wasn't fully featured," Darrah said. "It was getting long in the tooth from that perspective."

On top of that, the *Mass Effect* series used the third-party Unreal Engine, which made it difficult for the two BioWare teams to collaborate. Basic tasks like rendering a 3-D model required a totally different process on Eclipse than they did on Unreal. "Our technology strategy was just a mess," said Flynn. "Every time we'd start a new game, people would say, 'Oh, we should just pick a new engine.'"

Flynn and Darrah powwowed with one of their bosses, EA executive Patrick Söderlund, and came back with a solution: the Frostbite engine, which the EA-owned studio DICE, in Sweden, had developed for its *Battlefield* games. Although nobody had ever used Frostbite to make RPGs, Flynn and Darrah found it appealing for a few reasons. It was powerful, for one. DICE had a team of engineers who worked full-time on Frostbite's graphic capabilities, beefing up the visual effects that made, for example, trees sway in the wind. Because this was the video game industry, they also spent a lot of time making it look pretty to blow things up.

The other big advantage of Frostbite was that EA owned it. If BioWare started developing *all* its games on the Frostbite engine, it could share technology with its sister studios, borrowing tools from other EA-owned developers like Visceral (*Dead Space*) or Criterion (*Need for Speed*) whenever those companies learned cool new tricks for enhancing facial capture or making it look even prettier to blow things up.

In the fall of 2010, as the bulk of the *Dragon Age* team was finishing up *DA2*, Mark Darrah pulled together a small group to work on a prototype they called *Blackfoot*. This prototype had two major goals: to start getting a feel for the Frostbite engine, and to make a free-to-play multiplayer game set in the *Dragon Age* universe. The latter never happened, and after a few months *Blackfoot* fizzled, hinting at bigger challenges to come. "It wasn't making enough progress, ultimately because its team was too small," Darrah said. "Frostbite's a hard engine to make progress with if your team is too small. It takes a certain number of people to just keep it on."

By the end of 2011, with both *Blackfoot* and the *Dragon Age 2* expansion pack canceled, Darrah had a substantial team available to start working on BioWare's next big game. They resurfaced the old Inquisition idea and began to talk about what a *Dragon Age 3* might look like on Frostbite. By 2012 they had a plan in place. *Dragon Age 3: Inquisition* (which later ditched the "3") would be an open-world RPG, inspired heavily by Bethesda's smash hit *Skyrim*. It would take place all across new areas of *Dragon Age*'s world, and it would hit all the beats that *Dragon Age 2* couldn't. "My secret mission was to shock and awe the players with the massive amounts of content," said Matt Goldman, the art director. "People were complaining, 'Oh there wasn't enough in *Dragon Age 2*.' OK, you're not going to say that. At the end of *Inquisition*, I actually want people to go, 'Oh god, not [another] level.'"

BioWare wanted *Dragon Age: Inquisition* to be a launch title for the next generation of game consoles, the PlayStation 4 and Xbox One. But EA's profit forecasters, caught up in the rise of iPad and iPhone gaming, were worried that the PS4 and Xbox One wouldn't sell very well. As a safeguard, the publisher insisted that they also ship on the older PlayStation 3 and Xbox 360, both of which were already in tens of millions of homes. (Most early PS4/ Xbox One games followed the same strategy, except for a certain Polish RPG that we'll cover in chapter 9.) With personal computers added to the mix, this meant *Inquisition* would have to ship on five platforms at once—a first for BioWare.

Ambitions were piling up. This was to be BioWare's first 3-D open-world game and their first game on Frostbite, an engine that had never been used to make RPGs. It needed to be made in roughly two years, it needed to ship on five platforms, and, oh yeah, it needed to help restore the reputation of a studio that had been beaten up pretty badly. "Basically we had to do new consoles, a new engine, new gameplay, build the hugest game that we've ever made, and build it to a higher standard than we ever did," said Matt Goldman. "With tools that don't exist."

If an engine is like a car factory, then in 2012, as *Inquisition* entered development, the Frostbite engine was like a car factory without the proper assembly lines. Before *Dragon Age: Inquisition*, developers at EA had used Frostbite mostly to make first-person shooters like *Battlefield* and *Medal of Honor*. Frostbite's engineers had never built tools that would, say, make the main character visible to the player. Why would they need to? In first-person shooters, you see through the character's eyes. Your body consists of disembodied hands, a gun, and, if you're really lucky, some legs. *Battlefield* didn't need RPG stats, magical spells, or even save systems—the campaign kept track of your progress with automatic checkpoints. As a result, Frostbite couldn't create any of those things.

"It was an engine that was designed to build shooters," said Darrah. "We had to build everything on top of it." At first, the

Dragon Age team underestimated just how much work this would be. "Characters need to move and walk and talk and put on swords, and those swords need to do damage when you swing them, and you need to be able to press a button to swing them," said Mike Laidlaw. Frostbite could do some of that, Laidlaw added, but not all of it.

Darrah and his team knew that they were the Frostbite guinea pigs—that they were exchanging short-term pain for long-term benefits—but during early development on *Dragon Age: Inquisition*, even the most basic tasks were excruciating. Frostbite didn't yet have the tools they needed to make an RPG. Without those tools in place, a designer had no idea how long it might take to do something as fundamental as making areas. *Dragon Age: Inquisition* was supposed to allow the player to control a party of four people, but that system wasn't in the game yet. How could a level designer figure out where to place obstacles on a map if he couldn't test it out with a full party of characters?

Even when Frostbite's tools did start functioning, they were finicky and difficult to use. John Epler, a cinematic designer, recalled one internal demo for which he had to go through a Sisyphean ritual just to build a cut scene. "I had to get to the conversation in-game, open my tools at the same time, and then as soon as I hit the line, I had to hit the pause button really, really quickly," Epler said. "Because otherwise it would just play through to the next line. Then I had to add animations, and then I could scrub it two or three times before it would crash and then I'd have to start the process all over again. It was absolutely the worst tools experience I've ever had."

The Frostbite team at DICE spent time supporting Epler and the other designers, answering their questions and fixing bugs, but their resources were limited. It didn't help that Sweden was eight hours ahead of Edmonton. If one of BioWare's designers had a question for DICE in the afternoon, it could take a full day before they heard an answer.

Since creating new content in Frostbite was so difficult, trying to evaluate its quality became impossible. At one point, Patrick Weekes, a writer, had finished a scene between several characters and inserted it into the game. He then took it to some of BioWare's leads for one of their standard quality reviews. When they turned on the game, they discovered that only the main character could talk. "The engine would not hook up the nonplayer character lines," Weekes said. "You would say something, and then it would go 'blip blip blip blip blip' and then you would say something again, and you'd go OK, I don't know if I can judge the level of quality without any of the words that happen."

Engine updates made this process even more challenging. Every time the Frostbite team updated the engine with new fixes and features, BioWare's programmers would have to merge it with the changes they'd made to the previous version. They'd have to go through the new code and copy-paste all the older stuff they'd built—inventory, save files, characters—then test it all out to ensure they hadn't broken anything. They couldn't find a way to automate the process, so they had to do it manually. "It was debilitating," said Cameron Lee. "There'd be times when the build wouldn't work for a month, or it was unstable as hell. Because the new version of the engine would come in, the tools team would start doing the integration. All the while, the team is still working and moving ahead, so it gets worse and worse and worse."

The art department, meanwhile, was having a blast. For all its weaknesses as an RPG engine, Frostbite was the perfect tool for creating big, gorgeous environments, and the studio's artists took advantage to build out the dense forests and murky swamps that would populate *Dragon Age: Inquisition*. Under Matt Goldman's "shock and awe" approach, BioWare's environment artists spent months making as much as possible, taking educated guesses when they didn't yet know what the designers needed. "The environment art came together quicker than any other aspect of the game," said the lead environment artist, Ben McGrath. "For a long time there was a joke on the project that we'd made a fantastic-looking screenshot generator, because you could walk around these levels with nothing to do. You could take great pictures."

Great pictures didn't make for much of a video game, though. Mike Laidlaw, who headed the story and gameplay teams, had been working with the writers and designers to come up with basic beats for *Dragon Age: Inquisition*. Sketching out the story wasn't too hard. They knew the player would organize and lead an Inquisition of like-minded soldiers; they knew the big bad would be a demonic wizard named Corypheus; and they knew that, as always, there would be a crew of companions that the player could recruit and seduce. But the concept of *Dragon Age: Inquisition* as an "open world" game was stymying Laidlaw and his team. The art team had constructed all these sprawling landscapes, but what were players going to do there?* And how could BioWare ensure that *Inquisition*'s giant world remained fun to explore after dozens of hours?

In an ideal world, a big project like *Dragon Age: Inquisition* would have a dedicated team of system designers who were solely responsible for solving those problems. They'd devise quests, activities, and all the other encounters that could keep players entertained while exploring *Inquisition*'s massive world. They'd try to envision what designers call the "core gameplay loop"—what does a thirty-minute play session look like?—and then they'd keep prototyping and iterating until that gameplay felt good.

---

* One idea that BioWare never quite took seriously: rideable dragons. "[EA's CEO] John Riccitiello told us we should have the ability to ride dragons," said Mark Darrah. "That would make it sell ten million copies." (*Dragon Age: Inquisition* did not have rideable dragons.)

In the real world, Laidlaw and his team didn't have time for that. Frostbite wouldn't allow it. As they plugged away at the game, *Inquisition*'s designers found that they couldn't test out new ideas, because so many basic features were missing. Was there enough stuff to do in each area of the game? The camera wasn't working, so they couldn't tell. Were the quests interesting enough? They couldn't answer that yet, because their combat system didn't exist.

Laidlaw and crew came up with the abstract idea that the player, as the Inquisitor, would roam the world solving problems and building some level of power, or influence, that he or she could then use to affect events on a global scale. Yet for a very long time it remained unclear how that would look in the game. The team played around with the idea of "influence" as a currency, like gold, but that system didn't seem to click. "It really could've used more small-scale refinement and testing and 'Let's try three different ways of doing this,'" Laidlaw said. "Instead [we said], 'Let's build some levels and let's hope we can figure this out as we go.'"

One day in late 2012, after a year of strained development on *Inquisition*, Mark Darrah asked Mike Laidlaw to go to lunch. "We're walking out to his car," Laidlaw said, "and I think he might have had a bit of a script in his head. [Darrah] said, 'All right, I don't actually know how to approach this, so I'm just going to say it. On a scale of one to apocalyptic. . . . How upset would you be if I said [the player] could be, I dunno, a Qunari Inquisitor?'"

Laidlaw was baffled. They'd decided that the player could be only a human in *Inquisition*. Adding other playable races, like the horned Qunari that Darrah was asking for, would mean they'd need to quadruple their budget for animation, voice acting, and scripting.

"I went, 'I think we could make that work,'" Laidlaw said, asking Darrah if he could have more budget for dialogue.

Darrah answered that if Laidlaw could make playable races happen, he couldn't just have more dialogue. He could have an entire extra year of production.

Laidlaw was thrilled. "Fuck yeah, OK," he recalled saying.

As it turned out, Mark Darrah had already determined that it would be impossible to finish *Dragon Age: Inquisition* in 2013. The game was too big, and they had underestimated the length of too many tasks because of their Frostbite issues. To make *Inquisition* as good an open-world RPG as Darrah and his crew imagined it could be, they'd have to delay it at least another year. Darrah was in the process of putting together a pitch for EA: let BioWare delay the game, and in exchange, it'd be even bigger and better than anyone at EA had envisioned.

Sitting in a second-floor conference room overlooking the hotel promenade that shared a building with BioWare, Darrah and his leads hashed out an outline of new marketing points that included mounts, a sleek new tactical camera, and the big one: playable races. They put together what they called "peelable scope" proposals: here was what they could do with an extra month; here was what they could do with six more months; here was what they could do with a year. And, worst-case scenario, here were all the things they'd have to cut if EA wouldn't let them delay *Dragon Age: Inquisition* at all.

One day in March 2013, Mark Darrah and BioWare's studio boss, Aaryn Flynn, took an early flight to the EA offices in Redwood Shores, California. They were confident that EA would give them some leeway, but it was still nerve-racking, especially in the wake of EA's recent turmoil. The publisher had just parted ways with its CEO, John Riccitiello, and had recruited a board member, Larry Probst, to keep the seat warm while it hunted for a new top executive. It was impossible to know how Probst would react to BioWare's request. Delaying *Dragon Age: Inquisition* would affect EA's financial projections for that fiscal year, which was never good news.*

Darrah and Flynn arrived at EA's headquarters first thing in the morning. As they walked in, the first person they saw was their new boss, Larry Probst. "We walked in with Larry, and then we ended up leaving at the end of the day with him as well, which I think made a good impression on him," Darrah said. The meeting lasted around two hours. "You're talking over scenarios, you're talking over impact on finances," Darrah said. "There's some yelling."

Maybe it was a convincing pitch, or maybe it was the executive turmoil. Maybe the specter of *Dragon Age 2* had an effect on Probst and crew, or maybe it was that EA didn't like being called the "Worst Company in America." An Internet poll wasn't exactly causing EA's stock to plummet, but winning the *Consumerist* award two years in a row had made a tangible impact on the publisher's executives, leading to some feisty internal meetings about how EA could repair its image. Whatever the reasons, EA greenlit the delay. Moving *Dragon Age: Inquisition* back a year might hurt Q3 earnings, but if it led to a better game, that would be a win for everyone.

I first saw *Dragon Age: Inquisition* in a lavish suite at the Grand Hyatt hotel in downtown Seattle. It was August 2013, and the next day BioWare planned to show the game to fans at the Penny

---

* Ever wondered why so many big video games come out in March? There's an easy answer for that: the fiscal year, used for reporting financial performance to stockholders, which dominates the decision making of every publicly traded company. Most game publishers end their fiscal years on March 31, so if they're looking to delay a game but still fit it in the current fiscal year, March makes for the perfect window.

Arcade Expo (PAX) next door, so the studio had invited journalists to get a preemptive peek. Sipping from a complimentary water bottle, I watched Mark Darrah and Mike Laidlaw play through a beautiful thirty-minute demo set across two war-torn regions, called Crestwood and the Western Approach. In the demo, the player-controlled Inquisitor would rush to defend a keep from invading forces, burn down boats to prevent enemy soldiers from escaping, and capture a fortress for the Inquisition.

It all looked fantastic. None of it made it into *Dragon Age: Inquisition.*

That demo, like many of the sizzling trailers we see at shows like E3, was almost entirely fake. By the fall of 2013, the *Dragon Age* team had implemented many of Frostbite's parts—the tires, the axles, the gears—but they still didn't know what kind of car they were making. Laidlaw and crew had scripted the PAX demo by hand, entirely based on what BioWare thought *might* be in the game. Most of the levels and art assets were real, but the gameplay was not. "We did not have that benefit of rock-solid prototypes," said Laidlaw. "Part of what we had to do is go out early and try to be transparent because of *Dragon Age 2.* And just say, 'Look, here, it's the game, it's running live, it's at PAX.' Because we wanted to make that statement that we're here for fans."

Dragon Age 2 hung on the team like a shadow, haunting Laidlaw and other leads as they tried to figure out which gameplay mechanics would work best for *Inquisition.* Even after the PAX showing, they had trouble sticking to one vision. "There was insecurity, and I think that's a function of coming out of a rough spell," said Laidlaw. "Which of the things that were called out on *Dragon Age 2* were a product of time and which were just a bad call? Which things should we reinvent because we have an opportunity moving into this? It leads to a ton of uncertainty." There were debates over combat—should they iterate on the fast-paced action of *Dragon Age 2* or go back to the tactical focus of *Origins*?—and many, many arguments over how to populate the wilderness areas.

In the months after PAX 2013, the BioWare team ditched much of what they'd shown during that demo, like boat burning and keep capturing.* Even small features, like the "search" tool, went through dozens of permutations. Because *Dragon Age: Inquisition* didn't have a proper preproduction phase, in which the designers could fool around with prototypes and discard the ones that didn't work, Laidlaw found himself stretched thin. He had to make impulsive decisions. "I'm sure, depending who you ask, there are members of my team who would say, 'Wow, I think we did a good job in a rough situation,'" said Laidlaw, "and others who would say, 'That Mike guy is a giant asshole.'"

Previous BioWare games had been big, but none were as massive as this. By the end of 2013, the *Dragon Age: Inquisition* team comprised more than two hundred people, with dozens of additional outsourced artists in Russia and China. Every department had its own leads, but nobody worked in a vacuum. If a writer wanted to pen a scene about two dragons fighting, she would have to take it to the design team for a layout, then to the art team for modeling, and then to the cinematics team to make sure the cameras all pointed at the right places. They needed animation; otherwise the two dragons would just stand there staring at one another. Then there was audio, visual effects, and quality assurance. Coordinating all this work was a full-time job for several people. "It was a real challenge to get

---

* For years, video game developers have struggled with the question of what to put in demos. Is it lying to fans if an E3 feature never makes it into the final game? It's a nuanced topic. "When people get really mad—'Well, you showed this, and the final game wasn't like this,'" said Mark Darrah, "[we think,] well, it was supposed to be, or we thought it was going to be."

everyone working in the same direction," said Shane Hawco, the lead character artist.

"I think to get more specific on the complexities at this scale of game development, it's the dependencies," said Aaryn Flynn. "It's the things that have to happen for the other things to work and be successful." The common term in game development circles is "blocking," which describes when a developer can't get work done because he or she is waiting for someone else to send over some integral art asset or piece of code. "'OK, well I was going to do this today, but I can't because we have a crash, so I'm going to go to this other thing,'" said Flynn. "Good developers are constantly juggling these little tasks on a daily level."

Blocking was always an issue, but as engineers at both Bio-Ware and DICE added more and more features to Frostbite, work on *Dragon Age: Inquisition* became significantly less tedious. Tools started functioning properly. Levels began to shape up. People on the *Dragon Age* team who had been slowed down by Frostbite before, such as the systems designers, were finally able to implement and test ideas in the open world. They were running out of time, though, and another delay was off the table.

Every year at Christmas, each team at BioWare would send out a build of its game for the entire studio to play over the holiday break. Whichever game was closest to release became top priority, and over Christmas 2013, that game was *Dragon Age: Inquisition*. Darrah and his team spent long hours in November and December piecing together a playable version of the game. It didn't need to be perfect or polished (after all, nobody outside EA would see it) but Darrah saw it as an opportunity to size things up. This year's build would be "narrative playable"— people could play through the whole story, but big chunks were missing, and sometimes instead of a new quest, the game would just display big text boxes that described what was *supposed* to happen. When the rest of BioWare had played the demo and came back to the *Dragon Age* team with their feedback, Darrah realized that they were in trouble.

There were big complaints about the story. "Some of the feedback was that the game didn't really make a lot of sense and the motivations for the player weren't very logical," said Cameron Lee. At the beginning of *Inquisition*, a massive explosion would tear a hole in the Veil, a magical border that separated the real world from the dreamlike Fade. (In *Dragon Age* lore, this was bad news.) The original version of *Inquisition*'s story allowed the player to close this rift and officially take the mantle of "Inquisitor" during the prologue, which was causing some hang-ups. "It didn't do the story help," said Lee, "because you've closed the rift, so what's the urgency to keep going?"

The writers knew that fixing this problem would add extra hours to everyone's days, but what else could they do? Embarking on a mission that they called "Operation Sledgehammer," the writers revised the entire first act of *Dragon Age: Inquisition*, adding and tweaking scenes so that the player would have to go out and recruit aid from one of the game's warrior factions—the mages or templar—before closing the rift and becoming the Inquisitor. "[Sledgehammer] didn't destroy the story entirely; it just meant that you had to break some bones in order to reset them in the right kind of way," said Lee. "This happens very often in game development."

The other big piece of negative feedback from the holiday build was that the battles just weren't fun. In January 2014, in hopes of solving this problem, Daniel Kading, BioWare's lead encounter designer, began an experiment. Kading had recently joined the company after twelve years at Relic, a Vancouver-based studio best known for strategy games like *Dawn of War*, and he'd brought with him a rigorous new method for testing combat in video games.

Kading went to BioWare's leadership with a proposal: give him the authority to call up the entire *Inquisition* team once a week for an hour, four weeks in a row, for mandatory play sessions. The leads said yes. So Kading opened his own little laboratory, working with the other designers to construct a set of combat encounters that the rest of the team could test out. Because *Dragon Age*'s battles were composed of so many factors—player abilities, stats, monster strength, positioning, and so on—Kading saw his experiment as an opportunity to pinpoint where the problems were. After each session, the testers would have to fill out surveys about their experiences. Whereas the holiday build had been wide ranging, this was laser focused.

When surveys came back during the first week of Kading's experiment, the average rating was a dismal 1.2 (out of 10). Somehow, that was comforting to the *Inquisition* gameplay team. "Morale took an astonishing turn for the better that very week," Kading said. "It's not that we could recognize the problems. It was that we weren't shirking from them."

Over the next week, Kading and his team made several small tweaks to combat abilities, boosting cooldowns and changing animation speeds based on the feedback they'd received. "The individual responses came through in fits and starts," Kading said. "'Winter's Grasp is [much better] now that it's a four-second freeze instead of a two-second freeze.' 'This encounter was so much cooler now that I could wall off the behemoth reliably.'" Four weeks later, when Kading's experiment had finished, the average rating was an 8.8.

As 2014 went on, the *Dragon Age: Inquisition* team made significant progress, although many of them wished they didn't have to ship on those clunky old consoles. The PS4 and Xbox One were both significantly more powerful than their predecessors, particularly when it came to system memory (RAM), which is what allows a game to keep track of everything happening on-screen.* The PS3 and Xbox 360, which were running on graphics technology from 2004 and 2005, just weren't doing the job.

A console's RAM is sort of like a bucket. Displaying characters, objects, and scripts in a game is like adding varying amounts of water to the bucket, and if you overfill it, your game will slow to a crawl or even crash. The PS4's and Xbox One's buckets were nearly sixteen times as big as those of the PS3 and Xbox 360, but early on, Darrah and Laidlaw had decided not to add features to the next-gen versions that wouldn't be possible on the last-gen versions. They didn't want playing *Inquisition* on the PS3 and 360 to feel like playing a different game. That limited how much water they could put into their bucket, which meant the team had to find creative solutions.

"A lot of what we do is well-intentioned fakery," said Patrick Weekes, pointing to a late quest called "Here Lies the Abyss." "When you assault the fortress, you have a big cut scene that has a lot of Inquisition soldiers and a lot of Grey Wardens on the walls. And then anyone paying attention or looking for it as you're fighting through the fortress will go, 'Wow, I'm only actually fighting three to four guys at a time, and there are almost never any Inquisition soldiers with me.' Because in order for that to actually work on [the PS3 and Xbox 360], you couldn't have too many different character types on the screen."

"I probably should've tried harder to kill [the last-gen] version of the game," said Aaryn Flynn. It turned out that the safety net of older consoles wasn't even necessary. EA and other big publishers had severely underestimated how successful the PS4 and Xbox

---

* Confusingly, we also refer to the amount of space on a hard drive as "memory," because computers like to make everything more complicated than it needs to be.

One would be. Both new consoles sold gangbusters in 2013 and 2014, and the last-gen versions of *Inquisition* wound up composing just 10 percent of the game's sales, according to Mark Darrah.

Though the *Dragon Age* team was making progress, and they'd all become more comfortable with Frostbite, parts of the game were still way behind schedule. Because the tools had started functioning so late in the process, and because *Inquisition* was such a massive, complicated game, the team wasn't able to implement some basic features until the very last minute. "We were eight months from ship before we could get all of the party members in the party," said Patrick Weekes, who was trying to playtest the much-loved companion Iron Bull when he realized there was no way to *recruit* Iron Bull. "I went, 'Wait, we're eight months from ship and no one in the world has ever played the game with Iron Bull in their party?' So I have no idea if any line where he's supposed to say something, any line of banter, no idea if any of that is actually firing right. And it wasn't laziness on anyone's part. It's just reality: you're trying to make an engine. All of the programmers and scripters are at the time literally building the world."

Because everything was so far behind, the *Dragon Age* team could identify only some of *Inquisition*'s flaws during the last few months of development. Trying to determine the game's flow and pacing before that period was like trying to test-drive a car with three wheels. "You write the story and you do a review and you go, 'OK, we'll change some things,'" said Mark Darrah. "And then you put it in and you do a white box.* [You're] running around a level, and it's OK. And then you get the voice acting in and you go,

---

* A white box is an outline of a game's level without any art assets attached, used for quick testing and prototypes. At some studios, it's called a gray box. At others, it's called a black box. That even a concept as simple as this has no standardized name says a great deal about the youth of the video game industry.

'Actually, this doesn't work, it's totally terrible.'" Time was running out, and BioWare couldn't delay *Inquisition* another year—they needed to deliver this game in the fall of 2014.

This left Darrah and his team with two options. Option one was to settle for an incomplete game, full of rough drafts and untested ideas. In a post-*DA2* world, that wasn't an appealing thought—they couldn't disappoint fans again. They needed to take the time to revise and polish every aspect of *Inquisition*. "I think *Dragon Age: Inquisition* is a direct response to *Dragon Age 2*," said Cameron Lee. "*Inquisition* was bigger than it needed to be. It had everything but the kitchen sink in it, to the point where we went too far. . . . I think that having to deal with *Dragon Age 2* and the negative feedback we got on some parts of that was driving the team to want to put everything in and try to address every little problem or perceived problem."

The other option was to crunch. The *Dragon Age* team had gone through various periods of extended overtime during *Inquisition*'s development, but this would be the worst yet. It would mean months of never-ending late nights and weekends in the office. It would lead to, as Shane Hawco, put it, "a lot of lost family time." "I would love to have no crunch ever," said Aaryn Flynn. "I think it remains to be seen whether crunching actually works. Obviously a ton of literature says it doesn't. [But] I think everybody finds a time in their development careers where you're going, 'I don't see what options we have.'"

John Epler, the cinematic designer, recalled a bleary-eyed ritual in which every night he'd drive to the same convenience store, pick up a bag of Cheetos, and then go home and zone out in front of the television. "You get to the point where you've been at work for twelve or fourteen hours, you get on the road home and you think: all I really want to do is watch a TV show I've watched one hundred times and eat junk food I've eaten one hundred times, because those things are comfortable, and I know how they're going to end," Epler said. "Whereas every day is another something coming to the top of the pile, and, 'Oh shit, somebody needs to look at this.'" When the store's clerks started to recognize him, Epler realized he needed a lifestyle adjustment.

As they crunched through 2014, Darrah and crew finally finished off the features they wished they'd been able to nail down back in the first year of development. They completed the "power" system, which would allow the player to build up influence for the Inquisition by roaming around the world and solving problems. They filled *Inquisition*'s deserts and swamps with side quests, hidden treasures, and astrological puzzles. Ideas that weren't working, like reactive environments (destroyable ladders, mud that sticks to your shoes) were promptly removed. The writers blew up and rewrote the prologue at least six times, by one producer's count, although they didn't have time to give nearly as much attention to the ending. Just a few months before the game shipped they added some features that would turn out to be pivotal, like a "jump" button that would let the Inquisitor hop over fences and gradually scale mountains (through the time-tested video game tradition of leaping against the side of a mountain over and over until you make it up).

The team had originally scheduled *Inquisition* for October, but by the summer they'd bumped it back another six weeks for what game developers call "polish," the phase of development in which a game's content and features are complete and all that remains is optimization and bug fixing. "*Dragon Age: Inquisition* had about ninety-nine thousand bugs on it," said Mark Darrah. "That's the actual number. That requires a lot of context, because we file qualitative and quantitative bugs, so things like, 'Oh I was kind of bored at this point,' that's a bug."

"The number of bugs on an open-world game, I've never seen

anything like it," said Ben McGrath, the lead environment artist. "But they're all so easy to fix, so keep filing these bugs and we'll keep fixing them." For BioWare, it was far harder to discover them all. It required creative experimentation from the quality assurance (QA) team, who spent what felt like endless late nights testing everything from the intricacies of the crafting system to whether you could jump off the edge of a mountain and fall through the environment.

During those last few months, the writer Patrick Weekes would take builds of *Inquisition* home and let his nine-year-old son play around with the game. His son was obsessed with mounting and dismounting the horse, which Weekes found amusing. One night, Weekes' son came up and said he'd been killed by a bunch of spiders, which seemed strange—his son's characters were too high a level to be dying to spiders. Confused, Weekes loaded up the game, and sure enough, a group of spiders had annihilated his son's party.

After some poking around, Weekes figured out the problem: if you dismounted the horse in the wrong place, all your companions' gear would disappear. "It was because my son liked the horse so much more than anyone else had ever or will ever like the horse," Weekes said. "I doubt we would've seen it, because it takes spamming the button to figure out there's a one-in-one-thousand chance that if you're in the right place, it's going to wipe out your party members."

Mark Darrah, who was responsible for steering the *Dragon Age: Inquisition* pirate ship into its final port, had a knack for knowing which bugs were worth fixing (like the one where you could jump on your dwarf party member's head to get to areas that shouldn't be accessible) and which weren't (like the ones where your weapon's graphic would clip through walls). On an open-world RPG of this scope and scale, it would be impractical (and take way too much time) to fix every possible bug, so they had to prioritize. It helped that the *Dragon Age* team was full of veterans, and that over the years they'd developed a fair amount of chemistry as a team. "Muscle memory is incredibly influential at this point," said Cameron Lee. "Through the hellfire which is game development, [we're] forged into a unit, in that we know what [everyone's] thinking and we understand everyone's expectations and we know what needs to get done and just do it."

Eventually, they did it. On November 18, 2014, BioWare launched *Dragon Age: Inquisition*, successfully shipping the game despite Frostbite's many challenges. "I think at launch we *still* didn't actually have all our tools working," said Mark Darrah. "We had our tools working *enough*."

Almost immediately, *Inquisition* became the best-selling *Dragon Age* game, beating EA's sales expectations in just a few weeks. The combat was fun (if occasionally too chaotic), the environments were beautiful, and the companions were fantastic, thanks to top-notch writing and voice acting (including a breakout performance by the former teen heartthrob Freddie Prinze Jr. as Iron Bull). One standout scene, which unfolded right after the player's home base was destroyed, depicted the tattered remnants of the Inquisitor's army, singing a hopeful song in unison: "The dawn will come." *Dragon Age: Inquisition* was, in many ways, a triumphant game.

Look closely enough, however, and you can find lingering remnants of *Inquisition*'s chaotic development. One of the first things you'd see in the game was an area called the Hinterlands, a quilt of forests and farms that served as *Dragon Age*'s first open-world environment. The Hinterlands was full of fetch quests—"garbage quests," Darrah called them—that would send you off to deliver herbs and kill throngs of wolves. They were serviceable timewasters, but they felt like chores compared with *Inquisition*'s fascinating main story.

The problem was, too many people weren't going out and *seeing* the main story. Some players didn't realize they could leave the Hinterlands and return to their home base of Haven to trigger the next main story quest. Other players got stuck in a weird, compulsive gratification loop, forcing themselves to do every side quest in the Hinterlands before leaving. (One of my more popular *Kotaku* articles during the week of *Dragon Age: Inquisition*'s launch was titled "PSA: If You're Playing *Dragon Age*, Leave the Hinterlands.")

Internet commenters rushed to blame "those damn lazy developers" for this problem, but really, it was the natural consequence of *Inquisition*'s struggles. Had the *Dragon Age* team miraculously received another year to make the game, or if they'd had the opportunity to spend years building up Frostbite's tools before starting development, maybe those quests would have been more interesting. Maybe they would have been less tedious. Maybe they'd have had more twists and complications, like the ones found in *The Witcher 3* just a few months later. "The challenge of the Hinterlands and what it represented to the opening ten hours of *Dragon Age* is exactly the struggle of learning to build open-world gameplay and mechanisms when you are a linear narrative story studio," said Aaryn Flynn.

For BioWare, *Dragon Age: Inquisition* was nonetheless a victory. Aaryn Flynn, Mark Darrah, and the rest of the *Dragon Age* team had succeeded. "*Dragon Age 2* was the product of a remarkable time line challenge; *Dragon Age: Inquisition* was the product of a remarkable technical challenge," said Mike Laidlaw. "But it had enough time to cook, and as a result it was a much better game."

7

■ ■ ■ ■ ■ ■ ■ ■ ■ ■

SHOVEL KNIGHT

On March 14, 2013, a group of exhausted game developers sat in a cramped apartment in Valencia, California, surrounded by bulletin boards and Ikea tables. Sean Velasco, the messy-haired, charismatic leader of the team, took out a camera and started pointing it around the room, panning across three other tired faces: Nick Wozniak (the pixel artist), Ian Flood (a programmer), and Erin Pellon (the concept artist). On a call from Chicago was David D'Angelo (their second programmer), his head ever present on a laptop above the bookshelf thanks to Google Hangouts. A combination of anxiety and sleep deprivation was making them all jittery.

"Look, everybody," Velasco said to the camera. "We're going to fucking launch the Kickstarter right now. . . . Oh my god. OK. Here it goes. Ready to launch."

Nick Wozniak pressed the button.

"Oh my god, you have to confirm," Velasco said.

Wozniak pressed the button again. "It's launched," he said.

"Oh my god," Velasco said. "OK. All right. OK, you guys. All right. All right. Are you ready? We gotta get to work."

The *Shovel Knight* Kickstarter was now live, asking fans for $75,000 to make their dream game, although unlike Obsidian's *Pillars of Eternity*, this campaign didn't start skyrocketing right away. Few people were even paying attention.

"It was definitely nerve-racking," David D'Angelo said later. "We spent so much time thinking about it and planning for it and investing in it in our minds. Then you launch and no one notices, obviously, because how do you notice a Kickstarter the moment when it launches?"

If nobody ever noticed their Kickstarter, the five of them were in trouble. They had quit their jobs to be there, risking financial stability in hopes that enough people would look at their game and think, "I will pay money so this can be made." Velasco and crew had ambitious plans that they'd need way more than $75,000 to see through. They wanted to turn their blue-armored hero into an icon. With *Shovel Knight*, they didn't just want to make a game, they wanted to make the next *Mario*. Even if it meant going broke.

Up until a few months earlier, Sean Velasco and the rest of the team had worked at WayForward, an independent game studio around the corner in Valencia that was best known for cranking out an extraordinary quantity of console games every year. Some were licensed games like *Thor*, a tie-in to the Marvel movie, and *Batman: The Brave and the Bold*, based on the cartoon of the same name. Others were modern-day successors to NES classics, like the action game *Contra 4* and the platformer *A Boy and His Blob*, in which you maneuver a young boy around various obstacles, solving puzzles by feeding magical colored jelly beans to your amoebic assistant.

All these games had one thing in common: they didn't take

long to make. In other words, they were cheap. WayForward specialized in two-dimensional sidescrolling games that could be developed by teams of twenty to thirty rather than two hundred to three hundred, on schedules that would sometimes span less than a year—exceptionally short for a modern game. With each game, the company would shuffle people around, placing each developer where WayForward needed him or her the most.

Sean Velasco disliked this system, arguing that it devalued team chemistry. "I think we were strong people; we developed strong games," Velasco said. "So they thought, 'Well if we take this guy and put him here, this other guy put him here, then they'll be able to cede knowledge to everyone else.'" After working on successful sidescrollers like *BloodRayne: Betrayal* with the same core group of developers, Velasco wanted to stick with his buddies. "I always use the analogy of the [*Star Wars*] R2 unit," Velasco said. "Luke doesn't wipe R2, and so they work really well and really closely together. At WayForward, they would wipe the R2 unit every time and so you never got a chance to really get that level of cohesion."

WayForward was a "work for hire" studio, one that could survive only by juggling lots of contracts and making licensed games on very tight deadlines.* Keeping teams together wasn't the studio's priority, and in 2012, after they finished the brawler game *Double Dragon Neon*, WayForward's leadership split up Sean Velasco, Ian Flood, Nick Wozniak, and David D'Angelo, moving them all to different projects.

Upset that they were no longer together, the group started

---

* Recalled Ian Flood of their creative process: "It's like, 'That's really cool that you think that's what Batman should do, but you know what Batman really needs to do? Be out by Christmas.'"

meeting up outside work. On nights and weekends, they'd all go to Velasco's apartment and experiment with side projects, including a smartphone game that didn't get very far. None of them were really into the touchscreen—they preferred the tactile feel of proper buttons—and it wasn't the type of game they wanted to develop. What they really wanted was to work together on a proper platformer, one that you could play on Nintendo consoles like the 3DS and Wii U. "I remember saying, 'I got into the industry to make Nintendo games,'" said D'Angelo. "'Let's make a Nintendo game.'"

"And we all looked at each other," said Velasco. "And we said, 'Yeah, that's what we want to do.' We all want to make great gameplay-first games. We don't know how to have a touchscreen. We want to make gameplay games that use a controller."

Back in the office, Velasco pitched WayForward's leadership on a radical idea: what if he and his team did something new? WayForward had two buildings, one of which was currently occupied by the QA department. What if Velasco's team took over that second office and became its own semi-autonomous entity? WayForward's management had been thinking about launching a Kickstarter—what if Velasco's team handled that? What if they came up with something totally original, a Nintendo-style game that they could all be proud of?

After a few conversations, WayForward's management said no. It just wasn't how the studio operated. Moving people around helped the company crank out games more quickly. "Working at WayForward, you have that mentality of it's a 'work for hire' place," said Nick Wozniak. "They have to fulfill the obligations to the publisher first, at the expense of everything else."

During lunch one day at Dink's Deli, a restaurant near their office, Velasco started talking to Flood and Wozniak about what their dream "Nintendo" game would look like. It would be a 2-D game, they decided, both because that would be cheaper than 3-D and because it was what they all had experience making. It would look and feel like an NES game, minus the imprecise jumps and frustrating glitches that we saw so often during the 1980s. What Velasco and his friends really wanted was a game that felt like what people *remembered* about NES games, rose-colored glasses and all.

There would have to be a single core mechanic in their game, and the move that seemed most appealing was the "down-thrust" from *Zelda II: The Adventure of Link*. With this ability, Link could leap in the air and then stab toward the ground, destroying any enemies and obstacles in his path. "The down-thrust just seemed like such a fun, versatile move," said Velasco. "You can use it to break blocks, you can use it to bounce on things, you can use it to flip enemies over."

Someone suggested that the main weapon should be a shovel. Someone else asked: *What if it was a knight?* They all tried to picture it: A heavily armored knight, roaming the countryside and fighting off monsters with his big shovel. He could stab spiders with horizontal pokes or jump up and use his shovel like a pogo stick, hopping on bubbles, ghosts, and big piles of dirt. The image made all three of them laugh, and soon enough they'd agreed on both their game and their main character, who would share a name: *Shovel Knight*. It felt sufficiently iconic, like it could be slapped on T-shirts and lunchboxes.

As Velasco, Flood, and Wozniak sat there in the booth of the restaurant, batting ideas back and forth, they devised an entire structure for their game. Shovel Knight would battle against eight other knights, each with its own distinct theme, as in the old *Mega Man* games, in which the eponymous hero took on robot bosses with names like Crash Man and Metal Man. Shovel Knight wouldn't absorb his opponents' powers—they didn't want to rip off *Mega Man* that much—but each boss would have his own themed stage. Polar Knight would live in a frozen ship. King Knight would rule over a grand castle. Our hero, Shovel Knight, would conquer them all. "That was it," Velasco said. "He'll fight these eight guys. And each one will be cool. They'll have these unique silhouettes and then we'll have a big bad that you fight at the end. We just started from there."

Knowing that WayForward would never let them make *Shovel Knight*, they all decided to quit, gambling their savings on the game that they knew they had to make. Sean Velasco and Ian Flood filed resignation letters.* David D'Angelo, who had moved to Chicago while his fiancée attended graduate school, kept working at WayForward remotely but planned to moonlight on *Shovel Knight* and then eventually switch over full time.

Nick Wozniak wanted to stay at WayForward and save up more money before joining the new venture, but when WayForward's leadership found out he was planning to leave, they fired him. Recalled Wozniak: "[They said], 'You're going to leave, right? And I said, 'Well, eventually, yeah.' And they said, 'Why don't you just make today your last day?'" It was a tradition for departing WayForward employees to gather at the nearby Red Robin ("Not that we like Red Robin," said Wozniak. "It was just a thing that was terrible that we did.") and after finding out he'd lost his job, Wozniak called everyone for an impromptu trip there, including his wife. What nobody else knew was that Wozniak's wife

---

* Although the departure wasn't exactly amicable for some of them, the crew maintained a good relationship with WayForward over the years. "WayForward was so good to us," said Sean Velasco. "They lent us their tech, and they helped us with references, and we see them all the time at all the trade shows and industry events. I worked with them for seven years. They're great friends and they're good people, and there's no way Yacht Club could've existed or that I would exist as a designer without all the things I've learned at that place."

was eight weeks pregnant, and that the main reason he'd wanted to stay at WayForward was to save up money for their new kid. "She was freaking out," Wozniak said. "She was very nervous."

By January 2013, they were all in on *Shovel Knight*, which was exhilarating, yet terrifying. They were elated to be working on their dream game, but they knew they'd be working on it for at least a year before they started to make any money. Getting funding from investors or publishers seemed like a bad idea. A publisher would demand creative control, and worse, a publisher would oversee marketing. Velasco and crew had a specific vision for *Shovel Knight* as a brand, one that they wouldn't want to trust with a big publisher that was looking for profit above all else. The only real option was crowdfunding, not just to earn money for their game, but to start building a base of loyal fans. "We thought, Kickstarter is probably the best way we can grow a community that is behind the game the whole way through," said David D'Angelo. And so, like Obsidian and so many other independent studios, the *Shovel Knight* crew went to Kickstarter.

For the next two months they started preparing for the Kickstarter, the whole team living off their savings accounts as they drew bosses, sketched out levels, and tried to figure out what Shovel Knight would look like. He would have to be both unique and instantly recognizable. Everyone on the team had grown up in the late 1980s and 1990s, when a mustachioed plumber with a red shirt and blue overalls had taken over North America thanks to Nintendo's relentless marketing, and they wanted to do the same thing. They wanted *Shovel Knight* sweatshirts. *Shovel Knight* plushies. *Shovel Knight* magazines. "I wanted to make an eighties brand that created a character, where the name of the game was the name of the character," said Velasco. "That's a thing that didn't necessarily happen so much anymore."

When they'd finished designing Shovel Knight, he had light

blue armor, not unlike Mega Man. He always carried a shovel in one hand. His face was always masked, hidden behind a helmet with a T-shaped hole in the middle. Two pearl horns protruded from both sides of that helmet. Not only was he easy to recognize, he was easy to draw: sketch out the T helmet and a couple of horns, give him a little shovel, and you've got yourself a Shovel Knight. He didn't have a personality, which was also by design. "Shovel Knight can be all things to all people," said Velasco. "To some people, he's a cute knight going around. To some, he's a super badass *Dark Souls* knight."

Every day for the next two months, they all went to Velasco's apartment and worked on *Shovel Knight*, with D'Angelo's head watching them daily from a laptop monitor. (Although D'Angelo was technically still at WayForward, his mind was mostly on *Shovel Knight*.) They didn't sleep much. They'd decided to build King Knight's stage, Pridemoor, to share with fans as an early demo and proof of concept. That meant there was a ton of work to do: designing the level, conceiving enemy creatures, drawing sprites, animating everything, programming the physics, and oh so much more.

Helping fuel Velasco and crew was the fact that they were working for themselves, not for some other company's contract. Nobody enjoyed crunching, but spending long hours on *Shovel Knight* felt more rewarding than it had to lose sleep for Way-Forward's licensed games. "Before, we were talking about it on [nights and weekends], and now the fact that we got to do it full time felt refreshing," said Ian Flood. "I remember calling my dad and saying, 'Hey, I turned down a raise and quit my job.' And his response was, 'Why?' It's like, 'Oh, we're going to put together this project and it's going to be really great and we're going to put it up on something called Kickstarter, where we take donations.' His response was, 'Well, let me know when your begging site is up.'"

They called their company Yacht Club Games, perhaps because for a group of poor, tired, bleary-eyed developers, sitting in a one-bedroom apartment and working on Ikea furniture, it felt morbidly ironic.

And on March 14, 2013, they launched the Kickstarter. A brief trailer, scored by the well-regarded composer Jake Kaufman (who went on to write all of *Shovel Knight*'s music), showcased the art and levels they'd done so far. In a series of short clips, Shovel Knight would stab enemies and bounce around on his shovel. "We believe in *Shovel Knight*," they wrote in the Kickstarter description. "We know that the final game is going to be great. We're so sure of this that we quit our full-time jobs to work on it. We've poured a massive amount of time, money and effort into our labor of love, but it's not enough to finish the game. In order to make *Shovel Knight* a reality, we need you!"

That "you" didn't seem to be showing up, though. By the end of the week they'd raised only around $40,000 of their $75,000 goal, thanks to a handful of articles, including a feature on the gaming site IGN, and they were getting only a few thousand dollars a day.* As the Yacht Club crew kept powering through their ever-growing list of tasks, they started worrying that *Shovel Knight* wasn't going to make enough money. Or, perhaps worse, that it'd reach the absolute minimum goal. "You'd just have Kickstarter open on a second monitor or background, whatever you're doing," said Nick Wozniak. "You're constantly looking, trying to do the math, doing rough projections in your head." Even though they'd asked for $75,000, they were all hoping for way more than

---

* Before launching the Kickstarter, they contacted a writer at *IGN*, Colin Moriarty, who they figured would be a fan of *Shovel Knight* because he had started his career writing GameFAQs guides for games like *Mega Man* and *Castlevania*. Moriarty was indeed a fan, and he became a big supporter of *Shovel Knight* over the years.

that, because they thought they'd need closer to $150,000 to get *Shovel Knight* out the door. "If it hadn't funded, we didn't even have a backup plan," said Sean Velasco. "I guess we could've tried to stay as a team and pitch *Shovel Knight* to publishers. I don't know if they would've gone for it. It was kind of do or die."

They did have a plan to get more attention, though: they were going to PAX East. Earlier in the year, Yacht Club had booked a booth at Penny Arcade's annual Boston gaming convention, where they could show *Shovel Knight* to tens of thousands of fans, journalists, and industry colleagues. But they still hadn't finished the demo. In the following weeks, the Yacht Club crew worked sixteen-hour days in hopes of completing King Knight's stage for PAX, only taking breaks to hit F5 on Kickstarter.

At one point, nervous that they might not make it, the team panicked and came up with a backup plan. They'd set up some beanbag chairs and old Nintendo 64 games at their booth, then tell attendees to go home and fund *Shovel Knight*. "You can just come and hang out and we'll talk about our Kickstarter," said Velasco. "We were thinking that even a week or two before PAX. It was nuts."

Even on the day they flew to Boston in late March, the Yacht Club crew was putting the final touches on their demo. Hours before their flight, they all met up at Velasco's apartment to make some last-minute changes, like adding an arcade-style leaderboard so PAX attendees could compete over high scores. They'd printed out several thousand *Shovel Knight* flyers, but they couldn't afford to ship them to Boston separately, so they each had to stick giant stacks of paper into their luggage, then weigh it all to ensure they wouldn't have to pay extra at the airport.

Things got a little frantic. "About twenty minutes before leaving, I tried to make coffee and [Velasco's] sink started spewing up grounds of coffee," said Ian Flood. "I said, 'Hey your sink is going the wrong way.' He said, 'There's no time, we have to go to Boston.' I [said], 'OK great.' And so we just left it, and it was a floaty, chunky mess."

The five of them—Sean Velasco, Ian Flood, David D'Angelo, Nick Wozniak, and Erin Pellon—spent a total of roughly $10,000 on the PAX trip, with the promise that they'd each get their money back once the Kickstarter had funded. They all shared one room at night—"It was pretty horrible," said D'Angelo—and worked the PAX booth during the day, preaching about *Shovel Knight* to anyone who came within a few feet.

Their demo was flashy and eye catching, with bright 2-D graphics that immediately drew people's attention. Even from across the show floor, it was easy to tell what was happening in *Shovel Knight*: a little blue guy with a shovel was jumping around and hitting monsters. It looked like a modern take on an NES game, which appealed to plenty of nostalgic PAX-goers. "In just a few short days *Shovel Knight* has gone from a blip on my radar to one of my most anticipated titles of the year," a reporter for the video game website *Destructoid* wrote during the show.

Although PAX didn't lead to a sudden flood of money, it did help Yacht Club get the word out, and on March 29, 2013, with two weeks left on the Kickstarter campaign, they reached their goal of $75,000. They could still raise money until the campaign ended in mid-April, but now they were officially funded. "It was scary, because now we have to make this game, and it's going to be hard to do for $75,000," said D'Angelo. "We wanted it to blow up. We wanted to make the game for sure, but we didn't want it to be a horribly painful time. We didn't want to not eat the entire time we were making it."

At PAX, David D'Angelo talked to other developers who had successfully used Kickstarter and got two major pieces of advice. The first was to update their Kickstarter every single day, so backers could actively participate and spread the word about *Shovel Knight* rather than simply waiting around for the game. Right after PAX, Yacht Club started running daily Kickstarter updates with art contests, character reveals, and stretch goals. At $115,000 they'd make one of the boss knights playable. At $145,000 they'd add a second. If they hit $200,000, they'd add a multiplayer battle mode, and if they somehow got to $250,000, they'd create a third playable boss knight campaign.

The second piece of advice was that Yacht Club should send the *Shovel Knight* demo to popular YouTubers and Twitch streamers. Internet articles about the game were one thing; letting potential fans see *Shovel Knight* in action was quite another, and when huge YouTube channels like the Game Grumps later played through the demo, they reached hundreds of thousands of people. During the last few days of the *Shovel Knight* Kickstarter, the funding skyrocketed, going from a few thousand dollars to upward of $30,000 to $40,000 every day. It was enough to make Yacht Club wish they could extend the Kickstarter campaign an extra week, but alas, the site's rules wouldn't allow it.

When the Kickstarter ended on April 13, 2013, *Shovel Knight* had raised $311,502, which was more than four times their campaign goal but wasn't all that much money for a team of five people in Los Angeles. At the standard burn rate of $10,000 per person per month (which included not just salaries but equipment, legal fees, and expenses for the small new office they planned to rent), it would last them six months—maybe longer if they all took less money. Once they figured out how much they'd each need to pay bills and put food on their tables, they split up salaries accordingly. "Then we said we'd pay the difference for everyone afterward," said D'Angelo. "We really had to make the most out of every dollar." Knowing that they had to make eight stages, and that King Knight's stage had taken them around a month, Yacht

Club figured they could finish *Shovel Knight* in a year. It'd take from April to December 2013 to complete all the stages, with an extra three months as buffer. They'd have to finish the game by March 2014, or else they'd be out of money.

They also had to learn how to start a business, which was a time-consuming process involving signing up for health insurance, sorting out taxes, and finding a copyright lawyer who could help them protect the *Shovel Knight* IP. Eventually they decided to designate Tuesday as "business day" and spend the rest of the week making *Shovel Knight*, but the work became far more time consuming than they had expected.

Because their funds were so limited, the Yacht Club crew gave up on all semblance of work-life balance, knowing that if they didn't crunch on *Shovel Knight*, they'd run out of money. That March 2014 deadline was sooner than it seemed. "It would be best for us to kill ourselves on this than to fail," said Nick Wozniak. "The thing we sacrificed for that was ourselves. We knew we'd have to be working weekends. We knew we'd have to be working multiple-hour days. Time is a thing that you just give to the game."

For Nick Wozniak, that meant drawing and animating the many pixelated sprites that made up *Shovel Knight*, usually based on concept art drawn by Erin Pellon. For Sean Velasco, it meant designing levels, creatures, and mechanics. For David D'Angelo and Ian Flood, it meant writing the code that kept *Shovel Knight* running and fixing the code that wasn't working. For all of them, it meant trying to figure out how to make the game fun: iterating, fine-tuning, polishing, and holding daily meetings about pivotal decisions surrounding both their game and their company.

From the beginning, Yacht Club had made the unorthodox decision that nobody would be in charge. Sean Velasco was technically the director of *Shovel Knight*, and he led most of the meetings, but he wasn't the boss. They followed a simple, yet radical rule: If anyone said no to something, they all had to stop doing it. Nothing would happen until the entire team agreed on a singular way to proceed. It was the democratization of video game design. "We knew from the beginning we wanted to be equal," said Wozniak. "We saw ourselves as five partners, on paper and in act."*

In practice, this meant they spent a lot of time debating granular details. If one member of the team didn't like the way Shovel Knight's arm moved when he stabbed upward, they'd all have to talk about it. If someone at Yacht Club insisted that you should be able to replay levels after beating them, that would turn into a weeklong discussion. If Sean Velasco loved the visual of a blue, armored knight holding a fishing rod, then damnit, he was going to keep fighting until Shovel Knight could catch trout. (Said Velasco: "I kept bringing it up, kind of as a joke. Hey, let's do fishing, it would be stupid, it would be fun. Everyone's like, 'No, it's dumb, it's dumb, it's dumb.' Eventually I think I just wore them down.")

This sort of chaotic multilateralism might not have worked at any other company, but for Yacht Club, it just seemed to click. Part of it was their size, which kept them nimble—if they were fifty people instead of five, it wouldn't have been quite as easy to battle over every design decision. The other part was the chemistry they'd developed after years of making games together at Way-Forward. "When I give these guys my designs or when they give

---

* A sixth partner, Lee McDole, departed Yacht Club early after a dispute over the idea of a flat structure. He'd believed, based on earlier conversations and work he'd done in the previous months and years, that he and Sean Velasco would be 50/50 partners on the business. "I wrestled with the idea of continuing in this new arrangement for several days, but ultimately it didn't feel right moving forward," McDole said.

me their implementations of stuff, there's so much that doesn't even need to be said or doesn't need to be specced out, and there's this level of knowledge and trust," said Velasco. "It's like being in a band."

None of this would have been possible if they didn't have a single, unified vision. Everyone on the team knew that *Shovel Knight* was a two-dimensional, NES-style platformer with eight different stages. It wasn't getting any bigger. The fundamental gameplay wasn't going to change. Nobody was going to argue that they should turn *Shovel Knight* into an MMO or replace the down-thrust mechanic with a machine gun. There were no publishers or investors who could drop by the office and insist that Shovel Knight would look better if maybe he took off his helmet. Even when the team fought over creative decisions, they all agreed on the basics of where *Shovel Knight* should go.

If they were going to turn *Shovel Knight* into a massive franchise—make it the next *Mario*—then their first game had to be perfect. Throughout 2013, Yacht Club designed and argued and crunched, building out each of *Shovel Knight*'s eight stages gradually and meticulously. *Shovel Knight* had improved drastically from the demo they'd shown at PAX, and they'd added all sorts of cool graphic effects. They were all particularly enamored of parallax scrolling, a technique in which the background of a stage could move separately from the foreground, creating the appearance of depth. Now, when Shovel Knight walked on top of the golden towers of Pridemoor Keep, the pink clouds in the background would move along with him.

Sean Velasco had come up with a series of platforming design edicts, inspired both by his time at WayForward and by studying classic Nintendo games, that he used to envision every level in *Shovel Knight*. One edict, for example, was that the game should teach you how to get past each encounter fairly, not through dry tutorials but with actual gameplay. Say Velasco wanted to introduce the player to a new enemy: the plague rat, which would explode upon getting hit. If you could just walk up to a plague rat, hit it, and then die because you didn't know it would blow up, you'd get mad at the game. A better approach would be for the game to teach you the rules first, maybe by having the plague rat run back and forth next to a clump of dirt. "That way when you [hit] the dirt, the rat also has a good likelihood of getting hit," said Velasco. "Then you can see how he blows up."

One question Yacht Club had to debate over the course of development was just how challenging to make the game. Backers and fans would approach the team with different requests, some begging them not to make *Shovel Knight* too hard, and others asking that they not make it too easy. "Half the people who play this game are going to expect a really hard NES game, and that's part of what made those games fun," said David D'Angelo. "And half the people who play this game want the same feeling you get from an NES game but don't want it to be that hard. So how do you balance those two things?"

One solution was to add a variety of useful items, like a propeller dagger that would let Shovel Knight soar over gaps and a phase locket that you could use to gain temporary invincibility. Another solution—and one of the more elegant ideas in *Shovel Knight*—was to make checkpoints optional. Every time you found a checkpoint in a stage, you could either activate it (so that you'd restart there if you died and you wouldn't lose too much progress) or destroy it, gaining some treasure but raising the stakes for yourself.

By the end of 2013, all five of them felt like they were making a great game—they just didn't know how much longer it'd take. That $311,502, which was ultimately closer to $250,000 after taxes and fees, had dwindled quickly. (They'd also received $17,180 on

PayPal from extra pledges, but that didn't help much.) Yet finishing *Shovel Knight* by March 2014 seemed impossible. "I've always been late on every game I've ever worked on," said Sean Velasco, "and it's because I always want to revise stuff and do it again, or do it better, or put more polish on it." For months now they had been crunching, but there was still so much to do. The second half of *Shovel Knight* wasn't smooth enough, and they'd made some drastic changes to the ending, which they'd have to spend time tweaking and polishing. "I would say if we were at WayForward, we probably would've shipped it in March," said David D'Angelo. "It's probably the difference between good and great, or something. We really went over every pixel in the game and made sure it was what we wanted."

At WayForward, D'Angelo said, his teams had always released games when they were 90 percent ready. With *Shovel Knight*, they wanted to hit 100 percent, to be confident that they'd made as good a game as possible. But putting in any extra time would mean working without getting paid. As of March 1, 2014, they'd be out of money.

They delayed the game anyway. "We had no choice," said Sean Velasco. "And this was after we were balls-to-the-wall grinding on this game, didn't see the sunlight for sixteen months. All friends became strangers. . . . People would ask me how things were going and I was like, 'Everything is getting worse except for *Shovel Knight*. That's getting better.'" They all kept working, reaching into their savings accounts to pay for personal bills and whatever Yacht Club expenses might come up.

Nick Wozniak, who now had a newborn baby, had to borrow money from his parents. ("That was a really hard conversation to have.") At nights, he'd work through dinner and find himself driving home in the waning hours of morning, only for his stomach to remind him that hey, he was starving. The only open restaurant was a twenty-four-hour Jack in the Box, which he started patronizing every night. "You get to know the drive-through guys by name," Wozniak said. "I knew by voice which guy was going to fuck up my order, and so I wouldn't order certain things. It was ridiculous. When a new guy came, I almost was tempted to say, 'Oh, hey, you're new.'"

The lowest point for Sean Velasco was stopping at a gas station to buy coffee creamer one day toward the end of development. "I hand the guy my [debit] card and it's like *boop*. 'Oh sorry, your card is declined.' I started reaching in my pocket and grabbed my credit card, handed them that. And he did the same thing, he said, 'Sorry, this one's declined too.' So I had to walk out in shame, with no coffee creamer. That was the most desperate that it got."

The one thing that kept them going, as excruciating and demoralizing as those last months had become, was the feedback they'd keep getting from friends and family members who were testing *Shovel Knight*. "We got a lot of encouraging messages," said Velasco. One of his college friends sent him a kind note after playing an early version of the game, telling Velasco that this was it, that Yacht Club had pulled it off, that *Shovel Knight* was going to be great. Velasco kept reading, thrilled, until he reached the long list of problems that his friend had with the game. "We had to go back and hack at it and fix it again," Velasco said.

On June 26, 2014, after nearly four months without salaries, Yacht Club Games released *Shovel Knight*. They thought it was a good game, but really, there was no way to tell if anyone would care, or if it would be doomed to fall off the Steam charts with the other thousands of games that came out every year and faded away. They thought they'd done enough PR and marketing to get people's attention, but that was always a crapshoot. They'd been talking about merchandise and lunchboxes, but what if nobody even bought their game? There was a running joke around the office: if everything failed, they'd all just go off and start a bakery.

Then the reviews started coming in. People loved *Shovel Knight*. It was clever, challenging (but not unfair), and polished to pale blue perfection. It took a few days before the Yacht Club crew could sort out how many copies of the game they'd sold (outside the Kickstarter backers who had already paid), but when they got the numbers, they were stunned. In the first week, they'd sold 75,000 copies. By the first month, they were up to 180,000, exponentially higher than any game they'd developed at WayForward.

Shovel Knight was a critical and commercial success. For Sean Velasco, however, it was hard to relish. "It was really dark times," he said. After emerging from the hellfire of *Shovel Knight* crunch, Velasco had reentered the real world and found himself disoriented, like a felon going free after a long prison sentence. "It was emotions cranked up to twelve on every front," Velasco said. "The elation of putting out a game that people were excited about. The contentedness of actually having finished it and finally being done with it. And the thrill of going to all these different places and talking about the game and having such a good reaction. But then the downside of being so emotionally and physically drained from the whole thing."

Like many game creators, Velasco found himself dealing with a heavy dose of postproject depression and imposter syndrome. "I [thought], 'Oh, who even cares, we just ripped off *Mega Man*,'" he said. "We fooled people into liking this. I'm not even really good at this."

It would take a while before Velasco found his balance again, but at least now they were done. The crunch was over. Soon they'd be getting nice salaries—due to their flat structure, each of the cofounders would draw the same amount of money—and they'd be able to readjust their work-life balance. There were some bugs to fix, and they still had to wrap up those playable boss knights that they'd promised, but it was over. *Shovel Knight* was done. Wasn't it?

One of the first things you can see from the panoramic windows of Yacht Club Games' swanky twelfth-floor office in Marina Del Ray, California, is a dock full of luxury boats, which makes the company's name feel significantly less ironic. I went out to visit the studio in October 2016, nearly two and a half years after the release of *Shovel Knight*. They'd come a long way from the days of clogged drains and Ikea furniture.

By now the company had expanded from five to ten, and they were trying to hire more people, which had been a little difficult thanks to Yacht Club's unique structure.* They'd been trying to find a good QA tester, but nobody could get past the interview stage. "It's a little daunting to interview with us," said Nick Wozniak. "It's one interview with ten people." Since everybody at the company had to agree on every decision, they'd decided that prospective employees would have to take questions from everyone. Whenever they brought in a potential QA tester, he or she would have to take a job interview with all ten of them at once, in a single conference room.

That bizarre interview practice wasn't even the most remarkable thing about Yacht Club in October 2016. The most remarkable thing was that they were still working on *Shovel Knight*. Two and a half years later, Yacht Club Games still had Kickstarter promises to keep.

Those three boss knight modes that Yacht Club had promised

---

* Erin Pellon, the concept artist, left Yacht Club in 2015 after a falling-out with the other cofounders.

as Kickstarter stretch goals were taking far longer than anyone could have imagined. After shipping *Shovel Knight* and taking a few weeks to relax, fix bugs, and port the game to several consoles, Yacht Club began developing the first boss campaign, in which you'd get to play as the villainous alchemist Plague Knight. Early on, they decided they wouldn't just swap out Shovel Knight's character sprite and call it quits—they wanted Plague Knight to have his own abilities, like bomb hurling and burst jumping. And if he had his own set of abilities, they'd need to redesign all the levels to fit those abilities. What they thought might take a few months turned into a yearlong development cycle. After shipping the *Plague Knight* campaign in September 2015, they had two more boss campaigns to release: *Specter Knight* and *King Knight*. When I visited Yacht Club, both of those were planned for 2017. "If you had told me [in 2014] that I'd still be working on *Shovel Knight* now, in 2016, doing these other campaigns, I'd be like, 'Are you frickin' kidding me?'" said Sean Velasco. "But hey, here we are."

Years after shipping the game, Velasco was feeling better. He was spending less time at work. He was going to the beach, getting tan. After going through yet another grueling period of crunch in the weeks leading up to *Plague Knight*, Yacht Club's cofounders had all vowed not to do it again. "It's so draining," said David D'Angelo. "And it's especially hard because we crunched an insane amount already at WayForward, so we've gone through a lot. More than the average game studio."

Over lunch at a sandwich shop near their office, when D'Angelo mentioned that he never wanted to crunch again, Ian Flood sighed. Yeah, right, he said. Just wait until they had to ship *Specter Knight*. "I never want to accept that it's inevitable," Flood later told me. "I say that with more of a pragmatic attitude, less than an inevitability, like yeah, we're going to crunch, so get ready for it. Cancel all your plans."

There's no way to know whether Yacht Club's success would have been possible without a barrage of hundred-hour workweeks, but it was tremendous. By 2016, they'd sold well over a million copies of the game. They'd ported *Shovel Knight* to every gaming console possible, put out a physical version in retail stores (a rarity for indie developers), and even worked with Nintendo to build a collectible Amiibo toy based on their intrepid shovel wielder.* Publishers were approaching Yacht Club about distribution deals and even made offers to buy the company (that Velasco and crew politely declined). You could find Shovel Knight popping up in other indie games, too, making cameo appearances in the racer *Runbow*, the platformer *Yooka-Laylee*, and several others. He wasn't quite as ubiquitous as Mario had been in the 1990s, but Shovel Knight had become an indie icon nonetheless.

Despite this success, nobody at Yacht Club had thought they'd still be working on *Shovel Knight*. Even the company's most hardcore fans would send e-mails and comments to Yacht Club, asking them to stop updating *Shovel Knight* and just make something new already. But the team had committed to those Kickstarter stretch goals: three boss campaigns and a multiplayer mode. "That's been our biggest mistake, for good and for bad: we promised a lot of game," said David D'Angelo. "When we promise something, we want to blow it out of the water. So us promising anything is bad, essentially. Because we're going to go way overboard."

The other problem was that these boss knight campaigns weren't making them any money. They were investing cash—upward of $2 million, they estimated—into a bunch of campaigns that they were selling for a whopping zero dollars. After all, Yacht

---

* Remarkably, Shovel Knight was the first Amiibo from a third-party developer. All of Nintendo's previous Amiibo toys had been based on the company's own franchises. To make the toy happen, David D'Angelo told me he had simply bothered Nintendo representatives every month until they said yes.

Club had promised in the Kickstarter that *Plague Knight*, *Specter Knight*, and *King Knight* would all be free. Going back on that promise would be a bad look.

The optimistic view was that they were building a game and committing to updating it for the long haul, like Blizzard had done for *Diablo III*. "This is how you create a hit now: you make something and add to it," said D'Angelo. "And it's not about the day-one sales, it's about getting more and more people on board and invested in it."

The pessimistic view was that they'd spent millions of dollars—and years of their lives—on a game that should have been finished years earlier. And there was no way to tell whether people had even noticed all the additions. "You have no idea if it's actually working," said D'Angelo. "Our game sells well every month, but is it selling well because it's just *Shovel Knight*, or is it selling well because we added content to it?"

At first they'd planned to finish all three boss campaigns by the end of 2015. That became 2016. Then 2017. In January 2017, with the end finally in sight, Yacht Club made a bold move: They announced that they would (a) start selling all four campaigns separately and (b) raise the price of the overall *Shovel Knight* package, since buyers would now essentially get four games in one. After finishing *Specter Knight* and *King Knight*, Yacht Club would finally be done—which would be nice, because they'd all gotten sick of looking at *Shovel Knight*. "We were our own QA department, so we had to play the game hundreds of times," said Nick Wozniak. "We hired some friends to help out, but for the most part we were just playing constantly."

They all liked to fantasize about what they'd do next. The easiest next step might be a *Shovel Knight 2*, but after four years with their horned hero, Yacht Club's cofounders were craving something new. They talked a lot about emulating Nintendo. "I would love to have three tentpole brands that are huge," said Velasco. "And then just iterate on them." *Shovel Knight* would be their *Mario*, but that wasn't enough. Velasco wanted them to make another franchise that was as iconic as *The Legend of Zelda*. And a third that was as beloved as *Metroid*.

Coming from another developer, this might have sounded delusional, like the stoned fantasies of a film school student dreaming about his plans to make the next *Star Wars*. *Yeah, OK, you'll be the next Nintendo. Good luck with that.* But as I walked out of Yacht Club's beautiful offices, passing *Shovel Knight* T-shirts and *Shovel Knight* plushies and a large, ornate statue depicting a horned blue knight with a shovel in one hand, it somehow didn't seem that absurd.

8

■■■■■■■■■■

DESTINY

One day in late 2007, across the street from their offices in Kirkland, Washington, Bungie's employees sat in a rented theater, applauding raucously. They'd just won back their independence. After seven years under Microsoft's umbrella, they were free.

It wasn't that long ago that embracing corporate ownership had seemed like a good idea. Bungie, founded as an indie game studio in 1991, had achieved moderate success with games like *Marathon* (a sci-fi shooter) and *Myth* (a fantastical strategy game) but didn't really make it big until *Halo*, a first-person shooter set amid a galactic war between humanity and a theocratic alliance of purple-obsessed aliens called the Covenant. When Bungie unveiled *Halo* at the Macworld trade show in 1999, hype for the game reached feverish levels.

A year after that, Microsoft bought Bungie, turning *Halo* from a Mac and PC game to an Xbox exclusive.* When *Halo* launched

---

* *Halo* would wind up coming to Mac and PC in 2003, two years after the Xbox release.

alongside the Xbox in November 2001, it became an immediate cash cow for Microsoft, selling millions and helping turn the publisher's fledgling console into a device that could compete with products from the more-established Sony and Nintendo. *Edge* magazine called it "the most important launch game for any console, ever."

Over the following years, as they worked on *Halo 2* and then *Halo 3*, the developers at Bungie began yearning for independence. They were tired of having to run decisions up Microsoft's corporate ladder, and they wanted to make intellectual property that would belong to them rather than to some giant conglomerate. (Many were also frustrated that *Halo* was no longer theirs alone after Microsoft gave it to a certain RTS studio.) Bungie's leadership—including the company's top designer and cofounder, Jason Jones—began threatening to leave and start their own studio. Soon they were talking to Microsoft about a spin-out deal.

After months of negotiation, the two companies came to terms that everyone found satisfying. Bungie would finish *Halo 3* and then make two more *Halo* games. Microsoft would retain the *Halo* IP, but Bungie could hang on to the technology they'd developed over the past seven years. And, for the first time since 2000, Bungie would be independent.

On that day in 2007, as Bungie's management announced in the theater that they were breaking away from Microsoft, the whole studio was thrilled. "Everybody was cheering, and my first thought was 'Jeez, what did we do to you guys?'" said Shane Kim, the Microsoft vice president who had helped coordinate the spin-out. "Because I actually think we were pretty good. But I got it, too. At a real visceral level, I got it. They wanted to be independent."

High on the buzz of their newfound freedom, the Bungie staff wrote up a piece of parchment that they called the Declaration of Independence. Everyone at the studio signed it, then they hung it up in the common area. "We hold these truths to be self-evident," they scribbled in a font straight out of 1776, "that basically, we want to make games and create experiences our way, without any kind of fiscal, creative or political constraints from on high, since we believe that's the best way to do it. We want to benefit directly from the success of our endeavors and share that success with the people responsible for it."

Even as the Bungie staff celebrated, however, a wave of unease rolled over the studio. With this newfound independence came unprecedented levels of responsibility. There would be nobody else to blame for their mistakes. And nobody at Bungie knew what their first big non-*Halo* game in a decade, code-named *Tiger*, was going to look like. They were all confident that they could build something huge without Microsoft's resources, but there was still that nagging feeling: What if they couldn't?

"You have to be careful what you wish for," said Kim. "It's not everything it's cracked up to be. Running a big studio like that is complicated."

By 2007, Jaime Griesemer was sick of making *Halo* games. A Bungie veteran with curly hair and a meticulous eye for detail, Griesemer had been a top designer on *Halo*, *Halo 2*, and *Halo 3*, each of which had faced its own set of backbreaking obstacles and brutal crunch. Although every subsequent *Halo* game had brought new ideas to the table, they all had the same core rhythm: you, as the super soldier Master Chief, would shoot your way through a mob of aliens using a wide array of guns, grenades, and vehicles. There wasn't much room for innovation there. Ensemble Studios might get to play around with a *Halo* real-time strategy game down in

Dallas, but for the mainline *Halo* series, Bungie couldn't suddenly decide to, say, zoom out the camera and give *Halo 3* a third-person perspective. *Halo* brought with it certain expectations that Bungie was compelled to deliver.

"I felt like everything I'd ever wanted to do in *Halo*, we had done," Griesemer said. "There's two categories of features in *Halo*: the ones that Jaime liked, and the ones that Jaime didn't like. And we already did all the ones Jaime liked, so now we need to do all the ones I didn't like, and I'm not down for implementing something I don't like, so I need to get out of the way."

After Bungie released *Halo 3*, the bulk of the studio moved on to the last two games they were contractually obligated to make for Microsoft, spin-offs that would later become known as *Halo 3: ODST* and *Halo: Reach*. Griesemer, meanwhile, convinced Bungie's leadership to let him start dreaming up new ideas for the studio's next multimillion-dollar franchise. Squirreled away with a computer, Griesemer came up with a pitch for a multiplayer action game that he called *Dragon Tavern*. It wasn't quite an MMO like *World of Warcraft*, but it would be what he called a "shared-world experience." Each player would get his or her own tavern, a private area where players could put up decorations, hang out with friends, and congregate between quests. Then, when adventuring throughout the rest of the world, players would be able to cooperate and compete with one another as if they had just joined a big, public MMO.

Griesemer sat down with Chris Butcher, an engineering lead and top Bungie employee, who said he had some cool ideas for how the game could technically "matchmake" players and let them play together. It was all theoretical, but Griesemer was excited about the possibilities, mostly because it wasn't *Halo*. "What is *Halo*? That was sci-fi. OK, *Dragon Tavern* is fantasy," said Griesemer. "*Halo* was first-person? OK, *Dragon Tavern* is third-person.

I was just like: I've gotta get as far away from *Halo* as I can in order to have new ideas."

At the same time, Bungie's cofounder Jason Jones was planning his own vision for what the studio would do next. Jones, a reclusive but well-respected designer, wasn't technically in charge of Bungie—that role went to the CEO, Harold Ryan—but it was generally understood that whatever he wanted to happen would happen. It was Jones who had pushed hardest for Bungie to leave Microsoft, telling people that he'd start his own new studio if Microsoft wouldn't let them spin out. After years of hard work on another company's intellectual property, Jones no longer wanted to make games that Bungie (and, as Bungie's biggest shareholder, he) didn't own.*

Jones also wanted to move away from *Halo*, but for different reasons. One of his pet peeves had always been that the *Halo* games were too linear. Although the multiplayer modes remained fun no matter how much you played them, you had to play through a *Halo* game's single-player campaign only once to see everything it had to offer. Jones hated that. "I think the great tragedy of *Halo* is that for years and years it provided wonderful single-player and co-op content," he said in a 2013 interview, "and we provided people with almost no fun incentives or excuses, almost no reason besides their own enjoyment, to go back and replay it."†

For his next game—which he wanted to be a first-person shooter—Jones wanted to make something more open, with missions or quests that players could play, replay, and access in a nonlinear order. As with Griesemer's *Dragon Tavern*, Jones's ideas were also very theoretical. There was lots of Excel, lots of Vizio. "It

---

* Bungie (and Jason Jones) declined to be interviewed for this book.

† Ryan McCaffrey, "Bungie Cofounder, *Destiny* Creator on 'Halo's Greatest Tragedy,'" *IGN*, July 9, 2013, www.ign.com/articles/2013/07/09/bungie-co-founder-destiny-creator-on-halos-greatest-tragedy.

was, 'Here's what I think the natural evolution of the first-person shooter's going to be,'" said Griesemer.

Jaime Griesemer had clout at Bungie, but not nearly as much as Jason Jones. And Bungie didn't have the bandwidth to make both *Dragon Tavern* and Jones's project. "At some point," said Griesemer, "the studio leadership sat me down and said, 'Look, we're only going to make one game and it's going to be Jason's game, so you want to get in on that.' And I said, 'Yeah, but I really like this idea.' And Jason liked a lot of the ideas too, so we decided to—I won't say merge—it was more like Jason's project acquired the good ideas out of *Dragon Tavern*."

With that, they'd planted the first seeds for what they'd eventually call *Destiny*. For months, Griesemer and Jones collaborated on the project, trying to sort out how it would look and feel to play. There was an immense amount of pressure. Financially, Bungie was doing just fine—the *Halo 3: ODST* and *Halo: Reach* contracts gave them plenty of security—but there was a looming feeling that *Destiny* had to be the greatest thing they'd ever done. Bungie's staff needed to prove that, after all those years under Microsoft's authority, they could do even better on their own.

The good news was that unlike most video game studios, Bungie had plenty of time to iterate. In those early years, from 2007 until 2010, the game code-named *Project Tiger* took many different forms. At one point it looked like Blizzard's *Diablo*. At another point it looked like *Overwatch*.* Bungie spent a great deal of time debating core structural questions, like whether *Destiny*

---

* One early incarnation of *Destiny* looked a *lot* like *Overwatch*, according to Jaime Griesemer. "I went to Blizzard for a while, and played *Titan*," he said—*Titan* was the canceled MMO that was later reworked into *Overwatch*—"and I was like, 'Holy shit, you guys are working on the same game, down to character classes.'" The version of *Destiny* that shipped, of course, looked nothing like *Overwatch*.

should be a first-person game (one in which the player would see from their character's eyes), or a third-person game (in which the player would control the character's movements and actions from a camera above the world). This first- versus third-person debate would last for years.

Bungie, like many large studios, dedicated a great deal of time to what could technically be called "preproduction" but what was really just the act of figuring out what their next game was going to be. That was one of the most challenging parts of making any game—narrowing the possibilities down from infinity to one. "I think that's one of the things that plagued *Destiny*'s development," said Jaime Griesemer. "We would work for a while, spend a lot of money in one direction, and then because there was this sort of impossible ideal of, 'We're following up the biggest game of all time, and this has to be the new biggest game of all time,' there were several points in development where there was a total reset. And it wasn't a graceful, 'We go to prototype and that direction is wrong so we're going to backtrack a little bit and go in a different direction.' It was, I came back in from going on vacation for a week and everything I had worked on for a year was deleted. Unrecoverably, literally deleted. If I hadn't had a copy on my laptop, it would've been gone forever. With no warning, no discussion, no nothing."

Heightening the stress for Griesemer was the fact that with every reboot, *Destiny* seemed to get closer and closer to *Halo*, as if Bungie's iconic series was a gravity well that the studio just couldn't escape. Once *Halo 3: ODST* shipped, that team moved to *Destiny*. Once *Halo: Reach* shipped, that team moved to *Destiny*. Soon they had hundreds of people working on their next big game, which forced Bungie into making quick decisions just so they'd all have stuff to do (they, like Naughty Dog once Bruce Straley and Neil Druckmann took over *Uncharted 4*, had to "feed the beast").

At first Griesemer and the other developers had wanted *Destiny* to be a fantasy game. Over time, however, the castles began to morph into spaceships, the axes and swords into space axes and space swords.

"We have a huge team of production artists that mostly does sci-fi stuff, and they haven't done an orc or a sword ever, so maybe we have to do sci-fi," Griesemer said. "We want to do a third-person game, but we have a bunch of people who specialize in first-person game animations, and all of our code base is written assuming that the crosshair is in the center of the screen. And so now we're first-person. . . . Before you know it, we're basically making *Halo*."

Armed with ideas and presentations, Bungie's leadership started pitching the biggest publishers out there: Sony, Microsoft, EA, and even, by one former manager's recollection, Nintendo. Bungie didn't know exactly what *Destiny* was going to be, but they knew they wanted it to be massive, and eventually they reached a whopping ten-year, $500 million, multigame deal with Activision, the publisher of *Call of Duty*. By all accounts it was the biggest development deal in video game history. And although *Destiny*'s basic concepts were still in flux, Activision's executives signed the deal with the expectation that they'd get something like *Halo*. "The core [of Bungie's pitch] was very much what shipped," said one person involved in the contract negotiations. "It was a sci-fi space opera. Shooter meets MMO."

As part of the deal, Bungie would get to own the *Destiny* franchise, and Activision would give the studio creative freedom to develop *Destiny* games in whatever way it saw fit, so long as every milestone was met. Bungie's schedule would have a very strict cadence. Activision expected the studio to release *Destiny 1* in the fall of 2013, with an expansion called *Comet* following a year later. The next year would be *Destiny 2*, then *Comet 2*, and so on.

Jaime Griesemer began to realize that, as hard as he had tried to resist the *Halo* gravity well, they'd all been sucked in. Worse, he realized that most of the studio was just fine with that. "When I joined Bungie, there were eight guys working on *Halo*," Griesemer said. "When we shipped *Halo 1* [in 2001] it was maybe fifty guys. By the time *Reach* and *ODST* had joined the *Destiny* team, we were probably three hundred people. And the huge majority of them had been hired after *Halo 3* shipped. These are all people who love *Halo*. They wanted to work at Bungie because of *Halo*. So of course they wanted to work on something that was like *Halo*."

Frustrated at the direction *Destiny* was headed, Griesemer began picking fights with other Bungie staff. At one point, he e-mailed out a list of core design problems he thought *Destiny* was going to encounter. How were they going to handle the transition to next-gen consoles, he asked, without sacrificing cool features just to fit their game on last-gen hardware? How were they going to make content that stayed fresh no matter how many times people replayed it? And, perhaps most pivotally, how would they marry the precise shooting of an action game, in which your proficiency is based on skill, with the treadmill progression of an MMO, in which your character's strength is dependent mostly on levels and gear?

Eventually, Bungie's board of directors asked Griesemer to resign. "I kind of see it as a mark of honor," he said, "because I made a conscious decision: I don't like the way things are going, so I'm going to stand up and obstruct things to the point where they're either going to have to change [the way] they're going or get rid of me."

He wasn't the only one. In the coming years, a large number of longtime employees, including Vic Deleon, a senior environment artist; Adrian Perez, an engineer; Marcus Lehto, creative director of *Halo: Reach*; and Paul Bertone, design director, would all either quit or be forced out. Later, that list would grow to include Bungie's president, Harold Ryan.

"There was something about Bungie's trajectory from small and scrappy to king of the world to over-the-hill dinosaurs," said Griesemer. "They accumulated the negative traits of all of those stages. So there was the immaturity of being young and scrappy, the arrogance of being on top of everything, and then there was the stubbornness and inability to change from the dinosaurs stage."

Just a few years after regaining their independence, Bungie was facing serious growing pains. As Shane Kim had thought back at that raucous meeting: *Be careful what you wish for.*

In February 2013, Bungie invited journalists to its offices in Bellevue, Washington—where the studio had resided since leaving Kirkland in 2009—for the official unveiling of *Destiny*. A few details had trickled out in the previous months thanks to early leaks, but this was the big blowout—the event where Bungie would finally tell everyone what *Destiny* actually was. Speaking on a big stage, Bungie's top developers made fulsome, ambitious promises. They described *Destiny* as "the first shared-world shooter," a game where your character could seamlessly meet up with friends and strangers among the swamps of Chicago and the rings of Saturn. Jason Jones and other Bungie leads dissuaded members of the press from calling it an MMO, but the DNA was clear. *Destiny* was half *Halo*, half *World of Warcraft*. It was far less clear how those two halves would fit together.

The gist was this: *Destiny* took place in a futuristic version of our universe, where humans had thrived across multiple planets until an inexplicable cataclysm killed most of them. The remaining survivors fled to what was called the Last City, a safe area guarded by an enigmatic white orb called the Traveler. Playing as mighty galaxy protectors called Guardians, *Destiny* players would travel across the solar system, fighting aliens and hunting for loot on Earth, Venus, and other planets. And the story, as the longtime Bungie writer Joe Staten described it, would unfold over a series of episodes. "One lesson that's critical is that the most important stories we tell aren't going to be told by us," Jason Jones told the press. "They're going to be told by players—their personal legends built from shared adventures."

Staten then described a scenario in which two Guardians would fly together to Mars to investigate a buried city. En route, a group of hulking Cabal aliens would ambush the pair. A third player-controlled Guardian, who happened to be in the area, would fly in and annihilate the Cabal, then signal to the group that she wanted to help out their investigation. "Every time you run into another player, it's amazing," Staten told journalists in attendance. "It just doesn't happen in other shooters." In an instant, this third player would be able to join the party for a dungeon crawl through the catacombs of Mars. It wasn't clear just what *Destiny*'s "personal legends" would look like—Staten illustrated his story with concept art and videos rather than actual footage from the game—but in theory, they sounded wild. Plus, this was the company behind *Halo*. Everyone trusted that they knew what they were doing.

As 2013 went on, Bungie and Activision worked hard to build hype for *Destiny*, releasing a series of trailers and sizzle reels that made even more promises. During Sony's E3 press conference in June, Joe Staten and Jason Jones took the stage for a proper gameplay demo, grabbing controllers and awkwardly bantering as they shot their way through aliens in the hollowed-out walls of *Destiny*'s Old Russia. "There's something really magical about running into another player, especially when you don't expect it," said one Bungie staffer in a subsequent *Destiny* video. "You hear shots ring out, and you look to the left and there's your friend."

The most hyperbolic of hype came from Bungie's COO Pete Parsons, who told the website *GamesIndustry.biz* that he expected *Destiny* to become a cultural touchstone. "We like to tell big stories and we want people to put the *Destiny* universe on the same shelf they put *Lord of the Rings, Harry Potter* or *Star Wars*," Parsons said. "We were extremely proud of what we achieved with *Halo.* . . . I'm pretty convinced we are going to do it again with *Destiny* in a way that maybe even *Halo* never achieved before."

Behind the scenes, however, the weight of all this ambition was crushing Bungie. Since finishing *Halo: Reach* in 2010 and shifting full time to *Destiny*, the newly independent studio had been running into all sorts of problems. They still hadn't answered many of the questions that Jaime Griesemer had raised before leaving. What would the progression system look like? What would players do after finishing the game? How could *Destiny* tell a story that was both emotionally meaningful and endlessly replayable? And what exactly would it mean to give each player his or her own "legend"?

Sure, they'd done great things. Mouths were regularly left agape at *Destiny*'s stunning art direction: the rusted ruins of Old Russia; the pale swamps of Venus; the bloodred deserts circling Mars's buried cities. *Destiny*'s shooting mechanics felt even better than *Halo*'s did, and few actions in a video game were more satisfying than popping a Cabal soldier's head like bubble wrap. But those great individual pieces didn't seem to be coalescing into a great video game. Even as Bungie hyped up *Destiny* with videos throughout 2013, most of the developers knew their project was in trouble. They were way behind schedule, and that flashy E3 2013 demo, a level code-named M10 that had impressed so many fans when Jones and Staten played through it on stage, was one of the only finished parts of the game.

Perhaps the biggest problem was that *Destiny* still didn't have much in the way of an identity among Bungie's staff. "If you were to go to Bungie and ask people what they thought *Destiny* was," said one former employee, "half the studio would probably say it's a *Halo* shooter, and the other half would say it's *World of Warcraft*." The studio was growing rapidly, which made communication even more difficult. By 2013 there were hundreds of people working on *Destiny* in Bungie's unreasonably dark Bellevue offices. Not everyone played the game every day, and few of them could visualize what *Destiny* would ultimately look like, which led to, as a different former employee described it, "a bunch of great ideas that are all siloed off, and none of them actually complementing each other." Journalists had left the February event wondering exactly how *Destiny* would work. At Bungie, people were asking the same question.

In game development, one of the most important pairs of buzzwords is also the one you're most likely to see on a hacky marketing résumé: "unified direction." In other words, everyone needs to be on the same page. Because video games have so many granular moving pieces—sounds, user interface, visual effects, and so on—every department needs to have a strong, consistent idea of where a game is headed. The larger a team gets, the more important this concept becomes.

As with many video games, *Destiny* had pillars—mostly generic ideas like "a world players want to be in" and "a bunch of fun things to do"—but people who worked on the game said they found it difficult to visualize the final product, for several reasons. "The company grew faster than the management structure and leadership process," said one person who worked on the game, "which left many departments mismanaged with no clear understanding of the game's high-level vision." It was like they were fifteenth-century explorers leaving Europe: they knew how to steer a ship, and they knew they wanted to go west; they just didn't know where they were going to wind up. *Destiny*'s staff knew they were making a shooter—one that looked great, felt fantastic to play, and would let you team up with friends and strangers—but other areas of the game remained ambiguous, especially Joe Staten's story.

The project had gotten bigger than some at Bungie had ever imagined. The first *Halo*, which had been the work of around fifty people, felt like a lifetime ago. By mid-2013, *Destiny* was being developed by hundreds of staff. "When you played the *Halo* games, you really felt people's fingerprints on it; you could look at it and know a human made this project," said one former Bungie employee. "Because we had ballooned to such a large size, that just wasn't part of the program anymore."

Another major challenge was that Bungie had decided to rebuild its internal engine alongside *Destiny*, which was a whole lot of fun for the engineers, but made life far more difficult for everyone else. (As the *Dragon Age: Inquisition* team learned the hard way, building a new engine alongside a game is always a recipe for extra work.) Although Bungie's engineering team had devised impressive, cutting-edge technology to support *Destiny*'s matchmaking and other behind-the-scenes functions, the development tools that Bungie used to make the game were subpar, according to people who worked with them.

Whereas on *Halo* it might have taken ten to fifteen seconds for a design change to show up in the game, on *Destiny* it could take upward of half an hour. "Our content iteration times are pretty bad," Bungie's engineering director, Chris Butcher, admitted during a talk at the Game Developers Conference in 2015. "You can be looking at minutes for small changes and tens of minutes for big changes." What that meant was that for Bungie's artists and designers, basic tasks took way longer than expected, and the inefficiencies added up.

"The biggest differentiator between a studio that creates a really high-quality game and a studio that doesn't isn't the quality of the team," said one person who worked on *Destiny*. "It's their dev tools. If you can take fifty shots on goal, and you're a pretty shitty hockey player, and I can only take three shots on goal and I'm Wayne fucking Gretzky, you're probably going to do better. That's what tools are. It's how fast can you iterate, how stable are they, how robust are they, how easy is it as a nontechnical artist to move a thing."

Anyone who's ever screamed at a sluggish piece of computer software knows how frustrating it can be to have slow tools, whether it's Microsoft Word or a graphics renderer. "It's the least sexy part of development, yet it's the single most important factor there ever is," said the person. "Good tools equals better game, always."

A third problem, on top of the incohesive vision and inefficient tools, was Bungie's increasingly tense relationship with Activision. There's always some level of tension between a game developer and its publisher—creative people and money people make for uncomfortable bedfellows—but with *Destiny*, the stakes were enormous. It was the biggest gamble Activision had ever made, which was why some of the publisher's executives had gotten jittery when Bungie's "first playable" build turned out to be subpar. "They delivered a level that was playable but not to the standard we'd talked about," said one person who worked for Activision. (It was, that person said, repetitive and not very fun.)

So even as they hyped up *Destiny* to fans and journalists, Bungie was struggling. The size of the team had become unwieldy, the vision for the game was unclear, and the engine was a mess. Everyone knew something was going to give. They just didn't know when.

Marty O'Donnell likes to say he saw the meltdown coming. It was the summer of 2013, and the longtime Bungie audio director had just become entangled in a public feud with Activision over a *Destiny* trailer they'd published during E3. Much to O'Donnell's dismay, Activision had scored the trailer with its own booming music rather than the epic, sweeping choral suite that O'Donnell had composed for *Destiny* with his partner Michael Salvatori and the former Beatle Paul McCartney. Fuming about what he referred to internally as a "counterfeit trailer," O'Donnell sent out a series of tweets on E3's first day:

June 11, 2013, 12:33am: "I'm so proud of everything the Bungie team has created and produced. The trailer was made by Activision marketing, not Bungie."

June 11, 2013, 9:02pm: "To be clear, the 'Official Destiny E3 Gameplay Trailer' 2:47 was not made by @Bungie, it was made by the company that brought you CoD." [That'd be *Call of Duty*, Activision's popular series of military shooter games.]

June 11, 2013, 9:05pm: "@Bungie made the rest of all the other Destiny stuff at E3."

Activision's executives were infuriated at the breach of protocol. In the NDA-heavy video game industry, there's an understanding that creative conflicts should be handled privately, not on Twitter. Almost immediately, Activision's CEO, Eric Hirshberg, e-mailed Bungie's CEO, Harold Ryan, imploring him to "please put a stop to this as soon as possible before more damage is done." O'Donnell, who at fifty-eight was one of Bungie's oldest employees, now found himself at odds with people who had been his co-workers for over a decade.

Drama aside, Bungie had bigger problems than trailers and tweets. For the past few years, much of the *Destiny* team had wondered what the game's story would ultimately look like. They'd heard bits and pieces, sure. They'd recorded dialogue, directed cut scenes, and created character models based on the partial scripts that Joe Staten and his team were delivering. But few people at Bungie outside of Jason Jones and the writers had seen the entire story, and many at the studio, including Marty O'Donnell, were stressing about the fact that it wasn't finished yet. Plus, there was that lingering question: How would *Destiny* have both a grand, epic story *and* the "personal legends" that Bungie had been touting?

Back in the *Halo* days, O'Donnell would spend a lot of time talking about game stories with Staten and Jones. As audio director, O'Donnell was responsible not just for composing music but for directing and recording all the voice acting, so it was helpful for him to have an early grasp on what the overall plot would look like. On *Destiny*, things were different. Maybe it was the size of the studio, or the fact that Jason Jones was being pulled in multiple simultaneous directions and didn't have enough time to give the story his undivided attention—whatever it was, O'Donnell wasn't happy.

"Every time I worked with Joe [Staten], I said, 'Joe, I'm really out in the dark here on where the story's going—I don't understand what's happening with the story,'" O'Donnell said. "And he would say that he was frustrated too. And at least what he told me was that he was frustrated with the lack of commitment from Jason. Jason would say, 'Yes this is good,' then a month later say, 'No, we shouldn't do this.' So there was a lot of what looked like indecision coming from Jason."

In the summer of 2013, months after Jones and Staten had hyped up the story of *Destiny* to press and weeks after O'Donnell had feuded with Activision, O'Donnell went to the hospital to get sinus surgery. Just a few days after he got home, catastrophe began.

"I got a sort of panicked e-mail from [Bungie's production director] Jonty Barnes saying, 'Oh my gosh, Joe released this supercut thing, and everybody's up in arms and worried about the story,'" O'Donnell said. "And I was lying on the couch, in a drug haze from recovering, and I was just sort of like, 'You've got to be kidding me. This is horrible.'"

Said "supercut thing"—or, as it was more commonly called, the supercut—was a two-hour internal video that was meant to convey *Destiny*'s entire story. To most observers, it was a mess. Staten had compiled and edited the supercut almost entirely on his own, peppering it with incomplete dialogue, half-finished voice acting, and rough animation. People at Bungie, many of whom were already nervous about the state of the game's story, found it impossible to understand.

In the supercut's version of *Destiny*'s story, the player's main goal was to hunt down an artificially intelligent war machine named Rasputin, who had been kidnapped by the swarming, undead alien Hive. On the journey, the player would head to Earth, Venus, Mars, the Moon, Saturn, and a mystical temple on Mercury, where an Obi-Wan Kenobi-like wizard named Osiris would offer advice and words of wisdom. Along the way, the player would befriend and team up with characters like "The Crow," a suave alien with pale blue skin and slick hair.

Opinions varied on this story's quality, but almost everyone outside the writer's room agreed that the supercut itself was a disaster. "Joe's vision probably made tons of sense in his own mind," said Marty O'Donnell. "And Joe was just [thinking], 'Come on, everybody, we've all got to go in the same direction.

We've got to start now. Here it is. This isn't perfect but we can fix it. . . .' Instead it backfired completely. . . . Just about everybody in the studio thought, 'Oh my gosh, this is a train wreck.'"

Perhaps by putting out the supercut, Joe Staten had hoped to force the studio's hand. Maybe he wanted to make Jason Jones and the rest of Bungie's leadership commit to a singular vision for *Destiny*'s story and stick to it. One former Bungie employee said Jones had actually requested that Staten make a presentation so they could all assess the state of the story. (Staten declined to be interviewed for this book.) Few people at Bungie anticipated what would happen next.

Shortly after the supercut circulated, Jason Jones gave the studio a new edict: They needed to reboot the story. It was time to start over. Staten's story was too linear, Jones said, and too similar to *Halo*. Starting now, Jones told the studio, they were going to rewrite *Destiny*'s story from scratch.

Joe Staten, Marty O'Donnell, and others at Bungie pushed back, telling Jones that there was no feasible way to reboot the story this late in production. They'd already delayed *Destiny* once, bumping the game from fall 2013 to spring 2014, and this past year had already been terrible for their relationship with Activision. Overhauling the story *now*, less than a year before the game was supposed to come out, would either lead to a delay, a mediocre story, or both. Bungie had vowed that *Destiny*'s story could live up to *Star Wars* and *Lord of the Rings*. Suddenly they were going to throw it all away and start over?

Yes, Jones told his team. This wasn't up for debate. They were rebooting the story.

Over the following months, Jones put together a small group of people that he called Iron Bar. In this group were some of the lieutenants whom Jones trusted most, like the art director Chris Barrett and the designer Luke Smith, a former journalist who had started at Bungie as a community manager in 2007, then rose meteorically to the top of the company.* Also on board was Eric Raab, a longtime book editor whom Bungie had hired to help come up with *Destiny*'s lore.

Every day for several weeks, Jones held extensive meetings with this Iron Bar group, trying to figure out a new outline for *Destiny*. Then Jones took those ideas to a larger group of leads, which he called Blacksmith, to get feedback. (Bungie always had a flair for dramatic nomenclature; the Blacksmith was meant to "hammer" the Iron Bar.) Outside of Raab, few of Bungie's writers were involved in this process. As one former employee put it: "The writing team Joe put together was ostracized. The story was written without writers."

To some people at Bungie, this felt like a necessary Hail Mary, the type of last-minute drastic play that was oh so common in game development just as a project was nearing completion. To others, including Joe Staten, it felt like suicide. "[Joe] made a big push for sanity and rationality," said one former Bungie employee. "He basically said, 'People, the supercut can be saved, [but] if we try to re-create the game in six months, it's going to make a lot of people miserable.'" Staten's efforts failed, though, and by the end of the summer, he was gone.†

Marty O'Donnell also saw the writing—or the lack of writing—

---

* Not coincidentally, both Chris Barrett and Luke Smith went on to become the creative directors of future *Destiny* DLC and sequels.

† On September 24, 2013, Staten announced the news on Bungie's website with a gracious note: "After fifteen great years at Bungie, from the battlefields of *Myth* to the mysteries of *Halo* and beyond, I'm leaving to tackle new creative challenges. While this may come as a surprise, fear not. It's been my pleasure building *Destiny* these past four years, and after the big reveal this Summer, our hugely talented team is on track for greatness. I'll be cheering all of them, with all of you, when the game launches next year. Thank you for your support of me, and your continued support of Bungie. We couldn't have done it without you."

on the wall. "I saw that was the decision [Jason Jones] made, that's what he was proposing, and I said, 'OK, well, good luck with that, because you already know I completely believe that's impossible, and it's going to cause a death march, and it's not going to cause quality to happen," said O'Donnell. "Jason still wanted me to be part of Blacksmith, and I said, 'I think that's a mistake—I'm not on board with you on this. I don't believe in this plan.'" O'Donnell, who found the whole process miserable, wound up "the naysayer in the room," as he recalled it, shooting down many of the ideas that Jones and crew brought to the table. But he continued attending Blacksmith meetings nonetheless.

In the late summer of 2013, as gamers across the world eagerly waited for *Destiny*, Bungie's top developers spent marathon sessions locked in conference rooms, trying to piece together a new story. First they reduced the scope of the game, cutting out chunks like Mercury and Saturn (which they'd later use in downloadable content) and centering *Destiny* on four planets: Earth, the Moon, Venus, and Mars. (Sure, the moon isn't technically a planet, but in the parlance of *Destiny*, the two are interchangeable.) Rather than have players visit all four of those planets within the first few missions of the game, as had been laid out in the supercut, Bungie decided to treat each planet as a separate act, ramping up the difficulty as players progressed from area to area. On the Moon you'd meet the swarming Hive; on Venus, the ancient mechanical Vex. In the deserts of Mars you'd have to defeat hordes of militaristic Cabal.

Next, the Iron Bar and Blacksmith groups ripped into each mission of the game that Bungie had already created, splicing together old ideas and encounters to form the chimera that was *Destiny*'s new campaign. One old mission might get a brand-new premise; another might be split into three chunks and spread throughout three new missions. It was like tearing up a quilt, then stitching back together all the old squares in a new pattern, no matter how improperly they fit. Said one person who worked on the game: "If you were going from point A to point Z in the course of [the original, pre-reboot story], they would take out section H through J because it was really tight encounter design, and they'd put it off to the side and say, 'How do we get H to J in this other story line?'"

"It was literally like making Franken-story," that person said.

At the end of the Iron Bar meetings, *Destiny* had a new story, one that, coincidentally, seemed as if it'd been crafted by a committee of designers and producers. There were none of the "personal legends" that Bungie had promised. The plot of each mission would vacillate between vague and incoherent, strung together by meaningless proper nouns and baffling dialogue. One line, unconvincingly uttered by a robot called the Stranger (a rebooted version of a character from Staten's version of the story), summed up the plot rather definitively: "I don't have time to explain why I don't have time to explain."

Nowhere was *Destiny*'s rocky development more apparent than in the work of Peter Dinklage, the Emmy Award–winning actor best known for his role as the savvy dwarf Tyrion Lannister on *Game of Thrones*. In *Destiny*, Dinklage voiced Ghost, a pocket-size robot who served as the player's narrator and constant companion. Joe Staten and his team had planned for Ghost to supplement a large cast of characters who would talk to you during each mission. As you played, Ghost would interact with the environment and comment on your actions. But after the Iron Bar reboot, Ghost became *Destiny*'s main star, responsible for delivering the bulk of the game's dialogue—a role that Dinklage hadn't signed on for.

"He was not supposed to be the exposition guy and he certainly was never supposed to be the only voice you heard while you played the game," said Marty O'Donnell. Bungie had dished out big money for other celebrity voice actors like Bill Nighy, Nathan Fillion, and Gina Torres, but the story reboot had overhauled and minimized all those characters, leaving Dinklage and Ghost to shoulder the load.

As O'Donnell worked with the actors to record dialogue throughout the rest of 2013 and then 2014, the scripts kept changing. The studio was rewriting them constantly, sometimes up until the very last minute. Bungie had persuaded Activision to let them delay *Destiny* again, this time to September 2014, but the process hadn't gotten any more efficient. "I wouldn't have a script until just before walking into the session, so I didn't even know what it was," said O'Donnell. "Instead of having three hundred lines of dialogue to do in four hours, I was given one thousand. I'm like, 'OK this is just going to be like reading the phone book, this is bad, but I'll get it done.' It could sound like I was sabotaging, but I wasn't. I really was trying to make everything as good as I possibly could, but my spidey sense was telling me that this wasn't good. The story wasn't there. The characters weren't there." Combine an overworked voice actor with a disgruntled audio director and you had the formula for atrocious performances, particularly when *Destiny*'s dialogue included lines like: "The sword is close. I can feel its power . . . Careful! Its power is dark."

In April 2014, Bungie fired Marty O'Donnell, a move that felt both shocking and inevitable.* One of his first reactions, of course, was to tweet about it. (**April 16, 2014, 1:28am:** "I'm saddened to say that Bungie's board of directors terminated me without cause

---

* In the months to come, O'Donnell filed lawsuits against Bungie for failing to pay his wages and for confiscating his stock. An arbitrator ruled in O'Donnell's favor, giving him a nice payday.

on April 11, 2014.") It was the end of an era, both for O'Donnell and for the company he'd helped build.

Like many video game publishers, Activision tended to stick review score bonuses into contracts, offering extra payouts to developers whose games hit a certain threshold on video game aggregation sites like Metacritic or GameRankings. *Destiny* was no exception. Thanks to an early version of the *Destiny* contract that had leaked in 2012, it became public knowledge that Bungie would get a $2.5 million bonus if *Destiny*'s aggregated review score hit 90 or above.

In the weeks leading up to the launch, Bungie's employees would hang out in the kitchen and take guesses at *Destiny*'s Metacritic score. Some suggested they'd get a 90 or 95; other, more conservative staffers thought it might wind up in the high 80s, just below their bonus target. Their five *Halo* games had an average score of 92 on Metacritic, so they had good reason to be optimistic.

Destiny came out on September 9, 2014. A week later, once most of the reviews had hit, the Metacritic score landed at 77. Needless to say, Bungie missed its bonus.

Reviews called out *Destiny*'s frustrating, grindy mechanics and its repetitive mission structure. Critics slammed the stingy loot drop rates, the tedious endgame, and the lack of explanations for basic features. And most of all, people panned the story. The characters didn't make sense, key plot points were left unexplained, and the dialogue was hilariously clunky. Peter Dinklage's flat voice acting became the subject of memes and jokes across the Internet. One line, "That wizard came from the moon," had been so widely mocked during *Destiny*'s public alpha test that Bungie removed it from the game, but the rest of the script wasn't much better.

What was particularly frustrating was that *Destiny*'s lore was full of chewy, delicious sci-fi morsels. Many of the game's characters and weapons had compelling, intricate backstories; they were just hidden behind what *Destiny* called "grimoire cards," short stories penned by Staten's old writing team that were accessible only on Bungie's website. *Destiny* established tons of promising concepts, like the Black Garden, an area on Mars that had been "locked out of time" by the robotic Vex, but never quite delivered on their potential. Pete Parsons's old quote became a running joke. *Destiny*, sitting in the pantheon of great stories alongside *Star Wars* and *Lord of the Rings*? It could barely sit next to *Twilight*.

Morale at Bungie sunk. During a series of emergency meetings, the studio's leadership decided to overhaul their plans for the near future. In addition to fixing some of the biggest mechanical problems with free patches, they rebooted both of their planned downloadable content packs, *The Dark Below* and *House of Wolves*, remaking the missions and stripping out all the Peter Dinklage lines they'd already recorded.* *Destiny*, they decided, was done with Dinklage. In the coming months, Bungie's designers would devour feedback on forums like Reddit, trying to implement as many short- and long-term fixes as they could. In both *The Dark Below* and *House of Wolves* they experimented with new types of missions and leveling systems that players enjoyed far more.

At the end of 2014, a group of Blizzard leads, including Josh Mosqueira, the director of *Diablo III: Reaper of Souls*, flew up to

---

* One of the most inexplicable early *Destiny* decisions revolved around "engrams," the decahedral treasure chests that players could pop open for new loot. In the endgame, the only worthwhile gear was the rarest "legendary"-caliber weapons and armor, which were purple. You'd get a little rush of endorphins whenever you discovered a purple engram that might lead to a legendary piece of gear. But nearly 50 percent of the time, cracking open a purple engram would get you an inferior blue piece of loot—a bizarre decision that did nothing but infuriate players until it was changed in October 2014.

Bungie's offices for a pep rally. The parallels between *Diablo III* and *Destiny* were uncanny. Not only were both games published by Activision, they'd both launched with similar issues: a frustrating loot system, a punishing endgame, and way too much focus on random numbers. In a presentation to Bungie's staff, Mosqueira explained how they'd fixed *Diablo III*'s problems, telling the story of how they transformed their game over two painful years, from Error 37 to *Reaper of Souls*.

"It was like present us talking to past us," said Mosqueira. "They were afraid of all the same things that we were afraid of. . . . It was just amazing to be able to go up there and talk to them, and they got to see, 'Well, OK, all the things you guys did in *Reaper* were sort of moving in that direction. You guys are on the other side of the wall now. So there's life on the other side.'"

Bungie's staff said they found Mosqueira's talk invaluable. Despite *Destiny*'s many early stumbles—and despite Bungie regularly losing veterans who had been there since the *Halo* days—there was a belief that they had made something fundamentally solid. Despite everything, millions of people were playing *Destiny*. Most of them were complaining about *Destiny* as they played, but the game was addictive enough to keep them entertained nonetheless. The game's most important elements—the setting, the art direction, the way it felt to shoot guns—were all as stellar as you'd expect from the studio that had made *Halo*. If Bungie could fix some of the other problems, then maybe, just like Blizzard, they, too, could find redemption.

It'd have to start with *Destiny*'s first big expansion, the game code-named *Comet* that had been laid out in their contract. With this expansion, Bungie had originally planned to introduce a new planet, Europa, and several new zones across Earth and Mars, but production issues again forced them to cut down their scope.

When they'd finalized plans for the expansion, which they called *The Taken King*, they knew it would center on a single location: The Dreadnaught, an infested Hive ship floating near the rings of Saturn. Bungie also overhauled the leveling and loot systems, incorporating a great deal of fans' feedback to make *Destiny* feel more player friendly. (It helped that the director of *The Taken King*, Luke Smith, was an obsessive *Destiny* player who had racked up hundreds of hours in the game.)

Bungie also knew that if it was going to win back fans and critics, *The Taken King* needed a decent story. Under the writer Clay Carmouche, Bungie took a new narrative approach for *The Taken King*, one that felt far more focused. There was a clear villain—Oryx, the ruler of a phantasmagoric group of aliens called the Taken—and the game would give players ample motivation to track him down and kill him. Irritating characters like the Stranger disappeared for good, while the more charming members of *Destiny*'s cast, like Nathan Fillion's snarky Cayde-6, took on more prevalent roles. (Carmouche left the studio not long after shipping *The Taken King*.)

Bungie also made the remarkable, unprecedented move of wiping *Destiny*'s main star from the game. To play Ghost in *The Taken King*, they hired the energetic voice actor Nolan North, who lent his voice not just to new dialogue but to rerecordings of *every single line* in the original version of *Destiny*. Even Marlon Brando couldn't have done much with a line like "Careful, its power is dark," but by replacing the monotonous work of Peter Dinklage, Bungie was signaling to the world that it wanted to get things right this time. (Fans were pleased with Nolan North, but years later, there are those who miss the so-called Dinklebot and wish they could hear his dreary voice in *Destiny* again.)

When *The Taken King* launched on September 15, 2015, it

was universally lauded. Wrote my good friend and *Destiny* companion Kirk Hamilton on *Kotaku*: "After a year of missteps and half-recoveries, Bungie has found their firmest footing since last September. *The Taken King*'s creators have looked their players in the eye and confidently laid down a convincing vision of what *Destiny* has and will continue to become."

It would have been nice and neat if the story behind *Destiny* had ended there—if Bungie, like Blizzard, had fixed its mistakes then moved on to the next big thing. Even as they launched *The Taken King*, however, Bungie's leadership knew the road ahead would be rocky. Their ambitious ten-year contract with Activision stipulated that they'd have to release a sequel, *Destiny 2*, in the fall of 2016. That wasn't going to happen. Expectations were too high, plans were shifting too frequently, and their tools were too slow.

In January 2016, Bungie delayed *Destiny 2* another year, again renegotiating their contract with Activision to buy the team more time. (To replace *Destiny 2*, they put together a moderate-sized expansion pack called *Rise of Iron* that they'd release in September 2016.) Days later, Bungie fired its CEO, Harold Ryan, and throughout the year, dissatisfied veterans continued to leave the company, battling with Bungie's board of directors over office politics and a bizarrely long stock-vesting schedule.*

To some of those departed Bungie veterans, who had cheered so loudly back in 2007 when the studio announced that it was spinning out from Microsoft, going independent had been the company's biggest mistake. Ten years later, how many of the people who had signed Bungie's ostentatious Declaration of Independence were even left at the studio? "When we were working with

---

* At most tech companies, it'd take three or four years for an employee's stock to "vest" and fully belong to him or her; at Bungie, where the stock vesting schedule was tied to *Destiny* releases, it might take nearly a decade.

Microsoft, Bungie was like this little punk rock band who always shook their tiny little skinny fist at mom and dad," said one former employee. "And when we spun out, we didn't have anyone to shake our tiny fists at. We actually had to self-govern and run ourselves."

As I write this chapter, in early 2017, the story of *Destiny* is still ongoing. There are lingering questions, both within and outside Bungie, about the future of the franchise. How will people react to *Destiny 2*? What will happen to the series after that? Will Bungie remain independent, or will Activision find a way to buy it? By the time this book is published, some of those questions will be answered. Others might take a little longer.

"I think the real story of *Destiny*'s development is that just making any game is incredibly hard," said Jaime Griesemer. "Trying to make an ambitious game under a lot of pressure is staggeringly hard. . . . When you have just quantic explosions and craterings and huge assimilation and communication problems on a team, you end up wasting so many resources and so much time that you see it in the final game."

All things considered, it's remarkable that Bungie found a way to ship anything, let alone build something as popular as *Destiny* (a video game in which players travel through space, complaining about *Destiny*). Maybe the studio didn't quite make *Lord of the Rings* or *Star Wars*, and maybe they lost some of their soul—and a lot of talented employees—along the way. But *Destiny*'s challenges were many of the same challenges that nearly every video game production has faced over the years. The stakes were just higher. And the story of *Destiny*—more specifically, the story *around Destiny*—turned out to be fascinating for reasons Bungie could never have planned.

9

■■■■■■■■■■ ■

THE WITCHER 3

Marcin Iwiński grew up under the specter of Stalinism, which made it tough to play a lot of computer games. With light blue eyes and a face that seemed to be in a constant state of stubble, Iwiński was one of many teenagers in Warsaw, Poland, who wished he could just play the same games as everyone else in the world.

Until 1989, Poland was a Communist country, and even in the early 1990s, as the newly democratic Third Polish Republic began embracing the free market, there was nowhere in Warsaw to buy games legally. There were, however, "computer markets," open-air bazaars where the city's geeks would unite to buy, sell, and trade pirated software. Polish copyright laws were essentially nonexistent, so there was nothing illegal about ripping a foreign computer game to a floppy disk, then selling it for cheap at the market. Marcin Iwiński and his high school friend Michał Kiciński would spend all their spare time at the markets, bringing home whatever they could find to play on their old ZX Spectrum computers.

In 1994, when he was twenty, Iwiński started envisioning

a business that would import and distribute computer games throughout the country. He and Kiciński teamed up to start a company called CD Projekt, named after the industry-changing CD-ROMs that had just popped up in Warsaw. At first they imported and traded games at the computer market, then they started signing deals with outside companies like LucasArts and Blizzard to distribute those companies' games in Poland. CD Projekt's big break arrived when they convinced the publisher Interplay to give them the Polish rights to *Baldur's Gate*, one of the most popular role-playing games in the world.*

Knowing it'd be difficult to persuade their Polish brethren to buy proper copies of the game rather than pirating it online or at the market, Iwiński and Kiciński went all out. In addition to localizing *Baldur's Gate* in Polish (complete with authentic Polish voice acting), they stuffed the game's box with a map, a *Dungeons & Dragons* guide, and a CD soundtrack, gambling that Polish players would see the package's value as a justification to buy *Baldur's Gate* instead of pirating it. If you got a ripped version of the game, you wouldn't get all those goodies.

The tactic worked. On day one CD Projekt sold eighteen thousand copies, a massive number for a country where, just a few years earlier, buying games legally hadn't even been an option. It opened the door for Iwiński and his company to publish all the other big RPGs that were popping up, like *Planescape: Torment*, *Icewind Dale*, and *Fallout*.

This success in the distribution market allowed Iwiński to start pursuing his real dream, to make his own video games, and by 2002 he'd launched CD Projekt Red, a development branch of

---

* That *Baldur's Gate* was developed by BioWare (*Dragon Age: Inquisition*), localized by CD Projekt (*The Witcher 3*), and emulated by Obsidian (*Pillars of Eternity*) is testament either to the immense influence of that game or to the fact that I really like RPGs and wanted to cover three of them in this book.

CD Projekt. The question was, what kind of game was this new studio going to make? Someone at the company suggested that they start up a conversation with Andrzej Sapkowski, the renowned fantasy writer who was generally considered to be the Polish version of J. R. R. Tolkien. Sapkowski had written a series of popular books called *The Witcher*, a favorite of both adults and children throughout Poland. Starring a white-haired monster hunter named Geralt of Rivia, *The Witcher* mixed gritty fantasy with eastern European fairy tales, like a cross between *Game of Thrones* and the Brothers Grimm.

Turned out Sapkowski had no interest in video games, and he was happy to sell the rights to CD Projekt Red for a reasonable price. Iwiński and crew knew very little about developing games, but with *The Witcher*, they had an established property, which would be far easier than starting from scratch. It was also an appealing property, one that they thought might draw broad interest not just in Poland but across the world.

In 2007, after a tough five-year development cycle and multiple reboots, CD Projekt Red released *The Witcher* for personal computers. The game sold well enough to justify a sequel, and in 2011, CD Projekt put out *The Witcher 2*. Both games shared several traits: They were both dark, gritty action-RPGs. They both tried to make the player feel like he or she was making consequential decisions that had an impact on how the story would unfold. And they were both challenging, esoteric PC games. Although CD Projekt Red would later port *The Witcher 2* to the Xbox 360, both games were generally seen as PC-centric, which meant their audience was limited. Competing games like *The Elder Scrolls V: Skyrim* (November 2011) sold millions and millions in part because they were simultaneously released on both PC and consoles.

Also, *Skyrim* was North American. By the mid-2000s, as the

gaming industry became more globalized, role-playing games had formed their own sort of geographical divide. In the United States and Canada you'd find companies like Bethesda and BioWare, with big, critically acclaimed hits like *The Elder Scrolls* and *Mass Effect*, both of which sold gangbusters. Out of Japan came Square Enix's *Final Fantasy* and *Dragon Quest*, which weren't quite as trendy as they had been during the Japan-dominated 1990s, but still held their own among millions of fans. And then there were the European RPG publishers, which never drew as much respect as their American or Japanese counterparts. European RPGs like *Two Worlds* and *Venetica* were generic, janky, and critically panned.

With *The Witcher 2*, Iwiński and his studio had built a sizable audience outside Europe and even become a cultural icon in Poland, to the point where in 2011, when US president Barack Obama visited the country, prime minister Donald Tusk gifted him a copy of *The Witcher 2*. (Obama later admitted that he had not played it.) But the developers at CD Projekt Red were dreaming bigger. They wanted to prove that, even though they were Polish, they could compete with the Bethesdas and Square Enixes of the world. Iwiński wanted CD Projekt Red to be as much of a household name as BioWare, and he wanted that to happen with *The Witcher 3*.

To lead this third *Witcher* game, Iwiński and the other executives tapped Konrad Tomaszkiewicz, who had been a tester on the first *Witcher* before leaping up to become head of CD Projekt Red's "quest department," which they'd created during early development of *The Witcher 2*. Traditionally, an RPG studio would have separate writing and design departments, which collaborated to build all of a game's quests (Kill ten dragons! Defeat the dark lord and save the princess!). At CD Projekt Red, however, the quest department was its own entity, with a team of people who were each responsible for designing, implementing, and improving their own chunks of the game. As head of this department, Tomaszkiewicz had spent a lot of time collaborating with the other teams, which made him a good fit to be the director of *The Witcher 3*.

When he was told he'd be in charge of their next big game, an anxious Tomaszkiewicz started talking to CD Projekt Red's other executives about how they'd make the game appealing to as many people as possible. One of their immediate solutions was simple: make it huge. "We spoke with [studio head] Adam Badowski and the board and we asked [them] what was missing in our games to make them more perfect RPGs," Tomaszkiewicz said. "And we knew we missed the freedom of exploration and we needed a bigger world."

Konrad Tomaszkiewicz fantasized about a *Witcher 3* that wouldn't restrict you to one specific area per chapter, the way previous games had. Instead, this new *Witcher* game would let you explore a big open world, hunting monsters and undertaking quests at your discretion. ("Freedom" was the word Iwiński used most often as a pillar for what the game would offer.) They wanted it to be the best-looking game you could buy. And, this time, they would do a simultaneous release on both consoles and PCs. With *The Witcher 3*, CD Projekt Red wanted to show the world that Poland could make games just as critically and commercially successful as its competitors.

Right away Tomaszkiewicz and his team established some basic ideas. They knew they wanted to tell a story about the hero Geralt hunting for his adopted daughter, Ciri, a popular character from the *Witcher* books who could wield powerful magic. They knew that the primary villain would be a group called the Wild Hunt, a phalanx of spectral horsemen based on the European folk myth of the same name. They knew they wanted

The Witcher 3 to take place in three massive regions: Skellige, a group of Nordic-inspired islands; Novigrad, the largest and richest city in *Witcher* lore; and Velen, also known as No Man's Land, a poor, war-ravaged swampland. "We were terrified of the scope," said Konrad Tomaszkiewicz. "But at this company, [we] all want to create the best experience of games out there. And we are driven by challenges, [even] a huge challenge which is almost impossible to do."

As they entered preproduction, the design team started discussing and plotting out structural ideas, which were already getting complicated. "There were a lot of actually challenging bits in terms of paper design," said the lead quest designer, Mateusz Tomaszkiewicz (Konrad's younger brother). "For example, the original idea was that once you leave the prologue, you were supposed to be able to go to one of the three regions. Any of them." The goal of this decision was to allow for more freedom—Iwiński's watchword—but it left the designers in a tough spot.

CD Projekt Red had already decided that *The Witcher 3*'s enemies would have predetermined levels rather than scaling up with the player. Level scaling, most famously used in *The Elder Scrolls IV: Oblivion*, had been detested by RPG players, who'd complain that when enemies leveled up with you, it eliminated the feeling that your character was making real progress. (Few video game experiences were less pleasant than watching your high-level superhero get slaughtered by a gang of pitiful goblins.)

Without level scaling, however, there was no way to balance the difficulty in an open-world RPG. If the player could choose to go to Skellige, Novigrad, or Velen at the start of the game, all three of those regions would have to be populated with low-level enemies, or else they'd be too tough. But if all three regions had low-level enemies, you'd be able to breeze through them all once you'd gained some experience.

To solve this problem, CD Projekt Red went with a more linear structure. After the prologue, you'd go to Velen (low level), then Novigrad (midlevel), then Skellige (high level). You'd still have the freedom to move between regions, but progression would be a little more restricted. Besides, if the game was going to be as big as they hoped, they would need to funnel players a little bit. "We wanted you to feel like you're not lost, and basically you know more or less where to go, and what the structure is," said Mateusz Tomaszkiewicz. "When you are free to go anywhere, we felt that after the prologue, it was too much at once—that you would be overwhelmed."

Early on, the developers knew that they wanted *The Witcher 3* to be far larger than anything else out there. Most video games aimed for a campaign that was between ten and twenty hours long. The bigger ones, the RPGs and open-world games, usually set out for a range of forty to sixty. With *The Witcher 3*, CD Projekt Red wanted a game that would take at least one hundred hours to finish. To hit a number that absurd, *The Witcher 3*'s designers needed to start as early as possible, sketching and writing as much as they could during preproduction, before there was even a game to play.

Everything would begin in the writer's room. "We start with a very general idea," said Jakub Szamałek, one of the writers. "Then we expand it, then we cut it into quests, then we work closely with quest designers to make sure it all makes sense from their perspective. And then we iterate and iterate and iterate." The main quest would center on Geralt's hunt for Ciri, they decided, with interludes throughout the game in which you'd play as Geralt's adopted daughter. There would also be a series of important quest lines that were optional, but would have a major impact on the game's ending, like a potential regicide plot and a love triangle between Geralt and the sorceresses Triss and Yennefer, both of whom had appeared in previous *Witcher* games. Then there were the minor quests, which included an assortment of mysteries, monster hunts, and errands.

As head of the quest department (a role that he'd inherited from his brother), Mateusz Tomaszkiewicz would work with the writers to lay out a basic theme for each quest ("this one's about famine"), then assign it to a quest designer, who would plot out exactly how that quest would proceed. How many combat encounters would it have? How many cut scenes? How much investigation? "This whole logical chain of events would be done to come up with how this situation actually occurs, what are your objectives as a player, what are the challenges you have to face," said Mateusz Tomaszkiewicz. "The pacing is super important, because you can have a great story, but if it has too many dialogues or cut scenes it can drag. So you need good pacing, and that was a big part of our job in this process."

The workload ahead of them was overwhelming, and with plans to ship the game in 2014, their time was limited. By some accounts, *The Witcher 3*'s world would be thirty times the size of *The Witcher 2*'s, and as the quest team started looking at early art assets and plans for the map, they began to panic. "The first time they showed us the scope of the world, we were terrified because it was such a huge landmass," said Mateusz Tomaszkiewicz. "And since we didn't want filler content, we had to provide some worthwhile content in those regions so they were not empty, because that would be terrible."

During these early design sessions, Mateusz Tomaszkiewicz and other designers enacted a simple rule: don't make boring quests. "I called them 'FedEx quests'—the quests that are just fetch quests," said Tomaszkiewicz. "Someone says bring me the cup, or ten bear skins or whatever. You bring that stuff to them and that's it. There's no twist, no nothing. . . . Every quest, no matter how small it should be, should have something memorable in it, some little twist, something you might remember it by. Something unexpected happening." At one point in preproduction, worried that they weren't hitting this quality bar, Tomaszkiewicz cut around 50 percent of the quests they'd sketched out, "first of all because I thought we had no time to actually do all of them in time, and second of all because I just used this as an opportunity to filter out the weakest ones," he said.

They knew the way to make *The Witcher 3* stand out was to subvert people's expectations. One early quest, called "Family Matters," would introduce Geralt to the Bloody Baron, a noble with information about Ciri's whereabouts. To find out what the Bloody Baron knew, Geralt would have to help track down his missing wife and daughter. But as the quest continued, you'd find out that the Baron had driven his family to flee by drinking, abusing his wife, and acting like a violent piece of garbage to everyone. Now he appeared to be remorseful and apologetic. Would you forgive him? Try to help him reconcile with his family? Assist him in digging up and exorcising the demonic fetus of a stillborn baby he'd buried in the backyard? (*The Witcher 3* always took things to the next level.)

Other RPGs tended to draw strict lines in the sand when it came to morality—BioWare's *Mass Effect* trilogy, for example, separated your dialogue decisions based on whether they were good or evil—but in *The Witcher*, there were very few happy endings, which CD Projekt Red saw as a reflection of Polish culture. "That's how we Eastern Europeans see things," Marcin Iwiński said in one interview.[*] "My grandmother survived the Second World War. She escaped a Nazi transport and they hid in villages

* Chris Suellentrop, "'Witcher' Studio Boss Marcin Iwinski: 'We Had No Clue How to Make Games,' *Glixel*, March 2017, www.glixel.com/interviews/witcher-studio-boss-we-had-no-clue-how-to-make-games-w472316.

for a couple of months. This left an imprint on every single family of a big part of the team. Although the team is very international, the majority are Polish. This leaves something within you."

With quests like The Bloody Baron, *The Witcher 3*'s design team wanted to give players tough choices. They wanted to make you question your morality, and they wanted to leave you thinking about those ethical questions long after you finished the game. In the early days, when CD Projekt Red's writers and designers were trying to figure out how to pull off that sort of narrative complexity, they ran into the challenge that oh so many game developers have encountered: How do you determine whether a quest has an impact when you don't even have a game yet?

The writer Jakub Szamałek realized he was in trouble one day when he had to take a scene to get reviewed by some of his teammates. He'd written what he thought was a solid script, containing a funny dialogue exchange between hero Geralt and the sorceress Yennefer, then he'd implemented it into the game's engine to see how the scene looked. The art team hadn't finished Geralt and Yennefer's models, so Szamałek had to use a couple of generic fishermen as placeholders. There was no animation or lip movement in the game yet. In the background, what would eventually become detailed homes were currently big gray boxes. Occasionally, the camera would glitch out and fly into someone's head. There was no voice acting—they weren't going to record dialogue until it was final—so everyone had to read and imagine what the delivery would sound like. "And you sit there and you're trying to explain to them," said Szamałek. "'So listen, imagine that this happens here and Geralt makes this face and there's a pause here, and then they say this, and then we show Geralt's face and he winces.' It's supposed to be funny. And we have ten people in the room, and they're looking on the screen, and they say, 'I don't get it.'"

Szamałek, a novelist with a wry streak, had never worked on a game before *The Witcher 3*, so he hadn't realized how difficult writing a video game could be. During one quest, when Geralt and Yennefer would walk together through an abandoned garden on their hunt for Ciri, Szamałek had to write dialogue that captured the characters' complicated history. Geralt and Yennefer would snark and tease one another, but there was meant to be an undercurrent of warmth running under their banter. During early testing, it was impossible to convey that sort of subtle human emotion. "It all works when you have voice acting in, because a good actor can be both mean and warm at the same time," said Szamałek. "But when you just see letters at the bottom of the screen and you have two grey Skellige fishermen talking to each other, it's very difficult to get that and convince whoever's reviewing your work that it's going to work in the end."

For Szamałek and the other writers, one solution to this problem was to file draft after draft after draft, iterating on every scene as the rest of the team implemented more and more of the game. Once the game had basic character models and rudimentary animations, it was easier to tell how each scene was doing. People often wondered how CD Projekt Red sharpened the writing in *Witcher* games so well, especially when there was so much of it. The answer was simple. "I don't think there is a single quest in *The Witcher 3* which was written once, accepted, and then recorded," Szamałek said. "Everything was rewritten dozens of times."

In February 2013, CD Projekt Red announced *The Witcher 3*, revealing the game through a cover on the popular magazine *Game Informer* that showed Geralt and Ciri mounted on two horses. Konrad Tomaszkiewicz and his team made lofty promises: *The Witcher 3* would be larger than *Skyrim*. It'd have no loading times. It'd be out in 2014 and feature at least one hundred hours of gameplay. "We spoke about this cover for the game for a long time," Tomaszkiewicz said. "We knew what we needed to expose there [was] the open world." This was their coming-out party. By emphasizing that *The Witcher 3* was a game in which you would be able to go anywhere and do anything, CD Projekt Red would show the world that Poland could make pretty good RPGs, too.

The developers were purposefully ambiguous about the game's platforms, because Sony and Microsoft hadn't yet announced their next consoles, but everyone on *The Witcher 3* knew they were putting it out on PC, Xbox One, and PS4, skipping last-generation hardware. This was a big gamble. Some analysts believed that the PS4 and Xbox One wouldn't sell nearly as well as their predecessors, and most publishers were insisting on making their games "cross-gen" to reach the largest possible audiences, as EA and Activision did with *Dragon Age: Inquisition* and *Destiny*.

CD Projekt Red knew that the older hardware was too limiting for their goals. If they had to restrict *The Witcher 3*'s memory for last-gen consoles, they wouldn't be able to achieve the level of photorealism that they thought they could hit with this game. CD Projekt Red wanted to build a world with a functioning ecosystem and day-night cycle, with elaborate cities and grass that swayed in the wind. They wanted players to be able to explore the entirety of each region without waiting for parts of the game to load. None of this would be possible on the PlayStation 3 or Xbox 360.

Not long after announcing the game and showing their demo to *Game Informer*, CD Projekt Red's engineers made a drastic overhaul to the rendering pipeline that changed the way graphics would appear on-screen. The good news was that it made everything look significantly sharper, from the wrinkles on a leather bag to the characters' reflections in water. The bad news was that to make it work, the artists would have to change almost all the models they'd already developed. "This happens fairly often," said Jose Teixeira, a visual effects artist. "A big feature gets worked on, and if it's deemed important to the game—if the game will really benefit from it—then even if it is a big change and assets have to be redone and whatnot, it's worth doing it."

Teixeira, a Portugal native who was primarily responsible for visual effects like weather and blood splatter ("I had a very questionable browser history"), spent a great deal of time not just creating graphic enhancements but researching and experimenting with new technology that would make everything look better. He also had to find ways to optimize that technology. A single small village, for example, might have dozens of different light sources, like candles, torches, and campfires, all sucking away at *The Witcher 3*'s memory budget every time they flickered. "We had to work a lot with what we call levels of details," Teixeira said. "The further away things are, the less detailed they are. So we had to work very carefully to make sure that we're not, for example, using a really ridiculously complex particle system that's being spawned a mile away."

As development proceeded, *The Witcher 3*'s designers again began to panic that they didn't have enough content. They'd promised the world that this game would take at least one hundred hours to play. It might have been a ridiculous number, but it was the one they'd promised, and they felt compelled to hit it. "We had this feeling that the game might be too short, that we might not deliver on one hundred hours," said Mateusz Tomaszkiewicz. "And we were like no, we told everyone, we have to do it, we have to deliver one hundred hours." Tomaszkiewicz and his department kept churning out quests, trying their hardest to follow the edict that none should feel too FedEx-like, but the fear of emptiness lingered.

One fundamental conceit of *The Witcher 3* was that Geralt

would be able to own and ride a horse, which he called Roach. (A running joke in the *Witcher* book series was that Geralt gave all his horses the same name.) Horseback riding was not only significantly faster than walking, it was the main method of moving through *The Witcher 3*'s various regions. As a result, every area of the game needed to be big. Really, really big. Every day, the game's world would get bigger, requiring more and more content from the quest department. "We knew we wanted an open world, and we knew we wanted to have horse travel; we wanted to have a very big, realistic scope," said Mateusz Tomaszkiewicz, "and this basically caused the locations to grow and grow."

The most significant issue, and the cause of the most anxiety for the quest department, was how many of *The Witcher 3*'s core mechanics remained unfinished. Combat wasn't entirely complete yet, so the designers had to put Geralt into "god mode" during their testing, which meant he'd defeat every monster in one hit. This made it tough to judge whether quests were paced properly. "[It's hard] to estimate precisely how many hours of gameplay you will have when you don't actually have the gameplay balancing and mechanisms in place yet," said Tomaszkiewicz.

All these unknowns added up to a game that nobody knew how to properly judge. As Mateusz Tomaszkiewicz put it, "It's super hard to do quality reviews when you can't see the quality." And throughout 2013 and even into 2014, as CD Projekt Red sat through reviews and tested out various parts of the game, they remained nervous that *The Witcher 3*'s world felt too empty. They had pulled off some incredible technical accomplishments thanks to the new graphics renderer, and it was common for members of the team to gather around and gawk at how pretty everything looked. The foliage looked like it had come right out of a Polish forest. Geralt's ringmail was so elaborately detailed, you could identify each ring of metal. The leather looked sufficiently leathery. But the world was enormous, and the whole team grew anxious that they wouldn't be able to live up to that nagging promise of "one hundred hours."

Each of CD Projekt Red's major regions was bigger than most open-world games, and *The Witcher 3* had three of them, plus smaller areas like the keep of Kaer Morhen and the prologue area, White Orchard. To flesh out this world, a team of level designers combed the map and placed landmarks that they called points of interest (POIs) throughout each area. Each of these POIs would hold an activity ranging from minor (a group of marauding bandits) to major (a merchant wants you to find out who killed his assistant). Some POIs led to dumpy villages; others took you to ancient ruins filled with monsters and treasure.

The level design team was responsible for ensuring there were enough POIs to fill up the entire world. "We wanted to get an idea of the scope first: How many POIs feels good, how much is too much?" said Miles Tost, a level designer. "We'd just place them on the level. And then we would take the barely functioning horse and ride in between them and actually measure the time it would take, and then we would go, all right, so every minute we have a POI or whatever. We would even reference other games, like *Red Dead Redemption* or *Skyrim*, check how they did it, and then we wanted to figure out, all right, does this feel good for us, do we need it denser, or vary from that."

Tost's team didn't just want *The Witcher 3*'s world to feel like a collection of disparate quests—they wanted it to support an entire ecosystem. There would be a village that built bricks, connected to the city of Novigrad via elaborate trade routes. There would be manufacturing, agriculture, and all the other accouterments of a realistic medieval world. "If you look at the farming areas around Novigrad, all of these exist to support this huge city which believably could exist in this world," said Tost. "All of these people living there, they get support from different kinds of infrastructure around the world. This was something we put a really big focus on creating. There's even a village where they make carts."

As *The Witcher 3*'s staff grew larger, this insistence on realism led to some complications. At one point, Tost's team noticed a serious problem in Velen: there was too much to eat. "Velen was always supposed to be this famine-ridden land," said Tost, "where people don't really have a lot of food." For some reason, though, an environment artist had stocked up many of Velen's homes, filling the cabinets with sausages and vegetables. It bothered the level designers too much to leave as it was, so they spent hours digging through every village in Velen, taking food away from the people like twisted reverse Robin Hoods. "We had to go through all the houses in this area and make sure there was barely any food," Tost said.

It was this kind of attention to detail that CD Projekt Red thought could elevate *The Witcher 3* above the competition, not unlike Naughty Dog's approach on *Uncharted 4*. Most players might not have noticed the amount of food in a Velen cupboard, but those who paid attention would be rewarded. There was something special about realizing that the developers of a game actually took the time to make it so tree branches rustled and crackled when it was windy, and so the sun would rise earlier and earlier the farther north you went.

Of course, one of the problems with being a studio full of perfectionists is that you spend too much time on the little things. "From a player's point of view, you could almost never have enough detail," said Tost. "People like to explore a lot, and you can totally understand that. But of course at some point you have to consider the scope of the project, and whether this rock angled in a certain way actually adds something to the world. Or maybe you should instead go and fix another two bugs somewhere." Every second spent adding an extra detail to the game, every minute spent fine-tuning quests, and every hour spent wrangling with the unfinished world led to the schedule progressing faster than CD Projekt Red would've liked it to.

All those days added up, and as they entered 2014, the studio realized that they needed more development time. In March 2014, CD Projekt Red announced that they were delaying *The Witcher 3* an extra half year, to February 2015. "The board was really stressed, but they don't come in and try to influence the game itself because they trust us," said Konrad Tomaszkiewicz, the director. "It was really hard for me because I got on my shoulders all of this stress, this baggage. I knew that it could be catastrophic because we put a lot of money into this game, and it needs to be a success."

Since Marcin Iwiński had founded CD Projekt in 1994 (and CD Projekt Red in 2002), they'd made a total of just two games. *The Witcher 3* would be the third. The company was able to stay independent thanks to investors and other sources of revenue, like GOG, CD Projekt Red's successful online store, and Marcin Iwiński wasn't concerned that they'd go bankrupt if *The Witcher 3* flopped, but this was still a huge gamble for them. Thanks to the *Game Informer* cover and several big trailers, *The Witcher 3* was getting more buzz than either of its predecessors, and failing to live up to fans' expectations might be a deathblow for CD Projekt Red's hopes of competing with other big publishers. "This hype was really cool," said Konrad Tomaszkiewicz. "At the same time, when we were in the heart of the project, we got a lot of problems, like the engine would crash all the time and we didn't get streaming on time. On the PS4 and Xbox we could render one dot on the screen. And we knew that we needed to deliver, so it created this huge stress on the whole team."

What this meant was that 2014 would be a year full of crunch for the Polish company.* At E3 in June, CD Projekt Red planned to show a lengthy *Witcher 3* demo that featured Geralt exploring the swamps of Velen. During those long nights and weekends, when the crunch seemed like it would never end, what helped drive the development team was the fact that they'd be on the E3 stage alongside multibillion-dollar publishers like Ubisoft and Activision. Among the neon spectacle of the E3 show floor, where massive games like *Madden* and *Assassin's Creed* dominated everybody's attention, *The Witcher 3* held its own, winning E3 awards from major websites like *IGN* and *GameSpot.* CD Projekt Red were the underdogs, the outsiders, the guys from Poland who had made only two other games, yet fans thought *The Witcher 3* was one of the most impressive things at the show. "It's a source of motivation for us," said Piotr Tomsiński, an animation programmer. "We would like to be like the superfamous companies."

Throughout 2014, as the crunch continued and the development of *The Witcher 3* grew more intense, the game kept evolving. The quest team overhauled large swaths of the story after realizing that not enough of their quests involved the ongoing war between the Nilfgaardian Empire and the Kingdom of Redania, which served as a backdrop to the game. The engineers rebuilt the streaming system, spending months trying to make objects load seamlessly in the background, so the player would see no loading screens while riding his or her horse from area to area.

CD Projekt Red's programmers were also constantly trying to improve the game's tools. "There were times where the engine would crash twenty to thirty times a day," said Jakub Szamałek. "And actually that wasn't that bad, because we expected it to crash, so we'd save every five minutes." Every day, it seemed like

---

* It helped that at CD Projekt Red, unlike at most companies in North America, overtime was paid. Polish labor laws required it.

something new in *The Witcher 3* had changed. The artists decided to connect Novigrad and Velen, fusing them into a single big map rather than leaving them as two separate locations. The designers tweaked and modified and iterated on just about everything. "We used to read the forums and check what people are asking for, and we'd actually add elements in the game based on people's feedback," said the lead quest designer, Mateusz Tomaszkiewicz. "For example, there was this footage of Novigrad at some point. You could see the city in the distance. And there were some hard-core fans in the forums that were discussing the city. In the books it was said that the city has very solid, big walls. And in the trailer it didn't. So we said, 'Yeah, we probably should do that,' and we did build it."

Novigrad, a gigantic, detailed city with narrow streets and red-brick roofs, bore an uncanny resemblance to Warsaw's medieval Old Town. Both cities were intricate, cobbled, and full of life. Like Novigrad, Old Town was entirely fake, having been reconstructed brick by brick after it was destroyed by the German Luftwaffe in World War II. Unlike Novigrad, you could walk through Warsaw's Old Town without seeing beggars glitch out and start floating.

Toward the end of 2014, as the developers of *The Witcher 3* finally started to see the finish line, CD Projekt Red delayed the game another twelve weeks, from February to May 2015. The extra time would allow them to fix bugs, and the business department thought if they released in May, there would be fewer big releases next to *The Witcher 3*. "It was the perfect spot for us," said Konrad Tomaszkiewicz. "Actually, I think we were lucky. If we had released the game at the first date, we'd be competing with *Dragon Age* [*Inquisition*, released in November 2014] and other games. In May, people had finished all the games from last year and they were ready for a new big game."

Another compelling reason to delay, CD Projekt Red staffers said, was so they wouldn't turn out like *Assassin's Creed Unity*, a game that had launched a couple of months earlier and was widely derided for its graphics glitches, including one particularly horrifying bug that made an NPC's face explode. (Naturally, that face turned into an Internet meme.)

During these final months, some departments had to crunch more than others. The writers had already been through their brutal deadlines, and toward the end of the project, they could relax a little bit. In those final months, their job was to write all the letters, notes, and other various bits of text that you'd see in the game. "CD Projekt Red understands the position of writer very literally, because a writer is someone who writes," said Jakub Szamałek. "We're making sure that geese have 'goose' displayed over their heads and a piece of cheese is called a piece of cheese. And a 'legendary griffon trousers' diagram is called exactly that." The writers went through the entire string database to ensure all the names made sense. "We had times where the cat was called 'deer' and the deer was called 'cheese' and whatnot," Szamałek said. "After years of writing dialogue, that was actually very relaxing. We sat there and did things and nobody bothered us."

For other departments, however, the last few months were more brutal. Developers on the very end of the pipeline, like the audio team and the visual effects team, spent long nights at the office trying to finish up their work. The quality assurance testers had a particularly rough time. On a game as massive as *The Witcher 3*, with so many areas, quests, and characters, it would be physically impossible to find every game-breaking bug and glitch, but the testers still had to try. "You start realizing not just sheer size of the game, but the sheer amount of possibilities on how you can do things," said Jose Teixeira. "The game crashes, not if you go into a house, but if you talk to this person and if you get on a horse and then you go into a house. . . . [The testers] started coming up with these sort of 'what the fuck' situations." *The Witcher 3* ended up shipping with lots of bugs, as every video game does, but the extra three months helped them avoid an *Assassin's Creed Unity*–like catastrophe.

As the release date drew closer, the whole team started bracing for impact. Ever since the *Game Informer* cover, hype for *The Witcher 3* had been building steadily, but who knew what the world would think? The developers thought the game might be good, and they were particularly proud of the story and writing, but neither of their previous *Witcher* games had drawn much of an audience outside hard-core PC gamers. Would *The Witcher 3* really be able to compete with the likes of *Skyrim* and *Dragon Age: Inquisition*? They were hoping to expand their audience and sell a few million copies, but what if they were being too optimistic? What if the game wasn't big enough? What if nobody cared about this RPG from eastern Europe?

Then the praise started coming in. On May 12, 2015, when *The Witcher 3*'s reviews started going live on the Internet, the hype reached a fever pitch. Wrote a reviewer for the website *GameSpot*: "Make no mistake: this is one of the best role-playing games ever crafted, a titan among giants and the standard-setter for all such games going forward." Other reviews were equally adoring, and for the employees of CD Projekt Red, the next few days were surreal. Critics hadn't paid nearly this much attention to previous *Witcher* games, let alone lavished them with so many compliments. "It was such a weird feeling because looking back, you'd think people would be high-fiving each other like, 'Wow, we made it,'" said Jose Teixeira. "But we started reading these reviews and we're just looking at each other going, 'Holy shit, what do we do with this information?' Nobody worked that day, needless to say. Everybody was just on Google going 'Witcher 3 reviews' and refreshing. Suddenly this became the best year in our careers."

On May 19, 2015, CD Projekt Red released *The Witcher 3*. Somehow, the game was even more massive than any of them had anticipated. Perhaps to overcompensate for that persistent fear that they wouldn't have enough content, they'd wound up making too much. Their goal had been a maximum gameplay time of one hundred hours, but between quests, points of interest, and areas to explore, *The Witcher 3*'s final count was closer to two hundred hours. It could stretch out even longer, if you played slowly.

One could certainly argue about the merits of a game that long (and, in retrospect, some at CD Projekt Red felt like they maybe should have chopped 10 or 20 percent of the game), but what was remarkable about *The Witcher 3* was that very few of the quests felt like padding. Mateusz Tomaszkiewicz's edict to avoid FedEx quests had been successful. Every quest in *The Witcher 3* had some sort of complication or twist, as Tomaszkiewicz had requested, which was a design tenet that BioWare's developers would later tell me they were hoping to use in their own games after *Dragon Age: Inquisition*. CD Projekt Red, which had first found success when Marcin Iwiński got the rights to distribute BioWare's *Baldur's Gate*, had now made something that BioWare wanted to emulate. Who, now, could argue that European RPGs weren't as good?

Throughout the sleek wooden halls of CD Projekt Red's sprawling office on the east side of Warsaw, a series of posters displayed the long-running game studio's catchy, if slightly awkward slogan. "We Are Rebels," the posters said. "We Are CD Projekt Red."

It was fair to wonder, I thought while strolling through a maze of desks and computers during the fall of 2016, just how that slogan meshed with reality. These days, CD Projekt Red was a publicly traded company with nearly five hundred employees and offices in two cities. As I walked by one glass conference room full of people, my tour guide said it was an orientation for new staff. CD Projekt Red was hiring so many people, he added, that they had to start doing these orientations every week. After the company's astounding recent success, experienced game developers were emigrating from all over the world just to work here.

The word "rebels" implied counterculture. It conjured the image of developers going against the grain, working together to make games that nobody else would think to make. CD Projekt Red, on the other hand, was now the largest game company in Poland, and one of the most prestigious in the world. As of August 2016, the studio was worth over $1 billion. How, exactly, were they rebels?

"I think if you would've asked me this question a few years ago I'd say probably at this size we wouldn't have the spirit, but we still do," said Marcin Iwiński. They made a big show of giving out free downloadable content for *The Witcher 3*. They spoke out often against "digital rights management" (DRM), a catchall term for the antipiracy technology that restricts how games are used, sold, and modified. (CD Projekt Red's digital store, GOG, doesn't use DRM.) Iwiński liked to say they believed in the carrot, not the stick. Rather than try to make their games impervious to pirates, they wanted to convince potential pirates that a CD Projekt Red game was worth the money, as they had all those years ago during the era of Poland's computer markets.

"If you don't have the money to actually buy games, you have two options," said Rafał Jaki, a business development manager. "You won't play games, or you will pirate them. But then if you turn twenty, and you start earning money, maybe you start buying games, and you turn yourself into a consumer. But if you feel that all the industry is fucking you over, why would you do that? Why would you convert when you have the money and resources to actually buy something, when you feel that there is a DLC package with [costumes] for $25, and if you buy it at GameStop you will get the blue ribbon but if you buy it somewhere else you get the red one.* Why would you do that?"

Even during development of *The Witcher 3*, the team at CD Projekt Red thought of themselves as rebels, not just because they were competing against so many bigger, more experienced companies, but because they made decisions that they didn't think other people would make. "It means that we are breaking all the rules in game design to achieve some particular goals," said Konrad Tomaszkiewicz. "To achieve those goals, from the pre-alpha of the game, I'm sitting in the room and I'm playing all the quests all the time. Actually I played all the quests in *The Witcher 3* around twenty times to check if everything is correct, if the dialogue in this quest is consistent with the previous quest and the next quest, if we don't have any gaps there. Because immersion is really crucial in our games, and if you will find the gaps or things we don't fit in the game, you will lose this immersion."

As I sat in CD Projekt Red's cafeteria, poking at a plate of vegetarian lasagna, I wondered if *The Witcher 3* would have been possible anywhere else. The landscape outside Warsaw looked like a scene straight out of *The Witcher 3*, with its lush forests and frigid rivers. Poland's cost of living was low compared with that in North America and other European countries, which meant that

---

* Fans tend to hate "retail-exclusive" downloadable content, a practice used by publishers like Square Enix and Ubisoft that spreads preorder bonuses across different stores. Buying *Final Fantasy XV* at Amazon, for example, would get you a set of special weapons. Preordering it at GameStop would get you a bonus minigame.

CD Projekt Red could get away with paying its staff relatively low salaries. (That was changing, Iwiński told me, as they attracted more expats.) The game was also inspired heavily by Polish fairy tales, not to mention the ugly history of racism, warfare, and genocide surrounding Warsaw, all of which had crept into *The Witcher 3*.

More than that, though, it was the people who worked there who made *The Witcher 3* possible. In 2016, CD Projekt Red had a somewhat culturally diverse staff, with enough non-Polish natives that the studio had officially switched to English a while back, so they could all understand one another. But so many of them seemed to have chips on their tattooed Slavic shoulders. So many of them had grown up pirating games at the computer markets, where they'd score bootleg copies of games like *Stonekeep* and fantasize about one day making their own RPGs. "I think that in communism, many people's creativity was limited," said Konrad Tomaszkiewicz. "But after we were democrats, when everyone could do what they wanted to do, they started to fulfill the dreams they got in their heads." Even after the success of *The Witcher 3*, the developers at CD Projekt Red sounded motivated to keep proving that they were good enough to take the stage at shows like E3. Maybe that was what it meant to be rebels.

10

■■■■■■■■■■

STAR WARS 1313

F ew video games have seemed as much of a sure thing as *Star Wars 1313*. It was the perfect mixture: *Uncharted*-style cinematic gameplay, in which the player would blast enemies and careen off flaming starships, combined with the rich lore of *Star Wars*, a series with more fans than just about anything on the planet. When the iconic game studio LucasArts showed its flashy *Star Wars 1313* demo at E3 2012, people were stoked. Finally, after years of missed potential both on consoles and in theaters, *Star Wars* had returned to form.

On the morning of June 5, 2012, the first day of E3, a handful of *Star Wars 1313* leads set up shop in a small, dimly lit meeting room on the second floor of the Los Angeles Convention Center. They blew up their concept art on big posters and decorated the walls to make it seem like visitors were descending into the hives of Coruscant. Although they weren't on the main floor of E3, LucasArts wanted to make a splash nonetheless. The past few years had been awful for their studio, and they wanted to prove that they could make great games again. For three days, *Star Wars*

1313's creative director, Dominic Robilliard, and producer, Peter Nicolai, played through the demo, showing it to a new group of press and visitors every half hour.

The demo opened with two nameless bounty hunters walking through a rusty ship, exchanging quips about the dangerous cargo they were about to take underground. As the two partners bantered, a group of pirates led by a malicious droid latched onto their ship, sending in a flood of several dozen baddies to invade the cargo hold. From there, we saw *Star Wars 1313*'s combat in action as the player, controlling one of the bounty hunters, ducked behind a box and started shooting.

After taking out a few enemies—first with blasters, then with an impressive half nelson that wouldn't have been out of place in a Jet Li movie—the protagonist and his partner made it to the back of their ship just in time to watch the pirates steal their cargo. Following some theatrics (and a delightfully vicious moment in which the player's partner stuffed an enemy inside a missile pod, then sent him off with a bang), both bounty hunters leaped onto the pirate ship to get back their mark. The player character, landing on one flaming hull, climbed across the crashing ships to keep up with his partner, and as he leaped across the wreckage, the demo cut to black.

"It was one of the sharpest-looking demonstrations at E3 that year," said Adam Rosenberg, a journalist (and friend of mine) who got a backstage look at the game. "LucasArts tailor-made that clip to press the buttons of video game–loving *Star Wars* geeks everywhere, and it worked." Other reporters were just as thrilled, and fans started praising *Star Wars 1313* as one of the best demos they'd ever seen. With *Star Wars 1313*, LucasArts' stint of mediocrity finally seemed to be coming to an end.

What could possibly go wrong?

■ ■ ■

When the modern video game industry first started emerging in the early 1980s, film moguls stared over with a mixture of envy and consternation. How were these game makers, with their immature stories and wildly inconsistent product cycles, making millions of dollars off this strange, interactive new media? And how could Hollywood get a piece of this? Some movie studios licensed out their franchises or worked with game publishers to crank out cheap tie-in games like the infamous *E.T.*, best known for helping crash the video game industry.* Others decided not to bother. In future years, respected directors like Guillermo del Toro and Steven Spielberg would dabble in game development, but in the 1980s only one filmmaking giant had the foresight to build an entire company around video games: George Lucas.

In 1982, five years after the release of his smash hit film *Star Wars*, Lucas saw the potential of video games and decided to get involved. He spun up a subsidiary of his production company, Lucasfilm, calling the new studio Lucasfilm Games, and hired a squad of talented young designers like Ron Gilbert, Dave Grossman, and Tim Schafer. In the coming years, Lucasfilm Games found success not with movie tie-ins but with completely original "point and click" adventure games like *Maniac Mansion* and *The Secret of Monkey Island*. A reorganization in 1990 turned Lucasfilm Games into LucasArts, and over the coming years their iconic logo—a gold man holding up a shining arc—would adorn the boxes of beloved games like *Grim Fandango*, *Star Wars: TIE Fighter*, *Day of the Tentacle*, *Star Wars Jedi Knight*, and many more. Throughout the 1990s, the name LucasArts was a badge of quality.

---

* Released by Atari in 1982, *E.T.* is widely considered one of the worst games of all time. Its disastrous launch helped trigger the video game crash of 1983 and eventually led Atari to bury a truckload of unsold cartridges in the New Mexico desert. Thirty years later, in April 2014, excavators unearthed the cartridges. The game was still terrible.

A few years into the twenty-first century, something changed. As George Lucas and his company doubled down on the much-derided *Star Wars* prequel films, LucasArts became entrenched in office politics and unstable leadership. The studio became best known for publishing other developers' games, like *Star Wars: Knights of the Old Republic* (BioWare) and *Star Wars: Battlefront* (Pandemic), rather than making its own. Over ten years, Lucas-Arts went through four different presidents: Simon Jeffery in 2000, Jim Ward in 2004, Darrell Rodriguez in 2008, and Paul Meegan in 2010. Each time a new president took over, there would be a staff-wide reorganization, which always meant two things: layoffs and cancellations. (After one particularly massive layoff in 2004, LucasArts essentially shut down and then spun back up again, which was surreal for those who remained. One former employee recalled rollerskating around half of the building, which he had all to himself.)

As one former employee would later tell me, "The Bay Area is filled with people who have had their hearts broken by Lucasfilm or LucasArts—that sad legacy of multiple presidents, multiple layoffs. There's a lot of people out there who've been treated badly by the company."

Despite this, there were many at LucasArts who believed they could restore the studio to its former glory. LucasArts paid well and had no trouble attracting talented developers who had grown up on *Star Wars* and wanted to make games in that universe. In early 2009, under president Darrell Rodriguez, LucasArts began developing a *Star Wars* project with the code name *Underworld*. They envisioned it as a video game tie-in to the live-action TV series of the same name, which George Lucas had been developing for years. The *Underworld* show was meant to be an HBO-style take on *Star Wars*, set on the planet Coruscant, which was sort of like a cross between New York City and Gomorrah. The show would take place between the two *Star Wars* film trilogies, and there would be no CGI puppets or hammy child actors this time around. Instead, *Underworld* would feature crime, violence, and brutal conflicts between mafia families. Both the game and TV show were meant for adult *Star Wars* fans.

In meetings throughout 2009, a small group of LucasArts developers quietly began conceptualizing *Star Wars Underworld*, batting around ideas for what the game might look like. For some time they saw it as a role-playing game. Then they expanded their focus, knowing that George Lucas was fascinated by *Grand Theft Auto* (*GTA*). (His kids were into the games.) How cool would it be, the developers thought, if they could make a *GTA*-style open-world game within the scummy underworld of Coruscant? You, perhaps playing as a bounty hunter or some other sort of criminal, could traipse around the world, going on missions as a contractor for different crime families as you worked your way up through the ranks.

That idea fizzled fast. After a few weeks of research based on conversations with colleagues at *GTA's* developer, Rockstar, and *Assassin's Creed's* publisher, Ubisoft, the *Underworld* team put together a proposal of how many people they'd need (hundreds) and how much money it'd cost (tens of millions) to make an open-world game of that nature. Lucasfilm's executives weren't interested. "Of course there was no appetite to make that kind of investment," said one person involved with the game. "That idea came and went literally within the span of two months."

It was a running theme at LucasArts. To get anything done, the studio's management would need to go up the ladder to their bosses at Lucasfilm, who, for the most part, were old-school film-makers with little interest in video games. Sometimes, frustrated LucasArts managers would give elaborate presentations to Lucasfilm executives simply to explain to them how games were made.

Those Lucasfilm executives also served as gatekeepers to George Lucas, often giving LucasArts developers guidelines for how to talk to the legendary auteur. (One common directive: never say no.) Lucas, who owned 100 percent of the company, was still interested in video games, but seemed, to those who worked closely with him, to feel let down by LucasArts' recent history. Couldn't they be doing so much better?

By the end of 2009, the *Underworld* project had morphed into what the team snarkily referred to as *Gears of Star Wars*, a cooperative game focused on running, shooting, and taking cover, not unlike Epic Games' seminal *Gears of War* series. By this point, *Underworld* was much less of a secret. Over the next few months, the project expanded significantly, recruiting staff from elsewhere at LucasArts as they built prototypes and got online multiplayer functionality up and running. It was an interesting, albeit "much more conservative, less adventurous" version of *Underworld*, by one account.

In the summer of 2010, the wheel of LucasArts presidents spun yet again. Out went Darrell Rodriguez. In came a tough, ambitious new president named Paul Meegan. With this change in leadership came, as usual, big layoffs and project cancellations, including a massive technology shift: Meegan, who had previously worked at Epic Games, wanted LucasArts to switch from its own proprietary technology to Epic's popular Unreal Engine.

Meegan also thought *Underworld* was too conservative. He had a big plan for the future of *Star Wars* video games—a plan that included the gradual revival of the beloved *Battlefront* shooter series—and he wanted to see LucasArts make a big splash. By then, Meegan would tell people, it was too late to salvage the studio's output on the PlayStation 3 and Xbox 360. But for next-generation consoles, which were expected within the next two years, LucasArts could do something consequential. "LucasArts is a company with tremendous potential," Meegan later said in an interview.* "And yet, in recent years, LucasArts hasn't always done a good job of making games. We should be making games that define our medium, that are competitive with the best of our industry, but we're not. That has to change."

Shortly after taking over, Meegan sat down with Dominic Robilliard, the game's creative director, and the other LucasArts leads to talk about a new vision for *Underworld*. George Lucas's TV series was stuck in development hell, but Meegan and Robilliard still loved the idea of a *Star Wars* game set in the criminal underworld of Coruscant. They also loved Naughty Dog's *Uncharted* series, which blended the feel of an action-adventure game with the spectacle of a blockbuster movie. Making *Gears of Star Wars* wasn't all that appealing, but *Star Wars Uncharted*? Working under Lucasfilm had its challenges, sure, but LucasArts benefited from sharing a campus with Industrial Light & Magic (ILM), the legendary visual effects house that had produced special effects and graphics for the original *Star Wars*. For years, Lucasfilm and LucasArts had wanted to find ways to blend film technology with video games. What better way than with an *Uncharted*-style *Star Wars* game?

Out of these conversations came design documents and concept art, and by the end of 2010, LucasArts had come up with *Star Wars 1313*, named after the 1,313th level of Coruscant's underworld. The goal, as LucasArts' designers described it, was to evoke the fantasy of being a bounty hunter. Using a wide array of skills and gadgets, the player would hunt down targets for unsavory criminal families. "Nobody had quite nailed that in *Star Wars* games," said one person who worked on *1313*. "We wanted to do

* Michael French, "Interview: Paul Meegan, *MCV*, June 6, 2011, www.mcvuk. com/news/read/interview-paul-meegan/02023.

something—and this actually came from George—that didn't rely on the Force, or Jedi."

Part of this process meant pointing the entire team in a single direction, a somewhat vague but crucial goal. "When I started on the game, my goal was really to find out what everybody was thinking," said the lead designer, Steve Chen, a veteran LucasArts employee who moved to *Star Wars 1313* in late 2010. "Because I had seen it as an open-world game; I'd seen it as a buddy game; I'd seen it as more of a shooter. I'd seen it as many, many different things. It was all over the map."

When Chen started, he spent a few weeks sitting down with everyone on the team and asking what stood out to them about *Star Wars 1313*. What did they care about most? What did they want the game to be? "What I was trying to do was find the core, and get rid of the stuff that didn't feel like it was important," Chen said. "Here's an incredibly talented group of people with a lot of great ideas and a lot of skill but not a lot of focus."

One of Meegan's next big moves was to hire a new studio manager: Fred Markus, a grizzled developer who had been working in games since 1990. Markus was a loyal acolyte of what he'd refer to as the "Nintendo" approach to game design: keep fine-tuning your gameplay until it's perfect. "[Markus] joined the company and really made a huge change to the creative culture at LucasArts—a creative change much for the better," said Chen. "He was really quite a force to be reckoned with in the studio, and he made big changes from a culture standpoint from day one."

Markus, who had spent years at Ubisoft helping shape franchises like *Far Cry* and *Assassin's Creed*, would preach about adding structure to the chaos of game development by identifying every worst-case scenario as early as possible. For example, if they were making a game in the subterranean levels of Coruscant, they'd need to think about verticality. The player, while hunting for bounties, would have to ascend and descend different levels of the city. But moving upward tended to be less fun than moving downward, and chasing a mark up a flight of stairs could feel sluggish. As a solution, maybe they'd add high-speed elevators. Maybe they'd use grappling hooks. Whatever the answer, Markus wanted his team to solve the problem before they even entered production.

Not long after starting at LucasArts, Markus put the studio through what one former staffer described as "a boot camp" for controls, camerawork, and basic gameplay rhythms. Markus believed the best way to make a video game was to spend as much time as possible in preproduction, which meant lots of talking, prototyping, and answering questions both big and small. What exactly did it mean to live out the fantasy of being a *Star Wars* bounty hunter? How would the controls work? What kind of gadgets would you have? How would you traverse the underground of Coruscant? "He was really kind of a great influence on our team and on the studio in general," said Steve Chen. "Not necessarily the easiest person to deal with, because he was tough . . . but his effects on the studio and on the project were in my opinion a huge positive. He was really forcing us to take a good hard look at what the core of the game was."

Another of their principles was to avoid taking control away from the player. "One of the things that Dom [Robilliard] the creative director felt strongly about was, whenever possible, you want the player to be doing something that was cool, not watching something that was cool," said Evan Skolnick, the lead narrative designer.

For a while, preproduction proceeded nicely. The *Star Wars 1313* team started scoping for a fall 2013 or early 2014 release, with the hope of the game becoming a launch title for the still-unannounced PS4 and Xbox One. For months they played with prototypes and worked on the new story, which would revolve around their audacious bounty hunter. The engineers grew more familiar with the Unreal Engine, working closely with ILM to sort out how to make *Star Wars 1313* look as "next-gen" as possible.

As Fred Markus, Dominic Robilliard, and the rest of the team tried to sort out their vision for *Star Wars 1313*, George Lucas would sporadically check in and offer suggestions. "As I was going back and forth with him on story and gameplay details," Robilliard said during a panel discussion at the DICE Summit in February 2017, "he would allow us to use more of the locations that he had come up with and more of his characters." Occasionally, according to team members, he'd come in and say they could—and *should*—use new bits and pieces from the *Star Wars: Underworld* show.

"At first we were in the same universe," said one person on the team. "Then it was location. Then it was rewrite the story and start using more of the characters from the TV show." In theory, the developers of *Star Wars 1313* were thrilled about getting to use more of Lucas's canonical *Star Wars* universe, but in practice, it was incredibly frustrating. With every new character or setting, the team had to scrap and redesign large chunks of the game. "I don't think it's an exaggeration to say we probably developed thirty hours worth of focus-testable gray box content before we even started making the game that we ended up with," said a person who worked on the game.

It wasn't that George Lucas was trying to be malicious. People who worked on the game say he loved how *Star Wars 1313* was shaping up. But in Lucas's preferred craft, filmmaking, everything existed to serve the story, while in game development—at least on the type of game that Markus and Robilliard wanted to make—everything existed to serve gameplay. "One of the problems of working in a film company with somebody like George is that he's used to being able to change his mind and iterate on things purely on a visual level," said a person who worked on the game. "[He wasn't used to] the idea that we were developing [gameplay] mechanics that go along with these concepts, levels, and scenarios."

Star Wars 1313's leads theorized that as George Lucas saw more of the game, his trust in the developers grew, which made him feel more comfortable giving them more of his universe to play with. Besides, he could do whatever he wanted. It was his company. His name was in the title and he owned all the stock. As LucasArts employees liked to say: *We serve at the pleasure of George Lucas.*

"I've had the pleasure of presenting to George [on different projects] once or twice, maybe a handful of times in my years at LucasArts, and the first thing George will always say is, 'I'm not a gamer,'" said Steve Chen, who didn't work with George Lucas directly on *1313*, but had on previous games. "But he has really clear ideas about what story's like and what the experience should be like . . . If he made a request or made a suggestion about something in terms of story or character or gameplay, you feel like he's coming at it from his perspective, and you have to respect that as president of the company, and chief creative force for the company. The ripple effects, I don't know if that was necessarily the top of his mind like, 'Oh, is this decision I'm making going to change what the team does?' Maybe it does, maybe it doesn't. I don't think that's the highest priority for him. That was for us to worry about."

The most drastic of these changes arrived in the spring of 2012. Earlier that year, they'd decided to announce *Star Wars 1313* at E3, and the entire team was crunching on the flashy demo that would showcase their two bounty hunters. After all these years of development—and the poor recent output from LucasArts— the *1313* team felt big pressure to make a splash. Years of public layoffs, rushed games, and canceled projects had cost LucasArts whatever prestigious reputation it had in the 1990s. "We were at that point not super sure what the public's or press's impression of a LucasArts game was," said Chen. "I would say candidly it was probably spotty at best. So putting something out at that point had a lot of gravitas attached to it."

Two months before E3, George Lucas approached LucasArts' leadership with a new mandate: *Star Wars 1313* should star the bounty hunter Boba Fett. Lucas wanted to explore the backstory of the enigmatic mercenary, who had first appeared in *The Empire Strikes Back* and was revealed in the prequels to be a clone of Jango Fett, progenitor of the Republic's clone troopers. Instead of *1313*'s current hero, Lucas said, they should use a younger, pre-*Empire* version of Boba.

To the *Star Wars 1313* development team, this was like being told that they had to reroute an oil tanker. They'd already designed a protagonist, who had his own story, personality, and background. They'd cast the actor Wilson Bethel to play their hero, and the team had already recorded dialogue and captured many of Bethel's facial movements. Both Fred Markus and Dominic Robilliard pushed back, telling Lucas that changing the main character at this point would be a monumental undertaking. It would require the team to reboot everything, they explained. What if instead they added Boba as a nonplayable character, integrating him into the story without changing the hero they'd spent years developing? Couldn't they find some other solution?

The answer to those questions was no, and word soon came down from Lucasfilm's management that the decision was final. *Star Wars 1313* was now a game about Boba Fett. "We had a whole story planned out," said one person who worked on the game. "We were in full preproduction at that point. Every level for that version of the game had been planned and written. At that point we were on the fourth or fifth draft of the story. It was at the point where we were all super excited about it."

Word also came down that LucasArts couldn't talk about Boba Fett at E3, which meant that for the next two months, the *Star Wars 1313* staff had to build a demo around a character that they knew wouldn't be in the final game. On one hand, this made for a good opportunity to test out their new technological pipeline, which used ILM's film rendering techniques to create flashy smoke and fire effects, allowing for some of the most photorealistic spaceship crashes one could find in this galaxy. They could also experiment with facial motion capture, one of their most impressive (and most challenging) pieces of tech. "Human faces are the one thing that we as human beings are very tuned to know when something's right and something's wrong," said Steve Chen. "Getting that right took a lot of work. A *lot* of work. In terms of skin tone and lighting and surface texture and expression itself. Any tiny little thing where the face doesn't quite move in the right way or the eyes don't look quite right will set your mind off."

On the other hand, this E3 demo would take months of their lives; long days and late nights, all dedicated to characters and encounters that might never actually appear in their game. (Robilliard told the team they would try to salvage as much of the demo as possible, though they knew the story would be gone.) Maybe it'd be worth the stress, though. The *Star Wars 1313* team knew they needed to impress people. Even within LucasArts, there was a concern that the hammer might come down at any time—that the studio's parent company, Lucasfilm, would cancel the game; that they'd suffer more layoffs; that Paul Meegan might be another casualty of the cursed title "LucasArts president."

To Fred Markus, Dominic Robilliard, and the rest of the team, simply announcing *1313* at E3 wouldn't be enough. They had to be the best thing there.

▪ ▪ ▪

If you walked around downtown Los Angeles during early June 2012, you'd probably hear people talking about two games: *Watch Dogs* and *Star Wars 1313*. Both looked incredible. Both were planned for next-gen consoles that hadn't been announced yet. (Neither Sony nor Microsoft were pleased with Ubisoft and LucasArts for showing their hands so early.) And both games had stolen the show. Days of showing *Star Wars 1313*'s impressive bounty hunter demo had resulted in exactly the type of buzz that LucasArts needed that summer.

Critics wondered if, like many of the sizzling demos that game publishers brought to shows like E3, *Star Wars 1313* was all smoke and mirrors. Was this a "target render," demonstrating the type of graphics that the development team *wanted* to achieve rather than what they could actually make? Or would the game really look like that? "It was playable—I played it, and it was not the kind of thing where if you did one thing slightly incorrectly, the whole thing fell apart," said Evan Skolnick, the lead narrative designer. "All those mechanics you see are things that were working in the game."

After years of reboots and endless preproduction, the *Star Wars 1313* team had momentum. The press was excited, the public was hyped, and *Star Wars 1313* seemed *real*—even if nobody outside the studio knew that the main character was actually going to be Boba Fett. Some on the team still found it strange that Lucasfilm had barred the *1313* team from talking about Boba at E3, but seeing *Star Wars 1313* win E3 awards and leap to the top of press outlets' "Most Anticipated Games" lists was thrilling for them, especially those who had been at LucasArts for the past decade and watched the revolving door of presidents in action. Finally, it felt like they'd reached stability.

Once they'd flown back to San Francisco, the *Star Wars 1313* team gathered and started sketching plans for entering production. In the films, one of Boba Fett's most iconic accessories was his jetpack, which the development team knew they'd have to add to their game in some way. But they didn't know how to approach that. Would it be more of a jump pack, propelling the player forward large distances, or a hover pack, allowing you to hold down a button and gain altitude? Or something else entirely? "Just a simple decision like that can completely change what sort of levels you're going to build, what sort of enemies you're going to design, what it looks like on-screen, how it controls," said Steve Chen, who left the *Star Wars 1313* team after E3. "Something as simple as that has huge ramifications."

Either way, with Boba Fett in the starring role, the designers would have to reimagine all the encounters they'd planned. Enemies would need to be aware of the player's jetpack so they could take cover from attacks that came from above them, which, as one member of the *1313* team told me, was "a major pain in the ass."

LucasArts still had momentum, though. In the weeks after E3, as part of a planned hiring ramp-up, the studio recruited a dozen veteran developers from across the industry. The *1313* team was still relatively small—around 60 people, with hopes of expanding to 100 or even 150—but they had a great deal of experience. "Usually on a team there's a mixture of senior people, midlevel people, and juniors that would be learning the ropes and learning from the seniors who are mentoring them," said Evan Skolnick. "This team . . . it seemed like everyone was just senior level. Everyone knew their stuff really well, and were basically all-stars, so it was really amazing to be working with that caliber of talent across the board on that team."

Around September 2012, two strange things happened. First, Lucasfilm told LucasArts not to announce the other game they'd been developing, a shooter called *Star Wars: First Assault* that the studio had planned to reveal that month. Second was a studio-wide hiring freeze. Lucasfilm executives said it was temporary—LucasArts' president, Paul Meegan, had just quit, and the polarizing Lucasfilm president Micheline Chau was on her way out—but either way, it put the brakes on the *Star Wars 1313* team's plans. They needed more staff to enter full production.

To LucasArts, these moves made no sense. They were all feeling motivated after a spectacular E3 showing, and they had fans on their side, with video game news outlets everywhere publishing articles about how LucasArts might finally be "back." It was, as one LucasArts employee said, "a weird disconnect." Game development was so often about this sort of momentum, and LucasArts had struggled so much to get their projects revving over the past decade. Why wouldn't their parent company want to help them out? Why wouldn't they want to keep riding the *1313* train while it was at full speed?

The answer to all those questions was "roughly four billion dollars." On October 30, 2012, in a shocking, blockbuster move, Disney announced that it was purchasing Lucasfilm—and with that, LucasArts—for $4 billion. All the weird changes suddenly made sense. Lucasfilm wasn't going to make big announcements or hire dozens of new game developers when it knew Disney might have other plans in motion. And Disney's main interest was, as the company made clear when it revealed the deal, to produce more *Star Wars* movies. In the press release Disney sent out to announce its purchase, the word "LucasArts" appeared once. "Video games" did not appear.

To say that LucasArts' employees were stunned by this news would be like saying Alderaan was a little bit shaken up. For close to a decade, rumors had been floating that George Lucas might retire—he'd admitted to feeling traumatized by the fan backlash to his prequel films—but few people thought he'd follow through, even as he made his intentions clear. "I'm retiring," Lucas had told

New York Times Magazine in January 2012. "I'm moving away from the business, from the company, from all this kind of stuff." He had made comments like that in the past, though, so to see the legendary director sell his company was surreal for everyone who worked for him. "We just didn't know quite what to expect," said Evan Skolnick. "We were hopeful that it would mean good things for us, but . . . I think we were well aware that it might not mean good things."

To video game reporters, Lucasfilm representatives said the acquisition wouldn't affect *Star Wars 1313*. "For the time being all projects are business as usual," the company said in a statement, mirroring comments that Disney's CEO, Bob Iger, made internally to LucasArts' staff. *Business as usual*, he told them all in a meeting. But there was one giant, glaring red flag. Immediately after news of the acquisition broke, Iger said on a conference call that the company would look to license *Star Wars* to other video game companies rather than publish its own games, and that Disney was "likely to focus more on social and mobile than we are on console."

It was a "wait, what?" moment for LucasArts staff. They had two games currently in development, and both were on consoles. If Disney was going to make games for a more casual audience, where did that leave LucasArts? Some *Star Wars 1313* leads read the tea leaves and decided to call it quits, including Fred Markus, who resigned shortly after the acquisition. And the hiring freeze continued, which meant not only that the *Star Wars 1313* team couldn't expand, but that it couldn't replace the people who were leaving. LucasArts couldn't stop the bleeding.

Dominic Robilliard and those who were left on the *Star Wars 1313* team continued to work. They were optimistic that they still had the right combination of pieces to make something great: a good video game hook, a talented core staff, and top-notch technology. Plus, they figured their Boba Fett game would fit nicely with Disney's announced plans to make a new trilogy of *Star Wars* films. *Star Wars 1313* was set between the first two trilogies, so it wouldn't interfere with the newly planned episodes VII through IX.

In the weeks after the Disney purchase, *Star Wars 1313*'s developers put together a demo that they could show to their new corporate overlords, which Disney assessed with some interest. "They were interested in learning everything about the company they had just purchased, so they wanted to know about every project," said Evan Skolnick. "They were looking at the company holistically, as you would of a company you had just purchased for several billion dollars. So I think that *1313* was, along with every other in-progress project and planned project at the company as a whole, subject to evaluation, investigation, questioning, and eventually a decision based on every one of those analyses."

Disney stayed quiet, though, and as 2012 ended and the new year came around, LucasArts' employees still didn't know where they stood. Several people left for new jobs, and others started sending out applications, knowing that the studio wasn't making any progress. It felt like they were in purgatory, or maybe frozen in carbonite, as everyone at LucasArts waited to hear what Disney was going to do. Some thought Bob Iger might ax *Star Wars 1313* and *First Assault* in favor of a new slate of games, maybe tied to the movies. Others guessed that Disney would overhaul LucasArts, transforming it into a developer of casual and mobile games. All of them crossed their fingers that Disney would just let them keep doing what they were doing, and that it really would be, as Iger had promised, business as usual.

The next red flag came in late January 2013, when Disney announced that it had shut down Junction Point, the Austin-based studio behind the artsy platformer *Epic Mickey*. "These changes are part of our ongoing effort to address the fast-evolving gaming platforms and marketplace and to align resources against our key priorities," Disney said in a statement. In noncorporate speak, what that meant was that *Epic Mickey: The Power of Two*, the sequel to *Epic Mickey* that Junction Point had released in November 2012, had bombed.

Disney didn't offer sales numbers, but reports pegged *The Power of Two*'s first-month sales at around a quarter of what the first game's had been, which was especially atrocious considering that the first *Epic Mickey* had been a Wii exclusive while *Epic Mickey: The Power of Two* was on several platforms. As Iger had hinted, console games just hadn't worked out very well for Disney, which was inauspicious for LucasArts.

By February 2013, the whispers had grown louder. Both in and out of the studio, rumors flew that Disney was planning to shut down LucasArts. Employees would exchange knowing glances in the halls and sometimes even openly muse about the company's future. Still, there was a lingering sense at LucasArts that *Star Wars 1313* was untouchable. Surely, with all the fans talking about how exciting the game looked, Disney would have to finish making it. In the worst-case scenario, the developers thought, maybe Disney would sell *1313* to another big publisher. "I think there may have been a feeling that because we had built up so much anticipation for the game, and we had just done so well at E3 in 2012, having won and been nominated for so many awards, and really got the press and the fanbase excited, that we felt it might be enough to save the project," said Evan Skolnick. "That *1313* couldn't be canceled now, because there was so much anticipation."

What became clear to LucasArts' staff later, some said, was that Disney had given them a grace period. For several months, Disney allowed LucasArts to operate as if things were normal while it sought deals with other publishers for the future of both the studio and *Star Wars* video games. Of all the interested parties, there was one publisher that showed the most excitement: Electronic Arts. Throughout the early months of 2013, EA negotiated extensively with Disney, talking about all sorts of possible options for the future of LucasArts. Rumors began to float around the studio that hey, maybe LucasArts would be fine. Maybe EA wanted to buy them. All winter, LucasArts' management would proclaim that things were going to be OK, even telling employees not to bother handing out their résumés at the annual Game Developers Conference in March.

The biggest rumor, as conveyed by several LucasArts employees, was that EA had a deal in place to buy LucasArts and finish production on *Star Wars 1313* and *First Assault*. But then, the rumor alleged, the new *SimCity* turned out to be a debacle, which led to EA and its CEO, John Riccitiello, "mutually agreeing" to part ways, which caused the LucasArts deal to fall apart. Riccitiello, however, told me that these negotiations weren't as close as LucasArts' employees had believed. "Virtually everything gets discussed on some deal with somebody," he said. "Most of it is fantasy."

Then, everything collapsed.

On April 3, 2013, Disney shut down LucasArts, laying off nearly 150 employees and canceling all the studio's projects, including *Star Wars 1313*. It was the final act to a long period of turbulence at LucasArts, and the end of an era for one of the most treasured studios in gaming.

To those who remained at the studio, this felt both shocking and inevitable. Some left the building to go drink at a nearby sports bar (called, oddly enough, Final Final) and bemoan what might have been. Others stayed back and ransacked the place, using flash drives to grab half-finished trailers and demos off the LucasArts servers before they all disappeared. A few former employees even stole console development kits. After all, the employees figured, Disney didn't need them.

But there was still one sliver of hope. During the final hours of LucasArts, a top EA executive, Frank Gibeau, set up one last-ditch meeting to try to save *Star Wars 1313*. Gibeau told LucasArts to put together a strike team for a salvage mission at EA's headquarters. Dominic Robilliard gathered a small team of leads to meet at EA's sprawling campus in Redwood City, California. There they would give a pitch to Visceral, the EA-owned developer of *Dead Space* and *Battlefield Hardline*. If all went well, Gibeau said, Visceral would hire the core staff of *Star Wars 1313* and continue working on the project there.

Standing in front of a packed room of Visceral employees, Robilliard and his leads gave a lengthy presentation on *Star Wars 1313*. They talked about the story, describing in detail how you'd fight your way through the seedy hive of Coruscant, unraveling a spice trade conspiracy and watching your closest friends stab you in the back. They showed all the cool mechanics they'd prototyped, like the flamethrower and wrist-based rocket launcher. They walked everyone through the hours of levels they'd built in gray box, where there were detailed layouts of each stage (but no art). It was clear that (a) there was plenty of work left to be done and (b) *Star Wars 1313* had a lot of potential.

Then, as one person who was in the room recalled, nobody said anything. All heads turned to Steve Papoutsis, Visceral's longtime studio manager and the man who would ultimately get to make the final call. For a few seconds, Papoutsis just sat there, looking at the desperate faces of the *Star Wars 1313* team. Then he started to talk.

"He stood up in front of all the Lucas and Visceral people," said one person who was in the room, "and just said, 'Well, I don't know exactly what you've been told, but I can tell you that what you think is going to happen right now is not what's going to happen.'" Then, according to that person, Papoutsis said he had no interest in resuscitating *Star Wars 1313*. Instead, he and his studio would conduct interviews with all of *1313*'s key staff. If Visceral liked them, he said, the studio would hire them for a brand-new project.

The *Star Wars 1313* leads were shocked. They'd come to EA's campus in hopes of convincing Visceral to finish their game, not to get new jobs. Many of them had held on to the hope that even after everything they'd been through, they could still save *Star Wars 1313*. Even the most cynical of LucasArts' staff—the ones who thought that *Star Wars 1313*'s cinematic technology would never work properly in a video game—believed that the game had too much potential to fail.

Some leads left immediately. Others stayed and took interviews for what would eventually become a brand-new *Star Wars* action-adventure game directed by Amy Hennig, who joined Visceral in April 2014 after leaving Naughty Dog over *Uncharted 4*.

Later, a dejected Dominic Robilliard sent out an e-mail to the entire *Star Wars 1313* team. It opened:

> I had hoped that I could address you all face to face as usual, but it seems that we are already scattered to the winds and the chances of a well attended gong meeting are slim! It's probably for the best as I'm not sure I could get through what I have to say to you all and keep it together.

> When I look back on the last couple of years making this game I cannot believe what we achieved under the circumstances we had to deal with. It really is astonishing. Re-directions, interference, unstable management and studio leadership; sometimes I just can't believe you have stayed with me, and more importantly still deliver such an incredibly high quality of work. I cannot tell you

how proud I am of every [single] game-maker on this team. I will be
in your debt for the rest of my career.

Robilliard went on to compliment the team's work on gameplay ("The jetpack was the final piece of the puzzle") and visual
technology ("All of the effort and consideration that went into
our carefully and lovingly constructed look was so worth it"). He
praised the work they had done on the E3 demo ("I lost count
of how many publications and interviewers at E3 said that *Star
Wars 1313* was literally the 'best thing they had ever seen.'") and
lamented the fact that LucasArts would never get to deliver on the
game they'd promised.

"I have plenty more to say, and so much more gratitude to
show you all but right now it's too hard to articulate it," Robilliard
wrote. "I genuinely care for everyone on this team and hope desperately that we will work together again someday. . . . Until then
I will dedicate all my time and energy over the coming months to
making sure that anyone who is thinking of hiring a *Star Wars
1313* team member knows that they will be making an amazing
investment and the smartest decision of their career. You are the
greatest team I have ever known and I love you all."

Video games get canceled all the time. For every shipped
game under a developer's belt, there are dozens of abandoned
concepts and prototypes that never see the light of day. But
something about *Star Wars 1313* has always felt unique, not just
to fans but also to those who worked on it. "From my point of
view, the game was not canceled," said Steve Chen. "The studio
was canceled. It's a very different thing." Years later, members of
the *Star Wars 1313* team still speak of their time on the game in
revered tones. And many believe that the game might have been

a huge success if it had been given an opportunity to succeed. "If the phone rang," said Evan Skolnick, "and it was them calling to say, 'Hey, we want you to come back and make a new *1313*,' I'd be asking what time they want me there."

In one LucasArts meeting room there was a big bulletin board, adorned with beautiful illustrations and hundreds of colored Post-it notes. From left to right, these notes told the story of *Star Wars 1313*, laying out how Boba Fett would descend into the depths of Coruscant. There were ten missions, given tentative yet evocative titles like "Downfall" and "Scum and Villainy." The designers had plotted out every sequence in shorthand, lining up cards like "fight in back of casino" and "chase droid through subway tunnels" alongside brief descriptions of the powers you'd get and the emotional beats you'd hit. If you read them in order, you could visualize exactly what *Star Wars 1313* might have been. Eventually that board would come down, but as LucasArts closed its doors and its staff said their final farewells to the once legendary game studio, it was a story frozen in time. A snapshot of a game that would never happen.

EPILOGUE

Two years later, you've done it. You've made a video game. *Super Plumber Adventure* is out on all the big platforms—PC, Xbox One, PlayStation 4, even Nintendo Switch—and you can finally brag to all your friends that you turned your dream into a reality.

You might not tell your friends how excruciating the process was. Your plumber game was a year late, costing your investors an extra $10 million (which you swear they'll get back when *Super Plumber Adventure* becomes the hottest thing on Steam). It turns out you overscoped in preproduction—how were you supposed to know that each level would take four weeks, not two?—and you had to delay *Super Plumber Adventure* twice just to fix all the game-breaking bugs. Your team had to crunch for at least a month before each major milestone (E3, alpha, beta, etc.) and even though you bought them all dinners to make up for it, you still can't stop thinking about the missed anniversaries, the lost birthday parties, and the evenings they didn't get to spend with their kids because they were stuck in meetings about the best color schemes for your plumber's overalls.

Is there a way to make great video games without that sort of sacrifice? Is it possible to develop a game without putting in endless hours? Will there ever be a reliable formula for making games that allows for more predictable schedules?

For many industry observers, the answers to those questions are: no, no, and probably not. Game development is, as BioWare's Matt Goldman describes it, like being on the "knife's edge of chaos," where the sheer number of moving parts makes it impossible for anyone to find predictability. Isn't that one of the reasons we love video games in the first place? That feeling of surprise when you pick up a controller and know you're about to experience something totally new?

"Making a game . . . it attracts a certain type of workaholic personality," said Obsidian's audio director, Justin Bell. "It just requires a certain kind of person who's willing to put in more time. . . . Crunch sucks. It fucks your life up. You emerge from crunch and—I've got kids. I'll see my kids, and I'll look at them, and I'll [think], 'Wow, six months have passed, and you are a different person now. And I wasn't there.'"

In 2010, a Japanese company called Kairosoft released a mobile phone game called *Game Dev Story*. In it, you manage your own development studio, trying to release a string of popular video games without going bankrupt. You design each game by combining a genre and a style (example: "Detective Racing") and to make progress, you'll have to make a series of managerial decisions involving your studio's staff. It's a hilarious, if simplistic take on game development.

One of my favorite things about *Game Dev Story* is what happens during each game's production cycle, as you watch your pixelated minions perform and finish their tasks. When one of your designers, artists, or programmers is doing particularly well, they'll hit a hot streak and, quite literally, get set on fire. Their adorable, cartoonish sprite will sit there in the office, coding away, as they're engulfed in a giant ball of flames.

In *Game Dev Story* this is just a sight gag, but something about it rings true. These days, when I marvel at the incredible vistas of *Uncharted 4* or blast my way through *Destiny*'s addictive raids, or when I wonder how a bad video game turned out the way it did, that's the image that comes to mind: a room full of developers, setting themselves on fire. Maybe that's how video games are made.

ACKNOWLEDGMENTS

This book would not have happened without many, many people. First and foremost, thanks to my parents for their love, for their support, and for buying me my first video game. Thanks to Safta for more than I could ever list in one place. Thanks also to Rita and Owen.

I'm indebted to my agent, Charlie Olsen, who planted the idea for this book in my head with a single one-line e-mail and never looked back. My superstar editor, Eric Meyers, put up with my barrage of e-mails and shepherded this project from lunch conversations to finished book (no DLC required). Thanks to Paul Florez-Taylor, Victor Hendrickson, Douglas Johnson, Leydiana Rodriguez, Milan Bozic, Amy Baker, Abby Novak, Doug Jones, Keith Hollaman, and Jonathan Burnham at HarperCollins for all the support.

My dear friend and podcast cohost Kirk Hamilton offered sage advice, notes, and weather updates. My former editor Chris Kohler and my current editor Stephen Totilo both taught me just about everything I know. And my entire team at *Kotaku* makes work fun every day.

Thanks to Matthew Burns, Kim Swift, Riley MacLeod, Nathaniel Chapman, and several others (who asked not to be named) for reading early drafts of this book and giving crucial feedback.

Thanks to everyone who put up with my gchats, texts, e-mails, and nonstop chatter about this thing.

This book would not exist without Kaz Aruga, Chris Avellone, Eric Baldwin, Eric Barone, Justin Bell, Dmitri Berman, Adam Brennecke, Finn Brice, Waylon Brinck, Daniel Busse, Ricky Cambier, Steve Chen, Wyatt Cheng, Eben Cooks, David D'Angelo, Mark Darrah, Travis Day, Graeme Devine, Neil Druckmann, John Epler, Ian Flood, Rob Foote, Aaryn Flynn, Rich Geldreich, Matt Goldman, Jason Gregory, Jaime Griesemer, Christian Gyrling, Amber Hageman, Sebastian Hanlon, Shane Hawco, Marcin Iwiński, Rafał Jaki, Daniel Kading, Shane Kim, Phil Kovats, Mike Laidlaw, Cameron Lee, Kurt Margenau, Kevin Martens, Colt McAnlis, Lee McDole, Ben McGrath, David Mergele, Darren Monahan, Peter Moore, Tate Mosesian, Josh Mosqueira, Rob Nesler, Anthony Newman, Bobby Null, Marty O'Donnell, Erick Pangilinan, Carrie Patel, Dave Pottinger, Marcin Przybyłowicz, John Riccitiello, Chris Rippy, Josh Sawyer, Emilia Schatz, Josh Scherr, Evan Skolnick, Bruce Straley, Ashley Swidowski, Jakub Szamałek, Jose Teixeira, Mateusz Tomaszkiewicz, Konrad Tomaszkiewicz, Piotr Tomsiński, Miles Tost, Frank Tzeng, Feargus Urquhart, Sean Velasco, Patrick Weekes, Evan Wells, Nick Wozniak, Jeremy Yates, and the dozens of other game developers who spoke to me on background. Thank you all for your time and patience.

Thanks to Sarah Dougherty, Mikey Dowling, Radek Adam Grabowski, Brad Hilderbrand, Lawrence Lacsamana, Arne Meyer, Ana-Luisa Mota, Tom Ohle, Adam Riches, and Andrew Wong for helping coordinate many of these interviews.

And finally, thanks to Amanda. I couldn't ask for a better best friend.

ABOUT THE AUTHOR

Jason Schreier is the news editor at *Kotaku,* a leading website covering the industry and culture of video games, where he has developed a reputation for dogged reporting on a variety of tough industry subjects. He has also covered the video game world for *Wired*, and has contributed to a wide range of outlets including the *New York Times, Edge, Paste*, and the *Onion News Network*. This is his first book.